# THE COMMUNITY LAND TRUST HANDBOOK

*Coordinating editor,* Kirby White
*Graphics* by Bonnie Acker
*Book design* by Jerry O'Brien
*Book layout* by Darlene Schneck
*Photography* by Kerry Mackin and Bob O'Keefe

*Authors:* Marie Cirillo
John Davis
Rob Eshman
Charles Geisler
Harvey Jacobs
Andrea Lepcio
Chuck Matthei
Perk Perkins
Kirby White

# THE COMMUNITY LAND TRUST HANDBOOK

THE INSTITUTE
FOR COMMUNITY ECONOMICS

Rodale Press, Emmaus, Pennsylvania

*Printed in the United States of America on recycled paper, containing a high percentage of de-inked fiber.*

**Library of Congress Cataloging in Publication Data**

Main entry under title:

The Community land trust handbook.

Bibliography: p.
Includes index.
1. Land trusts—United States. I. Institute for Community Economics (Greenfield, Mass.)

| KF736.L3C65 | 343.73′025 | 82-9062 |
|---|---|---|
| | 347.30325 | AACR2 |

ISBN 0-87857-401-8 hardcover
ISBN 0-87857-439-5 paperback

*Lowest figure indicates number of this printing:*
2 4 6 8 10 9 7 5 3 1 hardcover
2 4 6 8 10 9 7 5 3 1 paperback

# Contents

# Acknowledgments

Helping with the preparation of this book were Lisa Berger, Virginia Farley, Louise Foisy, Mary Hillier, Nancy Jones, Ian Keith, Holly Ladra, Scott Ridley, Lou Robinson, Michael Swack, Ann Waterhouse, Nola White, and Ilene Wright.

The authors would like to thank all of the people who contributed to the CLT case studies: those who shared their experience in the interviews (whether their words finally appear in this book or not) and those who shared their homes and vehicles in helping to make the interviews possible.

The authors are also grateful for financial assistance from W. H. and Carol Bernstein Ferry, and the James C. Penney Foundation and its president, Carol Guyer.

# Preface

This book deals with a subject that is still very young. The idea of the community land trust (CLT), though it has very old roots, is new to America, and the community land trusts described in this book are even newer—most of them just a few years old. If our purpose as authors had been simply to report on the evolution of this new model for the control and use of land, we would have yielded to the temptation to wait awhile to let more experience accumulate, to let our subject define itself more clearly before we presumed to describe it. But we have also felt the pressure of the many hundreds of requests for information about CLTs that the Institute for Community Economics receives each year. So we have not waited. We have done our best to present a clear picture of something very much in motion.

The community land trust model was developed in the 1960s by Robert Swann and Ralph Borsodi. For some time Borsodi had been concerned with questions of land tenure and had been instrumental in founding several intentional communities that were, in some ways, forerunners of today's CLTs. The application of the model that emerged in the 60s, however, was not limited to intentional communities. Though such communities might still be founded on land held by a CLT, the community land trust itself was conceived as a democratically controlled institution that would hold land for the common good of any community, while making it available to individuals within the community through long-term leases. In the later 60s Robert Swann advocated the CLT as a useful tool for communities facing serious land tenure problems. At this time the emphasis was primarily on rural land, though the possibility of urban CLTs was recognized. In 1967 Swann and Borsodi founded the International Independence Institute (which has since become the Institute for Community Economics) as a vehicle for promoting the CLT idea.

The International Independence Institute prepared a book, *The Community Land Trust: A Guide to a New Model for Land Tenure in America,* which was published by the Center for Community Economic Development in 1972. After several printings, the text is still available and still in demand as an introduction to the CLT concept. At the time it was written, however, the subject remained almost entirely theoretical. The founding of one early community land trust was discussed at some length (New Communities, Inc., whose later history is presented in this book); otherwise, there was very little practical experience to report in 1972.

Since that time a number of CLTs have been established, including in recent years an increasing number of urban trusts. In providing technical assistance to CLTs and information to many other groups and individuals, the Institute for Community Economics felt an urgent need for a new, updated book.

An opportunity to address this need developed out of a gathering of people at Cornell University in the summer of 1980. At that time Cornell's School of Industrial and Labor Relations and the Department of City and Regional Planning sponsored an institute on economic democracy, which included week-long workshops on occupational health and safety, worker self-management, local economic policy—and community land trusts. The CLT workshop was led by Chuck Matthei of the Institute for Community Economics and Chuck Geisler of Cornell's Department of Rural Sociology. The 30 participants in this workshop represented a wide range of backgrounds and concerns. They included New York farmers, the director of a job program from a county Community Action Agency, a Black Muslim representative from New York City, a Franciscan priest involved in elderly services, the director of a housing cooperative of low-income Puerto Rican families in Detroit, a staff member of a state-wide food co-op warehouse, several students, an attorney involved in community development, and members of a church-related nonprofit housing corporation, among others. Some of these people had had experience with CLTs in their own communities, some had not. But all had had experience with the kinds of community problems that the CLT model addresses.

It was an engrossing week, and there was a strong appreciation of the opportunity that the workshop provided for people to share their experience and to begin putting together the practical information that it yielded. By the end of the week there was a general feeling that more of this sort of sharing was needed—and that there was also a great need to publish the gathering body of experience and information. Chuck Matthei and Chuck Geisler went on to organize "the CLT book project group," which included some of the Cornell workshop participants and several other interested people.

The group met for the first of a series of weekend meetings in January, 1981. Though our sense of what we could practically accomplish may have changed somewhat since that first meeting (as time ran short and the difficulty of working as a group of widely scattered individuals bore down upon us), the basic outline developed at that time has held firm.

This book was intended to provide three things: a general introduction to the CLT model as it is currently implemented, representative samples of existing CLTs, and a reasonably compact guide for people already establishing CLTs and those interested in doing so. The three major sections of the volume correspond to these three purposes.

Section I is a general introduction to the CLT model and the problems it addresses. The second of its two chapters describes the model itself. Readers who are unfamiliar with the CLT concept and have patiently read this preface in the hopes of learning *what a CLT is* might turn directly to the beginning of Chapter 2, but in organizing the book we felt the need to describe the problem before the solution. Chapter 1 is therefore a discussion of the serious, interrelated problems involved in contemporary American approaches to the use, control, and ownership of land. It will probably strike some people as an overly simplified discussion and perhaps others as overly complicated. We have been aware of a potential readership that includes both academically oriented people whose interest in CLTs involves a broad knowledge of land-related social patterns past and present, and, on the other hand, many people whose interest stems from immediate and practical needs. We have not wanted to disappoint either group. The problems are in fact very complicated and this complexity should be appreciated, but it is also true that the problems are experienced by people in ways that are often harshly simple. Both perspectives, we think, are important. We have tried to write a book that will be immediately useful while still acknowledging the complexity of its subject.

The second section of this book consists of case studies in which people involved with CLTs describe their efforts. Our only regret with this section is that there has not been more room for more material (both verbal and photographic) from more groups.

Section III provides guidance for communities interested in starting CLTs. It does not include all of the information that these groups will eventually need. Again our space and time have been limited, but more importantly, the variety among communities—and among CLTs themselves—is so great that we could not begin to offer specific advice for all possible situations even if we knew a great deal more than we do. This section is supplemented by a bibliography.

We hope that this text will be put to immediate practical use by many people—that it will help to increase the number and strength of community land trusts across the country. When it eventually becomes outdated, we hope it will be because the problems that the CLT addresses are being solved on a large scale so that the CLT's role in relation to these problems has changed. If our efforts can play a part in creating the kind of understanding of these problems that will be necessary for their solution, we will be happy.

# Section I

## Land Tenure Problems and the Community Land Trust

# CHAPTER 1

# Land and Property: Individuals and Communities

America once offered millions of people an opportunity they had never known before—access to land, and secure homes where they could enjoy the fruits of their labor. It offered them, also, an opportunity to shape and control communities.

Today much has changed. There is no longer a vast reserve of land waiting for settlement. Americans can no longer pull up roots, turn their backs on old problems, and make a new start on the frontier. The problems before American society today must be faced. And at the heart of many of these problems is the fact that an increasingly large number of Americans are being denied access to land and to the economic and social benefits of land.

**Urban America.** America is plagued increasingly by land speculation and absentee ownership of both land and buildings. Speculation often pushes the price of urban property far beyond the reach of the people most dependent on it—poor and moderate-income families in need of secure homes, small businesses in need of commercial and industrial sites, local residents in need of parks and open space for recreation and health. Absentee ownership has made matters even worse, particularly in neighborhoods with large concentrations of poor, minority, and working-class families. More than 75 percent of the land and housing may be owned by absentee landlords, leaving residents bereft of any meaningful control over local development or their personal futures. Frequently, all of the businesses and profitable property in an area are owned by people who live in other, more affluent communities, so that inner-city neighborhoods have little capital to reinvest in their own improvement. It is common to find row after row of abandoned buildings, left vacant by landlords who have taken all of the income tax deductions the law allows while deferring payments for property taxes and repairs. Until recently, when the problem was finally confronted by homeowner militancy and federal laws, banks often refused credit to certain "redlined" neighborhoods. Starved for financing for mortgages and home improvements, these neighborhoods deteriorated further each year.

Such scenes of disinvestment coexist in urban America with a new problem—gentrification. Inner-city neighborhoods of low-income and working-class people have begun to attract the interest of real estate brokers, luxury developers, and young, affluent professionals interested in moving back to the city. In neighborhoods long starved of capital, reinvestment of any

Robert O'Keefe

*The results of disinvestment.*

*A gentrified neighborhood in Cincinnati.*

Chuck Matthei

kind is initially welcomed with open arms. But enclaves of new, affluent city-dwellers tend to expand—changing the social, racial, and class composition of the entire area, displacing the original population, and destroying the community that was previously there.

Whether due to disinvestment or reinvestment, displacement has become an ever-present possibility for people who neither own nor control the urban land that is under their feet or the roof that is over their heads. The poor, of course, face the greatest threat, but they are no longer alone. All people who rent, all people who cannot afford to own their homes, face the possibility of being ousted from their homes by the sale of the property, by its conversion to condominiums, or simply by increases in rent to unaffordable levels. Homeownership, however, is a dream that is receding further and further away for most Americans. So little affordable housing is being built and remaining available that in 1980 the president of the National Association of Home Builders was prompted to write:

> Unless current trends are reversed soon, a housing cost crisis of unknown proportion could engulf this nation—pitting one generation of Americans against another and pushing from the mainstream of American society those who are being denied decent, affordable shelter—the young, the elderly, and the poor.

**Rural America.** The land and housing problems of urban America are paralleled by the speculation, concentration of ownership, absentee ownership, and housing shortages of rural America. Gentrification has its counterpart in the resort, vacation, and second-home development that is rapidly spreading across the country, displacing traditional occupations and indigenous families from the land they depend upon. Redlining has its rural equivalent in the reluctance of banks and government agencies to finance basic affordable housing that meets the needs of local people but does not meet the banks' idea of what is "marketable."

There are also serious problems that relate directly to farmland and farming. The United States has been converting agricultural land to

Kerry Mackin/Robert O'Keefe

nonagricultural uses at the rate of about three million acres per year. For the land that remains in agriculture, ownership is increasingly concentrated. One percent of the farmland owners possess 30 percent of the farmland, and 5 percent of the owners own nearly half of the land. A third of the land is owned by nonfarming landlords. These trends—farmland conversion, concentration of ownership, and ownership by absentee landlords—have been spurred by the rapid appreciation in land prices. Since land prices in recent years have risen faster than the general inflation rate, farmland has become an attractive investment for farmers and nonfarmers alike. As investors try to outbid each other for the available land, it becomes more and more difficult for small farmers and other local residents to retain access to land in their own communities.

If these trends continue, farms will become still fewer and larger, barring entry to more and more young, would-be farmers. *The Summary Report on the Structure of Agriculture,* issued in 1981 by the USDA, warned that public officials must act to slow these trends. Failure to act, concludes the report,

> will amount to a decision to accept greater and greater separation among the business functions of farming—ownership, management, labor, and operation—and greater concentration of landownership among fewer and fewer people, violating a long-held American principle and relegating the concepts behind "the family farm" to the status of museum relics.

Nowhere are the problems of speculation, concentration, and absentee ownership more obvious and more destructive than in the resource-rich corporate fiefdoms of Appalachia. In 1974 the editors of a West Virginia newspaper, the *Herald-Advertiser and Herald-Dispatch,* commissioned an investigation into who owns West Virginia. They discovered that absentee landlords—primarily a few dozen giant fuel, transportation, and lumber companies—own or control at least two-thirds of the privately held land in West Virginia. Six years later, the Highlander Center in New Market, Tennessee, asked a similar question for all of Appalachia, and set out to study landownership in 80 rural Appalachian countries. The center discovered that all 15 of the largest landowners in these selected counties were corporations, and that corporations owned 40 percent of the land and 70 percent of the mineral rights, while 75 percent of the land and 80 percent of the mineral rights were held by individuals or groups from outside the counties themselves. The center also discovered that property taxes paid by these absentee owners were extraordinarily low.

Corporate landowners have drawn tremendous wealth from Appalachia in essentially the same way that colonial powers draw wealth from their colonies. The land and resources of the region have not enriched the people of the region. The process of removing wealth from the region has impoverished a major part of the population, leaving them without access to land in their own communities, without the land they need to continue traditional forms of subsistence, to develop new economic opportunities for themselves, or even to provide secure homes for themselves. As a result, tremendous numbers of families have been forced to leave Appalachia in search of greater opportunities elsewhere.

But most have not found opportunities elsewhere. Like the black families of the Deep South who have been forced off their land by similar economic forces, the people of Appalachia have gone to northern cities. There they have found the urban problems described earlier in this chapter.

It is time to ask what has gone wrong. Our land still holds tremendous opportunities for those who control it. If millions of Americans are being denied the most basic kinds of oppor-

Mike Clark/*Southern Exposure*

*"Every problem Appalachia has—mine safety, black lung, strip-mining, pollution, the decline of farming, floods, substandard housing, welfare, every single problem—can ultimately be traced back to the question of who owns the land."* Mike Clark, Highlander Center

tunities, it is time to look at the ways in which American land is being controlled and used, and to ask in whose interest this is being done.

## INDIVIDUALS, COMMUNITIES, AND PROPERTY

**Land and property.** The problems do not spring from the land itself. They spring from the ways that the land is controlled, owned, and used. They are not land problems as such; they are *property* problems. The distinction between the words *land* and *property* is an important one, even though the words are often used as though they mean the same thing. People may speak of the same one-acre lot as either a "piece of land" or "a piece of property." When the lot is called "land" it is being described simply as an area of the earth's surface, something that exists independently of all human activity, all human laws and institutions; but when it is called "property" it is being described as a human possession, as something *owned* according to the laws of human society. Our concern here is with the arrangements whereby land is treated *as* property, and with the effects that these arrangements have on people.

**Public and private property.** For the most part, property is seen as falling into one or the other of these two categories. It is seen either as privately controlled by a private owner to serve the owner's "private interest," or as publicly controlled by one or another level of government in the "public interest." In fact, actual patterns of property ownership and control today are not nearly this easily categorized.

Nevertheless, these are the terms—"public" or "private"—in which current property problems are normally discussed, and they are very much the terms of current political rhetoric. As such, they are often surrounded with a great deal of emotion, and a great deal of confusion. In effect, the words have become banners flapping over an increasingly complicated field of controversy. These banners—"public" and "private" waved aloft—do not tell us much about the subject of the controversy; nor do they tell us much about the real interests of the people who wave them. We will therefore set the words aside for the time being. At the end of this chapter we will examine the complicated property arrangements that lie behind these words today, but we will approach the subject here in more basic terms.

**Individuals and communities.** The words we use to describe particular property arrangements are not as important as how these arrangements help or hinder people in getting the things they want and need from the land. These interests must be identified before the virtues and limitations of particular arrangements can be discussed.

People need and want certain things from the land as individuals, but they also need and want certain things as communities. The interests of individuals may be more obvious because they are more immediate. The interests of communities tend to be long-term interests, but in the long term they are no less important than individual interests. Though there are forces at work in our society that tend to undermine our *sense* of community, we do continue to live in communities and to depend on them in essential ways. Communities, in turn, depend on the land they occupy; if the community's interests in this land are ignored, the community will weaken until it can no longer provide those things that its individual members need from it.

## THE LEGITIMATE INTERESTS OF INDIVIDUALS

**Security.** Every person has a legitimate interest in having a secure home. In fact, the very idea of *home* calls necessarily for a degree of security. Home implies continuity and stability: it is the place we want to hang on to, the place we expect to come back to. It is also a *private* place; we think of it as our own whether we are technically homeowners or renters or squatters.

For many people this interest in security involves only the housing they occupy, but for others on homesteads or farms the interest extends to the land that they work and depend on for their livelihood. Here, too, continuity is essential. Those who work the soil want and need some assurance that they will be allowed to reap what they have sown.

**Earned equity.** People have a legitimate interest in keeping whatever value they put into their homes, or into the land they occupy and use, when this value is derived directly from their personal efforts. If they improve their property either directly through their own

labor or by spending on it what they have earned elsewhere, they have an obvious and legitimate interest in retaining as equity the value of these improvements.

**A reasonable legacy.** The development of a home, or of a farm or small business, is often a family effort extending over more than one generation. Families have a legitimate interest in protecting the continuity of such efforts—in seeing that members of a new generation can inherit the family homes, farms, or businesses in which they already have a stake.

# THE LEGITIMATE INTERESTS OF COMMUNITIES

**Community access.** A community has a legitimate interest in maintaining continuing access to its land for all of its members. The land and natural resources of a community are the necessary base for its economic and social well-being. Land must be available for housing, jobs, and social services if the community is to be healthy and secure.

**Community equity.** A community has a legitimate interest in retaining and utilizing for the common good whatever value it has created or nurtured. In other words, it has an interest in retaining value that accumulates not through the sort of individual efforts that create an individual's "fair earned equity," but through communal efforts that improve the community as a whole—whether these efforts involve obvious immediate accomplishments such as improvements in streets or parks or schools, or such long-term accomplishments as the nurturing of a stable and agreeable community character and a healthy local economy. It has an

interest as well in retaining a reasonable share of that value that has not been earned by anyone but that derives from the community's natural resources or from the larger economic process in which it participates.

**Community legacy.** A community has a legitimate interest in preserving its environment and guiding its own development in a way that will provide for the legitimate interests of future generations. Like individual families, communities exist over periods of time that span many generations. What is done to a community's environment by one generation will affect other generations far into the future.

## BALANCING INDIVIDUAL AND COMMUNITY INTERESTS

As isolated propositions, these statements of individual and community interests are relatively simple. But when the effort is made to protect both the legitimate interests of all of the individuals within a community and the legitimate interests of the community itself—all within one consistent set of property arrangements—the problems that must be faced are not so simple. What one individual does to secure his or her interests may interfere with the interests of either other individuals or the community. And what the community does to secure its interests may interfere with the interests of individuals. A satisfactory property arrangement must not advance the interests of one individual or group at the expense of another.

Any effectively balanced arrangement requires that there be agreement not only on what the legitimate interests are but on how they are limited by each other. It also requires that there be effective means of enforcing these limitations so that one interest does not overrun another. This is a task that grows more difficult as American society feels increasing pressures on its traditional property arrangements.

As this chapter has shown, our present property arrangements are not working well enough. It makes sense to look for alternative approaches that are based on respect for the legitimate interests of both individuals and communities and that provide an effective means of balancing these interests. The community land trust is one such approach.

Just how a CLT balances these interests will be described in the next chapter. Though it

Kirby White

*This is an Innuit (Eskimo) grave. The pieces of wood protruding from the rocks are the remains of a kayak paddle that belonged to the man whose bones lie beneath the rocks. Like the enamel cup, the paddle belonged to him so completely that it was buried with him.*

offers a real alternative to current arrangements, the CLT model is not a completely new invention; it is a fresh adaptation of some very old ideas. In fact, the view of land and property that has shaped the CLT is much older than our modern notion of private property.

## THE ROOTS OF A TWO-SIDED VIEW OF LAND

Throughout most of the time that human beings have lived on the earth there was little concept of land as private property. Private property consisted of such things as clothes and tools, which were direct extensions of the individuals who made and used them. But no human being made the earth, and the idea of owning a piece of land made no more sense than the idea of owning a piece of sky. Communities of people might identify themselves with their territo-

Kirby White

*This stone figure was erected by Innuits—not to mark a boundary or to establish anyone's claim to this hilltop, but as a humanizing landmark for all of the people who shared this vast, undivided land.*

ries—the large areas of land they knew and depended on for their survival—and they might be prepared to defend their territories against others. In this sense, community property can be said to have existed long before individual property, but these community lands were still not understood to be property in our modern legal sense. The association between a community and its territory derived from continuing occupancy and use rather than abstract legal claim.

These were originally the attitudes of more or less nomadic people, hunter-gathers who depended on access to large areas of land and on community cooperation in utilizing these large areas for survival. Our traditions of individual property can be traced to the emergence of agriculture. Though agriculture was practiced on a communal as well as an individual basis, it did raise new questions about individual interests. When people till the earth, they mix their labor with the land, and it becomes natural to think of them as having a special claim not only to the crops they produce but to the land they have improved with their labor. They also, of course, tend to establish permanent homes on or near the land they work, and in thus occupying a piece of land permanently they develop strong interests in it as individuals.

Yet as civilization has evolved away from the life of the nomadic hunter-gatherer, the sense of land as a common ground has not been completely left behind. No matter how preoccupied people may become with property—with their rights to specifically limited pieces of land—they continue to identify with larger areas as well. They continue to see the land around them not just as so many separate pieces of individual property but as the domain of their community, and, as we have noted, they continue to be dependent on this larger area as members of the community.

Thus our view of land has been two-sided from the very beginnings of civilization. This dual view is inherent not only in our social and legal institutions but in the Judeo-Christian tradition that underlies so much of our sense of what is right and what is wrong in the world.

The Old Testament has a good deal to say about both individual property interests and the ways in which these interests must be limited. The earth itself, we are told, belongs ultimately to God. It was given to humanity to use and to enjoy, but it was a gift with certain conditions attached to it. People must care for the land entrusted to them: they may not waste it, use it up, or trade it away permanently for short-term profits. The individual's right to take value from the land is clearly limited by the interests of the community and the interests of future generations. Many of these conditions are described in the Book of Leviticus—including the provision that after every period of 50 years all land must be returned to its original owners, so that its value can never be permanently lost to the community: "The land shall not be sold forever: for the land is mine; for ye are strangers and sojourners with me" (Lev. 25:23). If a traditional precedent is needed for the way in which a community land trust limits the rights of individuals to sell the land they use, it can be found in this passage.

Today the Old Testament's balanced approach to land and property is emphasized by many religious leaders. As Pope John Paul II has said, "There is a social mortgage on all private property."

## PRIVATE PROPERTY IN AMERICA

Since the first European settlers arrived in America, individual property has had a special importance in American society—as was noted

South Dakota Historical Society

by Alexis de Tocqueville, the shrewd French observer of nineteenth-century America.

> In no country in the world is the love of property more active and more anxious than in the United States; nowhere does the majority display less inclination for those principles which threaten to alter, in whatever manner, the laws of property.

This American "love of property" has been analyzed in various ways, but central to any explanation must be the fact that America offered the *opportunity* for individuals to own land—as many had been unable to do in Europe, where there was no abundance of land to begin with and where opportunities for acquiring land were severely limited by the feudal traditions that still affected much of European society. Settlers came to this country with a thirst for land, and they came with a profound dislike of these feudal traditions.

Feudalism was a system in which rights to land originated at the "top" of society, with monarchs and with powerful nobility, and were passed downward to those who actually used the land but who could not hold it in their own rights. Thus, feudal arrangements worked against the idea of private property except for a very few powerful individuals. By the time of American settlement, feudalism had been undermined in Western Europe by the increasing wealth and power of an urban "middle class," but opportunities for individual ownership of land, especially in rural areas, were still limited by traditional feudal arrangements.

Access to American land was not limited in this way, and the Americans who founded our nation had no intention of allowing it to become so. In America, property rights were to originate with individuals, not with kings. And the fact that there was an abundance of unsettled land made it possible for many people to acquire property. As de Tocqueville noted, the American love of property was not limited to a landed minority; it was a love felt by the majority of Americans, and it was a love that did not need to go unsatisfied as long as the vast "public domain" west of the Appalachians was being divided up and made available, year after year, to individual owners.

The conversion of this federally owned public domain to private ownership was an event unprecedented in human history. This is not the place for a thorough discussion of this long, variable, and often controversial process, but two large generalizations can be made. First, it is true that federal land policies were in some ways designed and manipulated to serve the interests of speculators who used their wealth and influence to acquire large tracts of land at low prices. As settlement proceeded and the value of this land increased, such people were able to sell it at great profit, often without having contributed anything to its improvement, and sometimes without even having seen it. Second, in spite of large-scale speculation in land, millions of people who had previously owned little or no property did acquire land in America. There were genuine opportunities for ownership for the people who actually settled and developed the land. Though there was risk and often failure, a great many people's basic interests in security, equity, and legacy were served by this land.

These generalizations suggest two distinct elements in the American love of property. On

Kansas State Historical Society

*Crowd in front of a Kansas land office.*

the one hand, private property has been valued as a source of profit. The best use of land has often been seen as the most profitable private use. On the other hand, we have continued to see private ownership of land as the basis of individual security, earned equity, and legacy. The idea of a secure place where one can enjoy the fruits of one's own labor continues to be a major element of the American Dream.

## COMMUNITY PROPERTY IN AMERICA

In spite of the American emphasis on private property, not all of the public domain was turned over to individuals. America does have a tradition of community land, going back to earliest colonial times when New England villages transplanted the English tradition of the "common." Originally set aside as community pasture land, some of these commons, like Boston Common, exist today as public parks. The unsettled public domain also served frontier communities as a kind of common, where people shared access to fish and game and other natural products of the earth—until this land, too, was divided into private holdings and the frontier moved on.

Federal land-distribution policies themselves addressed the needs of communities. The public domain was surveyed into townships containing 36 "sections" of one square mile each. In each township one section was set aside to help the new town establish a community school. Either the section was sold and the proceeds turned over to the town, or the land itself was turned over to the town. In either case, the policy involved a clear recognition not only of the need for local political structures but of the idea that communities should be able to draw on the land they occupy to meet community needs. Also, as new states were formed in the West, tracts of land were turned over to them by the federal government to help them finance the services they would need to provide, such as roads and law enforcement. Additionally, the 1862 Morrill Act granted a total of 13 million acres to the states for the purpose of endowing land grant colleges, which have since become some of our major state universities.

In spite of provisions such as these, federal land policy was weighted in favor of individual rather than community interests. One major reason for this emphasis was, again, the abundance of the public domain itself. As long as there was so much public land waiting to be settled there was relatively little pressure to deal with the long-range interests of the communities that were being created. Even in the older cities, people could look to new opportunities in the West rather than address the immediate problems of overcrowded city neighborhoods. At least it could always be argued that those who really wanted to could make new lives for themselves in the West.

## PRIVATE AND PUBLIC PROPERTY TODAY

Now much has changed. Americans may still move restlessly from place to place, but there is no longer a great reserve of unsettled land offering new opportunities. In this century millions of rural people have been forced to leave their land and move to the cities, where they often remain as landless tenants, dependent on others for housing as well as for jobs and community services. The problems of both rural areas and cities continue to grow. We can no longer turn away from these problems—for if we do turn from one troubled community, we are likely to find the same problems in the next.

In trying to deal with these problems we

have had to concern ourselves with the ownership and control of land in more complicated terms than applied in the nineteenth century when the central concern was that of converting the public domain to individual property. The meaning of "private" and "public" property has changed and is changing in America today.

**Private property—corporate property.** To most people, *private* is a very attractive word. It is strongly associated with the privacy and security of the home. However, much private land in America is not owned by people who live on it. Most land today is concentrated in the hands of a relatively small part of the population (75 percent of the privately held land in America is owned by 5 percent of the private landholders). And absentee ownership is increasingly common.

Some absentee ownership is still relatively private. When the narrator of Robert Frost's poem says, "Whose woods these are I think I know. His house is in the village though," he is speaking of an individual member of his own community who probably owns a few acres of woodland, a few miles from home, as his private source of firewood. But most absentee ownership today is not of this sort. Today if you stop by a woods in Maine or Georgia or Oregon, or by any area of extensive woodland not owned by government, and ask whose woods these are, the answer is likely to be International Paper or Georgia Pacific or Weyerhauser or some other giant corporate landowner. If you then ask where his house is, the answer must be "anywhere and nowhere." He is not a private individual. He is not a member of any community. In this case, private ownership does not necessarily mean individual ownership.

Corporate ownership is not limited to forest land, of course. As indicated at the beginning of this chapter, large corporations own a major share of the country's most valuable land. They own large areas of agricultural land. They have vast mineral holdings, often in the form of mineral rights beneath the surface of land belonging to others. They own residential and commercial property (buildings and the land beneath them) as well as land that is held for its *potential* value as residential or commercial property.

But large corporations are not the only factor separating our popular notion of private property from the actual property arrangements that surround us. People tend to think of property as something indivisible—either you own it or you don't. Yet legally, property must be understood as a bundle of distinct rights which can be separated and distributed among a number of parties. Our woodlot owner, for instance, may sell the timber rights to his land, or the mineral rights, or water rights, or development rights, or any number of rights-of-way. He may sell (or donate) these rights to other private parties or to public bodies. It is therefore possible—and increasingly common—to have property in which private and public ownership are mixed.

**Public control of private property.** Even more common than mixed ownership is the mixture of private and public *control* of property. Many Americans still cherish the idea that you can do whatever you want with your own property. In fact, this has never been entirely true. As has been noted, our view of property has always been two-sided. Even in America, community as well as individual interests in property have been protected. It was Benjamin Franklin, not some latter-day land reformer, who said, "Private property is a creature of society, and is subject to the calls of society, whenever its necessities shall require it." In the twentieth century, as these "necessities" of society have become more complex, the ways in which private property is "subject to the calls of society" have increased. Particularly since 1926, when the U.S. Supreme Court upheld the constitutionality of zoning laws, public control of private property has become more and more extensive.

Our woodlot owner may not have sold the timber rights to his land, but if the land is on a flood plain he may be prevented from cutting trees by a law designed to protect the community from the effects of flooding and erosion. He may retain mineral rights but still be prevented from engaging in certain kinds of mining operations that would endanger the community or its environment. He may retain development rights but the number and type of buildings that he is allowed to place on his land may be limited by local or state land-use ordinances. There are, in fact, a great many things that he may not do with his own property.

In cities, the public control of private property is likely to be even more elaborate. Zoning laws, building codes, health and safety regulations, and regulations defining the obligations of landlords to their tenants are among the many ways in which private control of property is likely to be limited in today's cities.

**Private control of public property.** Forty-two percent of the land in the United States is owned by one or another level of government—most of it by the federal government. All of this land is considered to be public property, but there are real questions concerning who controls its use and whose interests are served by this use.It is not our purpose to argue that there are no public benefits from this land, and it is certainly not our purpose to argue that there should be no public land, but we do want to emphasize that, as in the case of private property, public property is not altogether what the name suggests.

First, it should be said that most public land is not community land in the sense of a village common. Most public land is controlled by government agencies that are relatively remote from the communities in which the land is located. Even if these agencies are models of uncompromising public service, the public they serve is usually much larger than the communities in which they hold land. As a result, in communities where a great deal of land is owned by federal or state governments, or even by big city governments, there is often frustration and resentment at the community's inability to control the use of, and draw value from, its "own" land. In reality, of course, most public land-management agencies are heavily influenced by private interests that want to use the land for their own profit.

In the western United States, vast areas of land are controlled by the Bureau of Land Management (BLM), an agency within the Department of the Interior. Former Secretary of the Interior Cecil Andrus has observed that in practice BLM seems to stand for "Bureau of Livestock and Mining," for it is primarily livestock and mining interests that benefit from this land. BLM land is not *owned* by these interests. They do not need to own the land. In fact, they are often better off not owning it but letting it be maintained for them at public expense and paying in return only a small part of the value they derive from it. The same kind of situation is common with land owned by the other major federal land-management agency, the U.S. Forest Service, and with publicly owned land generally. This private use of public land may or may not be, ultimately, "in the broad public interest." The point is that, although public ownership does preserve the long-range possibility of public control and benefit, the immediate benefits and often a large portion of control are enjoyed by private entities—many of them the same large corporations that are coming to control more and more of our private land as well.

**Housing, public and private.** Until quite recently, housing was assumed to be an entirely private matter. In the last several decades, however, there have been a number of public efforts to help people in communities where private initiative and capital have not provided adequate, affordable housing. Most of these efforts fall into three general categories: public housing developed and owned outright by government agencies, rent subsidies for tenants in privately owned buildings, and subsidized financing for the purchase of private housing. All of these have been important attempts to balance public and private interests; they have helped many people. But as long-term arrangements, all of them have serious limitations.

Government-owned housing is the most direct means of providing for people who cannot otherwise afford decent housing. But like other rental housing, it gives these people only limited security and does not allow them to build equity in their own homes. As in other situations where government agencies own property within communities, the problem remains that the occupants and their immediate communities do not usually control the use of the property.

Rent subsidies, like government-owned housing, offer no opportunity for equity and only limited security. They can provide crucial assistance to individuals for as long as the payments are continued, but they do not help either these individuals or their communities to improve their basic situations.

Publicly subsidized financing has been made available both for individuals seeking to buy their own homes and for developers of rental housing. Prospective homeowners who qualify for subsidized low-interest loans do receive security and equity, but most low-income people cannot qualify for these loans. Furthermore, when these homes are sold in the open market they may not be affordable for the next generation of prospective homeowners. To keep housing affordable for potential homeowners in a low-to-moderate income community, it may be necessary to provide subsidized financing each time a piece of residential property changes hands.

Perhaps the most basic problem with both rent subsidies and subsidized financing is that the public money put into them flows quickly into the hands of private interests—not only as remuneration for services rendered, but often as very large profits for landlords, developers, speculators, and other investors. Thus the value of public efforts to improve the community is not retained by the community. It passes to people who are for the most part outside of the community.

We do not want to suggest that these public efforts are wrong from the start. There is a tremendous need for assistance to communities that lack the resources to deal with their own increasing problems; private efforts are not likely to solve these problems, which are, in fact, often the result of private interests having diverted capital away from the community. The question is how to apply these subsidies so as to serve both the shorter-term interests of needy individuals and the longer-term interests of their communities. Today, as public subsidies are being reduced and those that remain are being closely scrutinized, there is a rapidly increasing awareness of the importance of this question. City administrators, in particular, are looking desperately for answers.

**In search of new property forms.** It is no longer meaningful to describe property as either public or private. As simple labels, the terms do not fit the complicated property arrangements we have been discussing, and they divert attention from the dynamic nature of these modern arrangements. If the problems facing American individuals and communities are to be solved, a new understanding of property is needed—an understanding based on a clear view of the ways in which individual and community interests are related. Only through such an understanding can property arrangements be designed to balance and protect these interests.

The need for new and balanced arrangements is urgent. Unstable economic conditions and the rapidly increasing costs of land, housing, and financing are putting conventional homeownership out of the reach of more and more people. In an effort to stimulate a flagging market, private real estate interests and lending institutions are attempting to reduce the purchase costs of homes through new kinds of property arrangements. With shared-appreciation mortgages, for instance, homeowners no longer receive the full amount of any increase in the value of their property; the holder of the mortgage receives part of it. Perhaps even more significant is the fact that some private developers have begun setting up landholding companies in order to separate the ownership of homes from ownership of the land and thus reduce the purchase price of the homes themselves.

These are piecemeal efforts designed to serve the interests of lending institutions and developers. They may be helpful to those people whose incomes and credit ratings qualify them as potential homeowners in today's market, but they do not address the basic problems of communities or the needs of people who do not qualify.

Some of these new arrangements have similarities to some of the distinctive features of the community land trust. But they do not represent the balanced approach that the CLT provides. Given current market trends, conventional access to land- and homeownership will continue to tighten, and the nature of ownership will continue to change. The question is no longer whether there will be new approaches to property. The question is whose interests they will serve.

CHAPTER 2

# The Community Land Trust Model

## WHAT IS A CLT?

A community land trust is an organization created to hold land for the benefit of a community and of individuals within the community. It is a democratically structured nonprofit corporation, with an open membership and a board of trustees elected by the membership. The board typically includes residents of trust-owned lands, other community residents, and public-interest representatives. Board members are elected for limited terms, so that the community retains ultimate control of the organization and of the land it owns.

The CLT acquires land through purchase or donation with an intention to retain title in perpetuity, thus removing the land from the speculative market. Appropriate uses for the land are determined, in a process comparable to public planning or zoning processes, and the land is then leased to individuals, families, cooperatives, community organizations, businesses, or for public purposes.

Normally, the CLT offers lifetime or long-term leases, which may be transferred to the leaseholders' heirs if they wish to continue the use of the land. Leaseholders must use the land in an environmentally and socially responsible manner, but the CLT may not interfere with their personal beliefs, associations, or activities. Leases are given only to those who will use the land. Priority in leasing is usually given to those whose needs are greatest, though individual needs must, of course, be matched with the capacity of a particular piece of land. Leaseholders pay a regular lease fee—based on "use value" rather than "full market value" of the land—but they do not need to make down payments and do not need conventional credit or financing to gain access to the land.

While leaseholders do not own the land they use, they may own buildings and other improvements on the land. In many cases the CLT can help leaseholders to acquire ownership of buildings and improvements by arranging affordable financing, and in some cases by organizing volunteer labor to assist in construction. Where the CLT has purchased property that includes existing housing, the housing may be sold to leaseholders over an extended period of time, either with the CLT holding the mortgage or through a land contract arrangement.

If leaseholders leave the land and terminate the lease, they may sell or remove the improvements which they own. Typically, the

Mary Beth Lewis

*House construction on land owned by Covenant CLT in Maine.*

CLT retains a first option to buy the improvements at the owner's original invested cost, often adjusted for inflation, depreciation, and damage during the ownership period. This property can then be sold to the next leaseholder. Thus, the first leaseholder is guaranteed equity in the improvements, and the succeeding leaseholder is able to buy the improvements at a fair price. No seller will profit from unearned increases in market value, and no buyer will be priced out of the market by such increases. Any increase in value that is not due to a leaseholder's efforts will remain with the CLT.

Thus, neither the CLT nor the leaseholder holds the land itself as a commodity. The CLT holds it as a basic resource in which the community and individuals within the community are acknowledged to have certain legitimate interests. In this situation the lease agreement becomes the specific, flexible, legal means by which the legitimate interests of both the community and the individual leaseholder are explicitly described and protected in accordance with the policies of the CLT.

## INDIVIDUAL INTERESTS

**Security.** CLT leaseholders have the same basic security of land use that in our society has been traditionally enjoyed only by landowners. The CLT provides and guarantees this security through the long term of the lease and a variety of specific provisions detailing the respective rights and responsibilities of the CLT and the leaseholder. As a nonprofit organization, the CLT does away with the common conflict between the profit motives of some individuals and the security rights of others, and it does so without bringing into being a remote "public landlord." As members of a democratically structured organization, leaseholders are directly represented on the CLT's board; they are assured that the lease agreement will be administered by a group which includes their peers. Should any disputes arise between a leaseholder and the CLT concerning the terms or performance of the lease, a process for arbitration is provided in which each will have equal standing with the other and a fair opportunity to present their cases to a jointly established arbitration panel.

The CLT makes both long-term land use and homeownership possible for people who could not otherwise afford them. These people enjoy security in both their long-term lease and their title to their homes. They have the assurance that they will never be forced from their homes, or from the land they use, by a landlord who finds he or she can make more money by using the property in some other way or by renting to other parties. Such security stands in stark contrast to the vulnerability of most renters, especially in a "landlord's market" of limited housing and high inflation, where leases become less available and their terms shorter, and displacement is a common threat.

As these same economic pressures weigh more heavily on many present and prospective owners of land and homes, they too may find greater security in a CLT. By joining together, CLT members assure themselves of more support from others and greater access to financing than they could command as individuals. As a group they can give support and assistance to one another, both in daily land use and property maintenance as well as in times of hardship and special need. With its broader financial base, the CLT may be able to reduce its lease fees or provide direct financial assistance at such times.

**Earned equity.** CLT leaseholders normally have equity for their own investments in buildings and other improvements on their leaseholds. Once again, this is a far better situation than that of ordinary tenants, who rent their housing and other improvements as well as the land beneath them, and have neither equity nor any way of developing equity. By law, any improvements made to land or housing by conventional tenants belong to the owner and remain with the property. The tenant has no permanent claim to them—no security in their use and no return for this investment—regardless of what they have cost her or him in effort or money. Yet most low- and moderate-income people have no choice but to accept the role of tenant. They cannot get the financing necessary to purchase property of their own. They are told by banks and other lending institutions that they cannot afford to own their own land or their own homes. They cannot afford an arrangement that would allow them to keep some of the fruits of their own labor and thus improve their own lot. Ironically, they can only afford to pay rent that will continue to rise as the market permits, and that, in a lifetime, may amount to many times what it would now cost them to purchase the property that they are renting. They are stuck with an arrangement that will not yield them one cent of equity. The CLT offers an alternative to this renter's dilemma.

Some renters of moderate income cling to the hope of owning land and a home. If their luck holds, if they can save enough for a down payment, if interest rates fall, if inflation is checked, this may one day be possible. The CLT can offer them an earlier and more certain opportunity to realize the benefits associated with ownership.

For those with sufficient financial resources to purchase land and housing, becoming a CLT leaseholder may represent an economic sacrifice. As leaseholders, they will build equity only through their own investment in improvements, not through increases in market value due to other factors. Such people may choose to become CLT leaseholders because of lower financing costs required through the CLT, or for the sake of the community of support and friendship which it offers, or out of concern for providing affordable properties within the community for future use by their children, friends, and others.

Kerry Mackin

*This building has been offered to the Central Roxbury CLT in Boston.*

**A reasonable legacy.** The CLT provides the assurance that not only the leaseholders' property (the buildings and improvements which they own) but the leasehold itself (the right to continue the use of the land) may be passed on to their heirs. Obviously the right to bequeath property means nothing to someone who has no property to bequeath. The CLT first makes it possible for many people who could not otherwise do so to acquire property that they can leave to their heirs. Children who have grown up in homes on CLT land can continue to live in the homes that they know and have helped to maintain, or they may realize the value of the improvements through liquidation of the estate. Children who have grown up in families that farm CLT land can continue to work the land in which they already have a real stake. The parents of these children can live their lives with the knowledge that the fruits of their labor will not wither when they die.

## COMMUNITY INTERESTS

Because a community is a collection of individuals, it is true that the advantages for individuals outlined above tend, at least indirectly, to be advantages for their communities. Certainly a community is healthier when its people enjoy security and can earn equity and leave it to their children. These opportunities are not only important in themselves but foster the development of supportive social relationships and services, providing personal benefits to community residents and reducing the burden on public agencies and appropriations. However, a community does have certain legitimate interests, as stated in the first chapter, that must be protected and balanced with the interests of individuals.

**Community access.** Increasing numbers of communities are suffering from a lack of access to their own lands and therefore a lack of security for present and future generations of residents. For many communities, access is severely limited by high rates of absentee ownership. This has long been true for communities with a substantial base of valuable resources. It is increasingly true for agricultural communities. It is true for urban neighborhoods where a large percentage of the housing stock is owned by absentee landlords, or sometimes city governments and redevelopment agencies, and is made unavailable or unaffordable for neighborhood residents. Always, it is low-income communities whose needs are most consistently neglected and denied.

When land, housing, and commercial developments are offered for sale, they are subject to a market which recognizes only the potential for profit, not the needs of the people whose security depends on this land and property. Confronted on the one hand by monopolization and absentee ownership, and on the other by tight credit and the financial barriers of a speculative market, communities are becoming more and more aware that their security depends on community acquisition or control of land.

The CLT can be an important tool for communities seeking to regain control of their own lands. As a flexible nonprofit organization it can utilize a variety of acquisition techniques. It can receive donations of land from people and institutions motivated by sympathy with the CLT's goals and by an interest in the tax savings resulting from the donation. It can arrange to acquire land from elderly people who want to live out their lives in their own homes but can no longer maintain these homes. (CLT acquisition can both help these people to stay in their homes and secure long-term community control.) In purchasing land, a CLT can draw on a wide range of both conventional and nonconventional sources of financing. It can utilize private grants and a variety of public grants and subsidies. It can borrow from conventional private and public sources of capital and from the growing number of individuals and institutions that are seeking socially responsible ways of investing their savings and endowments.

The lease fees that a CLT receives for the

use of its land can be utilized to acquire more land and, as the value of its accumulated resources increases, the CLT's ability to borrow in order to finance further acquisitions will also increase. Thus for the long term a CLT can become a powerful means of acquiring land for the community.

But the importance of the CLT is not simply as a community land-acquisition tool. It is designed to hold in perpetuity the land that it acquires, and to provide secure access to that land for individuals within the community—particularly for individuals who have previously been denied the access to and the benefits of land. For the land that it holds, the possibility of absentee ownership and monopoly is eliminated. In its leasing policies, the CLT typically offers use rights only to those who will use the land themselves, or to organizations that will manage the land for the direct benefits of community residents. Land is allocated only in the amounts required for use.

The CLT also provides a means of assuring that the benefits of access are fully realized by those to whom the land is leased. Its resources can be utilized in developing housing on its land, and in helping leaseholders to maintain their homes and use their leased land effectively.

It goes without saying that a community land trust cannot be the sole means of assuring access to land and resources for all members of a community. In this effort it must be a partner with government as well as with other community organizations. Public legislation is still extremely important. Civil rights legislation has prohibited discrimination in housing and in the workplace. State and local laws give tenants a greater degree of security—and in some cases help them to purchase their own buildings. Such laws represent real progress, though a great deal remains to be done in enforcing them. As an active community organization concerned with questions of access, a CLT can work effectively to see that such laws are enforced, and that further necessary legislation is passed. It can be particularly effective in these efforts if it works in cooperation with other community organizations.

**Community equity.** No element of a local economy is more basic than the community's land and natural resource base. On this land, and from this land, the wealth of the community and most of its individual members is produced. The community's land is the original "commonwealth." Yet present patterns of landownership and transfer often render land and resources and their economic value unavailable to the communities that occupy them. In these situations the economic benefits of community development are continually captured by a privileged few or drained away by outside interests. In other words, the community is deprived of its equity.

The community's claim to this equity rests on two principles: that the inherent value of the land is not of human creation and thus cannot rightfully be regarded as personal income for any individual, and that the appreciated value of the land (as opposed to the value of improvements made to the land) is the result of the activity and efforts of individuals, organizations, and public agencies throughout the community, and economic forces outside the community. By holding land permanently in trust, a CLT preserves for the community both the original, inherent value of the land and any value that is added to it by the efforts of the community or larger economic forces. Individuals who use the land may retain the value of what they invest as individuals, but they may not claim or remove for themselves what belongs to the community as a whole.

As outlined here these distinctions are necessarily abstract, but the importance of the CLT as a means of preserving community equity is not merely a matter of abstract justice. What is at stake in this matter is the survival of whole communities and the basic well-being of their residents. Contemporary problems such as those described at the beginning of this book are directly related to the loss of community equity.

The process of gentrification, for instance, stems from recent drastic increases in the costs of transportation and home heating and from changes in family values and lifestyles that make urban living newly attractive. Both of these changes have encouraged speculation by investors who themselves had no role in making these neighborhoods more attractive, but whose financial resources and access to credit allow them to profit greatly from them. In such situations the existing community retains little of the increased value of its land base, and may be powerless to prevent the large-scale displacement of its members.

Even more ironic is the grim paradox faced by many low-income neighborhoods—and by an increasing number of middle-income communities as well—when residents try to improve their community and the quality of their lives in it, for if they succeed in this effort they will make the community's land more attractive for speculation. By making their streets cleaner and safer, creating community gardens and playgrounds, renovating their homes, and building a stronger local economy, they may initiate or accelerate the market forces which will increase property values, raise property taxes and rents, and ultimately drive them from the community.

The loss of community equity is also a problem in rural areas, where the concern is often less with housing than with preserving the community's economic base. Many rural communities whose land has been cultivated by generations of family farmers are losing control of the land necessary to local enterprises. At the same time that new technology and marketing systems are driving small farmers out of business and depressing the economies of farming communities, the market value of land in these communities has tended to rise sharply as it is sought sometimes by agribusiness but in many cases by people seeking vacation homes, and by developers, speculators, and other outside investors. With the increase in market value, taxes often increase and resident landowners find that not only is it difficult to make a living from their land, but they can no longer afford to own it. As properties change hands, the community also changes. Social networks are broken. As land is withdrawn from cultivation, agricultural support services may be lost, further increasing the difficulty for those still trying to farm their land. The result may be increased control of the community's land by absentee owners. Community equity is again eroded.

In all of these situations, urban and rural, the CLT offers a means of preserving community equity. Any increase in the value of the CLT's land is retained and residents need not be displaced by real estate market forces. On

Kirby White

*New houses on land owned by Monadnock CLT in New Hampshire.*

the contrary, the increased value of the community equity held by the CLT can be used, judiciously, as collateral to leverage financing for further land acquisitions, to meet the needs of some of those who may be displaced from other community land. From this equity base the CLT will also receive direct income in the form of lease fees.

Lease fees represent the fair return to the community from those who have been given use of the community's land and resources. They reflect the value of the land as it appreciates through community investment and development. They are similar in principle to local property taxes which landowners now pay, but with a significant difference: The lease fee is based on the value of the land alone, with no consideration for the value of the improvements which the leaseholder may construct upon the land. In contrast, many local property tax structures not only tax improvements, but tax them at a higher rate, while undeveloped land and extracted natural resources are often taxed at considerably less than their full value. Such a tax structure tends to discourage constructive development and to encourage the monopolization of potentially productive land and resources.

Typically, the CLT makes an effort to base lease fees on the use value of the land, so that leaseholders are not penalized for land uses which are consistent with the interests of the community but are less profitable than the "highest and best use" of the market. This practice is similar to the "current use" taxation policies of many local governments, which allow farmers and owners of forest land to pay lower taxes on productive land that has a higher market value based on its development potential.

The CLT may also choose to lease land for less than a full-value fee, to facilitate access to the land by low-income families or to respond to a situation of personal hardship for the leaseholder. When the real value of its land has in fact increased, the CLT can afford to hold lease fees at a level below real value, thus providing a form of subsidy for needy members of the community and reducing their dependence on public assistance and subsidies. This use of increases in community equity to assist needy residents reduces the public expenditures necessary to meet the basic needs of these people; and, since many of those assistance funds have come from federal or state governments, it reduces the uncertain dependence of local communities on policies and appropriations beyond their direct control.

However, when government subsidies *are* provided to a community, the CLT can be the most effective recipient and administrator of these subsidies. Many current government efforts to subsidize housing and other facilities within a community can be likened to an attempt to help a hemorrhaging patient by administering repeated transfusions without any action to stop the bleeding. Transfusions of public money—in such forms as acquisition and development funds, or rent and interest subsidies—offer short-term benefits to individuals and communities, but the value of the subsidy normally passes *through* the community, often quite rapidly. It is not retained, so the transfusions must be repeated over and over again at increasing expense or, as is the current trend, the community must be abandoned to its own limited resources. Through the CLT, public funds can be retained within the community for repeated use with multiple effect. They achieve their original purpose and still remain in the community as a type of revolving fund. The benefits pass on to a succession of individual recipients, and the need for further transfusions is reduced.

**Community legacy.** Every community has a legitimate interest in its development over time and in the preservation of its natural environment for both present and future generations. At present, many critical land-use decisions are made by individuals and interests outside the local community, by people who are leaving the community, and by the operations of the commercial market. Through a CLT, while leaseholders have secure tenure and considerable freedom in their use of the land, decisions about redistribution and long-term community planning and development are made by the community.

Using its ownership of the land and its power to grant or withhold leases, the CLT exercises effective community control over development. Specific land-use plans can be formulated through democratic procedures and with expert advice where needed. The stability and character of established neighborhoods can be protected. Undeveloped land can be divided, appropriate building sites identified, roadways, sewage systems, and other facilities mapped out, all with a concern for the long-range effects on the land and on the community. Sites that are appropriate for commercial or industrial use can be identified, and the use of these sites allocated to enterprises that will offer long-term benefits to the community. Productive agricultural land may be reserved for agricultural purposes. Forest land may be preserved and the forest itself managed so as to provide a continuing supply of firewood, timber, and jobs for community residents. Limited fragile areas such as wetlands may be protected in an undisturbed state; other areas may be kept in a relatively natural state for recreational use or for aesthetic reasons.

Of course, one may ask why control of present and future land use should not be left to established local governments, which are already involved in such matters as zoning and community development. Zoning boards and planning commissions have made efforts to evaluate and regulate development in their own communities. But in many instances, the initiative is in the hands of the owner/developer; land-use hearings take on the character of adversarial proceedings, and the community lacks a firm economic base from which to offer or implement alternatives.

Certainly the CLT does not replace local government in these matters. It is itself, as a landowner, subject to prevailing regulations. Ideally, the CLT should work in partnership with local government for the good of the com-

Pam Roberts

*Betsy Corner and her daughter Lillian outside their home on land owned by the Valley CLT in Massachusetts.*

munity. In the complicated process of land-use planning and environmental protection, such a partnership can provide a valuable additional layer of protection.

However, there are some ways in which the CLT offers distinct advantages. Land owned by the CLT is removed from the market. Community control over its future development is direct and long-term; the potential for speculative gains is removed as an incentive for land acquisition and development. CLTs are also more likely to avoid the sort of "public versus private" or "owner versus regulator" controversies that often paralyze attempts to establish or implement public ordinances affecting private land. In planning the use of CLT land, community members are more likely to come together as equals, rather than adversaries, to do what is best for all concerned. The land is theirs; it will remain theirs; and ultimately, they all have an equal interest in it.

As an association of community members, the CLT may also be able to promote sound policies beyond the boundaries of the land it actually owns. The CLT's outreach and educational programs can contribute importantly to public understanding of land and development issues, and the organization can exert a degree of influence that its members as individual citizens may not be able to muster. The CLT can mobilize community members to respond to these issues, and can serve as a critical vehicle for community-based voluntary initiatives when there is not yet an effective public policy or a political consensus to support governmental action. This may be particularly important in low-income communities whose members typically lack the economic and political power necessary to protect the community from exploitation by outside interests. Even indirectly, a CLT can have a healthy effect on local politics as people realize that through the CLT they really can influence the future of their community.

## ROOTS OF THE CLT

The CLT is both a practical, multipurpose tool for dealing with immediate problems and an institution based solidly on deeply rooted and durable assumptions about the land and our relationship to it. As a specific model, the CLT is still new in America; the earliest developments in the CLT movement occurred only some 15 years ago, and only in the past few years has the model begun to achieve rather wide recognition. As a basic approach to landownership and control, however, the CLT model is very old—far older than the property institutions that surround us today.

In its basic approach, the CLT model stems from the ancient view of the earth as something naturally given, or God-given, to all people in common—something which, like the air above it, can never be owned in any absolute sense by individuals. The principle that people can never own land absolutely and the recognition of the duality of individual and community interests in land are deeply embedded in the Judeo-Christian tradition, as they are in other major religious and ethical traditions. In this sense the CLT is a deeply traditional approach to land.

In its approach to the economic significance of land, the CLT model draws on Henry George, the author of the influential book *Progress and Poverty* (published in 1880). George reaffirmed the principle that land is a common trust, and traced the origin of much of the poverty and social distress of his times to the maldistribution of land and the failure of society to claim its economic value. To remedy the situation—to make land available to all, and to retain for the community the value which it created through municipal development and services—George proposed having a single tax on the full value of land (known as site value, or land value, taxation), and no tax on private improvements. This "single tax," as it was commonly known, is comparable to the lease fees charged by CLTs, although most CLTs take other factors into account along with the value of the land in determining their fees.

Based on George's analysis and proposals, a number of "single tax enclaves" or communities of "economic rent" were established in Alabama, New Jersey, Delaware, Massachusetts, and other states. In the wake of the Depression, the social philosopher Ralph Borsodi (who is sometimes called the grandfather of the CLT) assisted in the development of several new communities based in part on Georgist principles. Some of these single tax communities are still flourishing, although in several instances an element of speculative gain has been allowed to creep into their methods of operation.

As a practical tool, the CLT has been influenced or inspired by more recent land reform policies in several other countries. Vinoba Bhave, a close co-worker and successor to Mahatma Gandhi, initiated a voluntary land gift program in India known as Bhoodan. In a series of long walks across the Indian countryside, Bhave and his companions collected gifts of land from landowners, and distributed the land to landless peasants. When it became clear that many of the new landowners soon lost their land—to creditors or the temptations of cash offers—the program was changed to Gramdan, or village gift. A Gramdan village acts as trustee of the lands, which are made available for individual use but not individual ownership.

The Jewish National Fund of Israel is a land trust on a national scale. Founded in 1901, the JNF is a nongovernmental public institution which predated the founding of the state of Israel. It currently owns most of the productive land of Israel and considerable additional land in both rural and urban areas. The land is held in trust and leased out for use. Improvements on the land may be owned by the leaseholders.

In Mexico and Tanzania, government land reform policies have given trusteeship of local land to village communities, which grant use rights to individuals but retain a degree of control, so that these individuals cannot sell the land and wealthy people cannot reacquire large landholdings.

In a number of western countries, local and regional governments have created land banks. A land bank is a public agency which acquires land, holds the land for varying lengths of time, and sells or leases the land to private or public parties for a variety of purposes. The technique had developed largely as a response to the perceived failure of planning strategies and land-use controls in regulating metropolitan growth, and in anticipation of the problems often associated with the rapid increases in land prices which result from development. Metropolitan land banking has been successfully used in Sweden since 1904, and in a number of other countries as well. In recent years rural land banks have been established in the Canadian provinces of Saskatchewan and Prince Edward Island to purchase and lease farmland in an effort to preserve family farming and reverse the trend toward greater absentee ownership of rural land. In the United States, public land banking has remained a relatively undeveloped technique, despite early programs of public acquisition and planning which played important roles in the development of such cities as Washington, Austin, Savannah, Detroit, and Chicago. Currently, public land banks in Puerto Rico, New York State, and Massachusetts are operating with an emphasis on job creation and economic development.

## COMPARISONS AND CONFUSIONS

The CLT bears some resemblance not only to the forerunners mentioned above but to a variety of other contemporary landholding entities. In some instances the apparent similarities are deceiving. In other instances they are real and significant. In any event, it is important to understand the similarities and differences, and to avoid the likely confusion.

**Real estate trusts.** A CLT is a trust in the basic sense that it holds land in trust for the entire community, but it is not a trust in the traditional legal sense. A CLT is a nonprofit corporation. A legal land trust or real estate trust, on the other hand, is a private entity with private purposes. It is a means of holding property for the good of certain specified "beneficiaries," and it is controlled by specified trustees. The legal land trust is a closed arrangement, while the CLT is open and democratic.

Real estate trusts may be relatively small, established to manage a fixed amount of property for the benefit of a very limited number of individuals; or, they may be quite large and commercially active. In the past few years, an increasing number of private land trusts (legal trusts and other legal entities) have been created by major financial institutions turning to land as a sound investment, and by private developers seeking to reduce the sales price of their properties, increase sales, and realize long-term speculative gains.

**Enclaves and communes.** There is a long history in America of intentional communities and cooperative settlements in which land is held in common. Some of these communities may be regarded as forerunners of the CLT, particularly those which have focused on land as a basic economic issue and have distinguished between land and human improvements on the land. For the most part, however, these communities have been enclaves, or private trusts created by and for groups of people who share a specific philosophical commitment or personal affinity. Their memberships are not open to all members of the larger communities in which they are established, and they are not designed to relate to the various needs and interests of these communities.

A CLT is not a commune. Communes, or intentional communities, may lease land from a CLT, or choose to put the land they already own into a CLT; but the two are not synonymous.

**Conservancy trusts.** Conservancy or land conservation trusts seek to prevent the development of certain undeveloped lands so that their natural characters can be preserved. They provide maximum protection for particularly distinctive or fragile natural areas and ecosystems. With a history in the United States that reaches back over a century, the local land conservation movement has grown tremendously in recent years—as environmental problems have grown and as the economic trends which now oppress individual families and communities also pose new threats to environmental protection efforts. Currently, there are more than 700 local conservation trusts across the country.

The organizational structures and land acquisition techniques of conservancy trusts and CLTs are often quite similar. Most, though not all, conservancies are local organizations, and many, though not all, have open memberships. Their obvious and principal difference lies in the goals of their land acquisition programs. Conservancy trusts normally withhold their lands from all human use except for limited scientific or educational field study and some carefully regulated recreational use. CLTs, on the other hand, are usually concerned with housing, agriculture, economic development, and other basic human land uses.

The purposes of these two types of trusts are surely not mutually exclusive, and should be complementary. Conservancy lands can offer recreational, educational, and psychological benefits to local residents and can often protect water supplies and other vital resources. CLTs frequently do set aside or protect natural land areas and they work to develop land-use plans to protect both social and natural characteristics of local communities.

Some communities now include both types of trusts. It is natural to assume that the two would be allies, and in some communities this is the case. In others, however, differences of orientation and strategy, or differences in the backgrounds of the respective memberships, have prevented them from becoming effective partners. As with many other environmental groups, conservancies are often associated (whether in fact or in the public mind) with more affluent communities, while many (though by no means all) CLTs are based in low-income communities whose members face a daily struggle to meet their basic needs. When communication between the two groups is weak, some community residents may see a conservation organization's concern with "wilderness" as disregard for human needs; others may worry about the effect of conservation acquisitions on property values, access barriers, and tax rates throughout the community.

But the real differences between conservancies and CLTs need not prevent cooperation or cause tension between the two. There is a strong basis for common effort, and each has resources which can be critically useful to the other. With current economic problems so often used to justify environmental compromises, environmentalists need a broader grass-roots base of public and political support, in local communities as well as on the state and national levels. CLTs can help to provide this kind of community support for conservancy trusts. At the same time, as economic problems raise traditional access barriers even higher for low- and moderate-income people, they and their local CLTs may need the help of the frequently greater technical skills and financial resources of the conservancy trusts.

**Limited equity cooperatives.** As legal entities, cooperatives differ from nonprofit corporations in that co-op members each own an equity share of the co-op's assets, while the assets of a nonprofit corporation cannot be held by or distributed to its members. In a housing cooperative, each member owns a share of the value of the co-op's building and land; in a CLT, members and leaseholders never have personal ownership of the corporation's land. Both organizations are democratically structured, with boards elected by their members.

The value of a traditional housing co-op's assets increases with the market value of its property holdings, and the value of each share appreciates accordingly. As with other real estate on the commercial market, this inflation in the price of co-op shares may threaten the future availability of its housing units to lower-income people. As a result, a number of co-ops—particularly those composed of low- or moderate-income people—have chosen to limit the value, or the potential for inflation in the value, of each member's share. These co-ops retain an option to purchase and resell the share of any departing member at the established value. These are "limited equity" or "low yield" co-ops.

Obviously, limited equity co-ops and CLTs share the same basic social commitments and function in a very similar manner, though they normally differ in the scale and diversity of their landholdings. Most limited equity co-ops include only one or a limited number of buildings, in a single location, and these buildings are limited to housing. The CLT, on the other hand, may own land throughout a much larger area and its land may be put to a variety of uses.

Limited equity co-ops do not necessarily separate the ownership of their housing from ownership of the land on which it is situated.

Normally, cooperatives own both in the traditional way, but the separation of landownership may serve the purposes of a limited equity co-op very well when there is a CLT that can take title to the land. In fact, there are important opportunities for collaboration between the two organizations.

When a limited equity co-op turns its land over to a CLT, or when it is established on CLT land, the CLT retains ownership of the land and its value, while the co-op holds a renewable lease to the land and its members each own an equity share in their building. The co-op will control the resale of shares and the admission of new members. Only in the event that the co-op proposes to sell the entire building will the CLT exercise its option to purchase the improvements on the land. Such an arrangement gives greater stability and security to the co-op. In a number of legal jurisdictions, a co-op's provisions for equity limitation cannot be made perpetual—thus the CLT's option provides an additional layer of protection, an assurance that these housing units will continue to be available to those who need them most. At the same time, co-ops offer a strong organizational base for CLT members, particularly those who live in multiunit buildings. Such co-ops can effectively provide both maintenance and personal services for buildings and people, and reduce the administrative burdens of the CLT. While each co-op normally includes a limited membership who share common circumstances, the CLT can link a number of co-ops together across the community, forming a larger "cooperative" of shared purpose and resources.

## ONE MODEL—A VARIETY OF ACTUAL FORMS

If a representative group of people involved in starting CLTs were brought together in one place, it might be hard to say what they had in common. They would be urban and rural people; low-, middle-, and upper-income people; farmers, factory workers, public officials, professionals, and unemployed people. They would be people concerned with preserving traditional communities, and people concerned with bringing about changes in afflicted communities. They would be philosophically oriented people with a theoretical interest in the question of property, and pragmatically oriented people looking for practical ways of meeting immediate needs. The group would consist of all sorts of people, from all sorts of communities. Members would have a common interest in community land trusts, but the CLTs with which they were associated would vary widely.

Because communities vary, CLTs vary both in the emphasis that they place on specific issues and interests and in the strategies and techniques that they use to realize their goals. CLTs in rural areas are working to provide access to land and decent housing for low-income people, to preserve family farms and farmland, and to facilitate sound, long-term land and forest management. Urban CLTs have formed to combat speculation and gentrification, to preserve and develop low- and moderate-income housing, and to maintain useful urban open spaces.

Some CLTs have been created in response to specific and pressing needs, others in response to long-range concerns with land-use planning and future management of community resources. Some are concerned with a strictly defined locality, others with a larger and less clearly defined area. Some have moved rapidly to acquire substantial amounts of land; some own only a little land and are moving slowly toward long-range goals; some have focused on the acquisition of partial interests in land.

CLTs also vary in the kinds of roles they adopt in relation to their communities and to

Robert O'Keefe

*A meeting of the Community Land Cooperative of Cincinnati.*

other community organizations. In some cases, a CLT may be *the* organization in a community that is concerned with giving people access to land and with helping them preserve and take advantage of this access. In such cases the CLT may initially play an active and varied role as the primary organizing force in the community and as the planner and developer for the land it acquires. It may even serve to enfranchise people in a community that lacks its own representative government, as in unincorporated rural areas and some urban neighborhoods.

In other situations, however, some or all of tnese functions will be performed by other specialized community organizations, and the CLT's role may be limited essentially to land stewardship—simply acquiring, holding, and managing the transfer of land, making sure that it is used appropriately and in the best interest of the community. In fact, the CLT is often initiated by other organizations that have been active in the community and have come to appreciate the underlying importance of landownership as a community concern. It may also be the initiator of other organizations as it comes to feel the need for them. The case studies presented in the next section of this book illustrate a number of possible community roles and relationships that CLTs may develop.

## PROSPECTS AND POSSIBILITIES

Community land trusts have many important capabilities; they can undoubtedly make critical contributions to the stability and responsible development of many very different communities, on their own and in partnership with other organizations. They are not, of course, a panacea. As with any other institution or program, CLTs hold a potential for failure or abuse. They are subject to the same organizational problems—problems of both initial organization and efficient operation—that other community groups face. While they are democratically structured to provide an opportunity for broad participation and a fair representation of the different interests in the community, their members can (like the members of other groups) become less active or vigilant, and the CLT can become less truly representative and democratic.

CLTs also must struggle within the limits of their resources: human resources, technical skills, and financial resources. The most obvious problem to date has been limited access to affordable financing for land acquisition and development. In the past several years, as interest in CLTs has grown, considerable progress has been made and new sources have been opened. But social problems are growing also, and in many communities CLTs may not be able to acquire sufficient resources soon enough to meet pressing human needs and to prevent displacement of the existing community. Also, while they are founded on traditional values and utilize conventional legal forms, CLTs may some day face legal or political challenges.

Nevertheless, the CLT is one of the best tools available to local communities in their efforts to meet land and housing needs with respect for both individual and community interests. CLTs do meet the strategic criteria required of a land and housing program for success in our current economic circumstances, and they offer greater security and long-term benefits than many other models. With the collective resources they assemble, the advantages of a nonprofit corporation, and their own base of collateral and income potential, CLTs can offer access and equity to people in need today. By limiting individual equity to the value of the leaseholder's own investment and retaining an option to purchase and resell these improvements, the CLT can insure that this land and property will remain available to those who need it, regardless of the forces of a speculative market. And ultimately, through its landownership and lease fees, a CLT will enable the community to re-create, and to retain, its own economic base.

As neither "public" nor "private" institutions, CLTs incorporate some of the best features of each with considerable flexibility. In some communities they may be able to build new bridges between individual and community interests, and may help to overcome traditional political dichotomies. As voluntary local initiatives, they may be able to effect community control and land reform without the controversies and uncertainties that surround new public land-use policies. In any case, CLTs offer incentives and opportunities for responsible community development, and discourage or prevent inappropriate development.

Implementation of the CLT idea in America is still experimental, still evolving. Most of the CLTs examined in the second section of this book are only a few years old. None of them can yet stand as proof of the long-term effectiveness of the model. One thing that they all do demonstrate, however, is the stimulating effect that the idea has had in communities where it is being tried.

Ours is a time in which most people feel helpless before the powerful and often paralyzing economic forces that affect their lives. They may sometimes benefit from these forces and sometimes suffer from them, but in either case they feel little or no hope of altering the forces themselves. As a result, they are often encouraged to look out for themselves, as individuals, as best they can—to take what profit they can get when and where they can get it, regardless of the effect on a community which they may expect to leave before long anyway. In this way community relationships are weakened. People are alienated from their neighbors and from their localities.

The community land trust offers opportunities for reversing this tendency. By joining together to form a CLT, people find that they can affect the economic structures that surround them. By seeking control of land *as a community* they can hope to benefit as individuals *without* sacrificing community interests. In fact, they can hope to benefit through promoting community interests. It is an exciting discovery—one that nourishes the roots of community life, that stimulates the side of human nature that needs community and wants to work for it.

It is true that in the long run CLTs must acquire significant amounts of land if they are to be seen as important institutions. For the present, however, we can best measure the success of newly formed CLTs not in terms of

total acreage or total housing units but in terms of the constructive community activity being generated. Without this sort of activity—and the sense of community that goes with it—no amount of institutional change can solve our problems. The open and democratic structure of the CLT is thus a centrally important feature of the model. A community land trust cannot succeed as something created merely *for* a community. It must represent an effort *of* and *by* the community. The case studies that follow are examples of this kind of effort.

# Section II

## Case Studies

## INTRODUCTION

In the first six chapters of this section we present case studies of six community land trusts. The first three of these are rural CLTs, the next three are urban. Different as they are in many respects, these CLTs are all located in communities where people have suffered from a lack of access to land or affordable housing, or where they have been threatened with the loss of such access. All six CLTs are centrally concerned with helping these communities to provide land and housing for these people. In the last chapter of the section, we offer three shorter case studies of organizations that are primarily concerned with the preservation of agricultural and forest land. We grouped these organizations together at the end of the section not because the issue of preserving productive land is truly separate from the issue of giving people access to productive land, but because as a practical matter the emphasis of these groups does differ from that of the first six, and because the organizations diverge in various ways from the basic CLT model.

In selecting the nine organizations presented here we did not try to choose the nine best or the nine most important or most inspirational. All

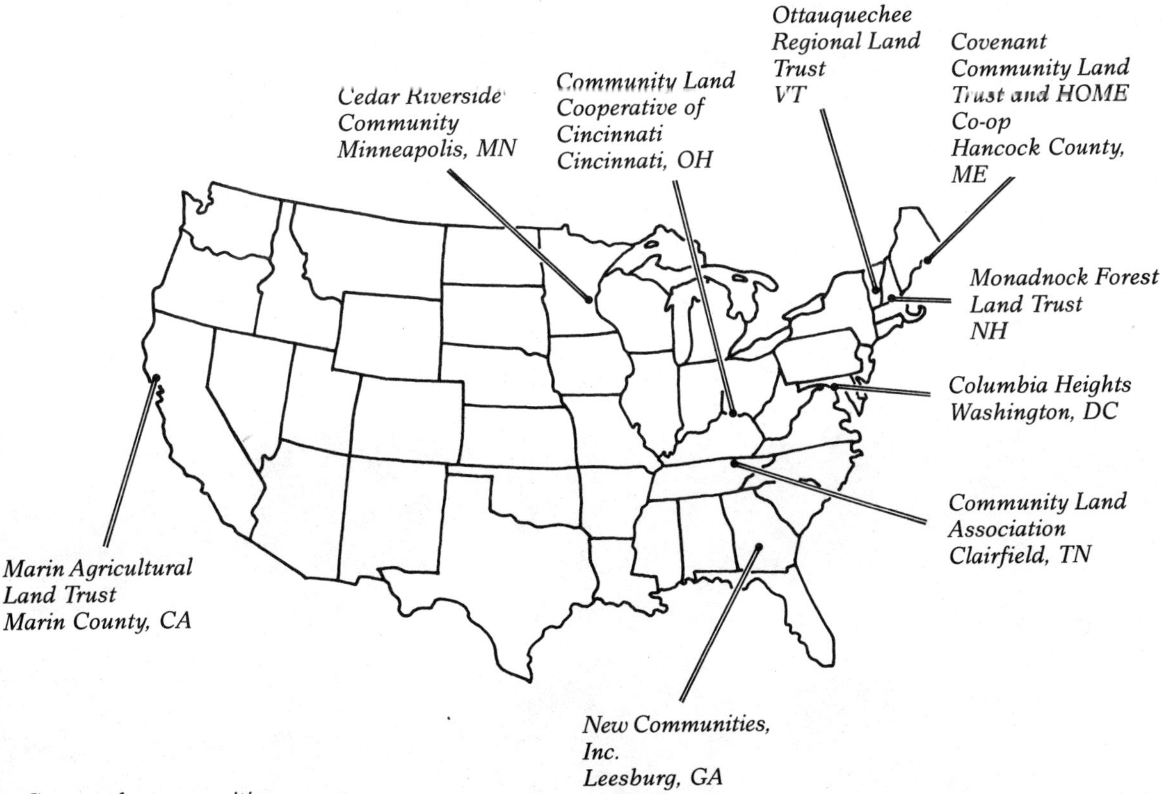


*Case study communities.*

of these organizations are interesting and important in their own right. Rather, our first concern in making this selection was to illustrate the wide range of CLTs that have been established in recent years around the country. Certainly there is much that is inspirational in these stories, but there is also much that reveals the complications and frustrations that these CLTs have faced. These are real people in real communities, working with limited resources to solve very large problems. The institutions they are creating are for the most part without precedent. None of them can yet be judged as a success or failure in any final sense, and it is not our purpose to try to judge them. It is our purpose to show what kinds of land-related problems they have addressed, how they have approached these problems, what their experiences have been, and what they feel they have learned from that experience.

Our intent was to let people tell their own stories; therefore the case studies consist primarily of edited excerpts from interviews. We supplemented these with editorial introductions, transitions, and summaries as they seemed necessary to present the stories clearly, but we strove to avoid the kind of interpretation that would involve passing judgment from a distance.

CHAPTER 3

# New Communities, Inc. Leesburg, Georgia

Incorporated in 1968, New Communities was the first American institution to be shaped by the CLT concept as it was being articulated in the 60s. Soon after its founding the organization acquired a single, very large tract of agricultural land near Albany in southwest Georgia—a total of 5,735 acres, for a price of $1,080,000. Most of this sum was borrowed. Since that time the organization has been forced to sell a portion of the land in order to reduce this very large debt and relieve the burden of annual interest payments; however, the remaining tract of 4,387 acres still makes New Communities by far the largest landholder among American CLTs.

Another significant way in which New Communities, at least in its origin, differed from most recent CLTs is that it was not created by a single, geographically limited community. In fact, New Communities was founded by a group of people—most of them widely involved in the southern civil rights movement—who were concerned with the land issue as it affected the security and opportunities of rural blacks throughout the South. As the name of the corporation suggests, the original ambition of these people was to acquire land and found new communities wherever they could throughout the region. In this ambition they were influenced by settlement policies in Israel, where a number of new communities have in fact been founded on land held in trust by the Jewish National Fund. However, the very large commitment that the group made to its single acquisition in southwest Georgia has effectively planted the organization in that one locality, so that today, as a practical matter, it can be viewed as an individual CLT.

Indeed, it seems to us that New Communities is an appropriate and useful subject with which to begin this series of case studies not only because of its historical significance but because it is in some ways a very simple and direct application of the CLT concept: The founders simply acquired as much land as they could, to make it available to people and to use it as a base on which to develop economic opportunities for these people. From the beginning, the fate of the organization has been tied to the initial acquisition. It is a situation that continues to hold both important possibilities and serious limitations.

The details of New Communities' early history have been published elsewhere (*The Community Land Trust,* International Independence Institute, 1972). The following interview with director Charles Sherrod concentrates on the founding of the organization and the opportunities and limitations that it faces today.

Dawn Makarios

*Charles Sherrod.*

*

*QUESTION:* You were associated with the early civil rights movement. Would you talk a little bit about the evolution of your thinking—of how you went from working for civil rights to this interest in land and the founding of New Communities?

*CHARLES SHERROD:* I guess the thing that prompted me to think in terms of self-sustaining capacity more than anything else was knocking on doors all over the country—whether it was in Mississippi, Alabama, Georgia, or in Virginia where I was born. I was hearing people say the same thing time and time again. "What you going to do if I'm kicked out of my house? You young people are talking a good talk—this is a good thing you're doing—but I live on this man's land, and what am I going to do if they take my job, take my house? What am I going to do with my children?"

This was when I was organizing in the field and that was a resounding echo in my mind for years and years, a question that I was never able to answer: Who shoulders responsibility when it happens? It wasn't as if it was a hollow question, because right there before my eyes every year were examples of people getting kicked out of their houses, people losing their jobs and all security, contracts dishonored, children not being able to eat. So what could I do? There they were. And there I was—with my commitment, but no power; my love, but no bread. And with all my tenacity and strength of mind, I couldn't employ nobody. So years of that—on dusty roads, thinking and talking, riding through and looking at people's homes on plantations, getting kicked off plantations myself, perilling other people's houses and sustenance myself, just being on their plantation. The only solution that one could come to would be that we have to own land ourselves.

Most of these people have gone to every known agency possible. FmHA [Farmers Home Administration] wasn't giving any housing loans—only for white people. The Federal Land Bank people weren't about to give any—they were controlled by the white farmers. The ASCS [Agricultural Stabilization Conservation Service] committees were all controlled by the white farmers, who were the same people who were part of the establishment which gave birth to the Ku Klux Klan. So we didn't look to the existing structures of government, or government programs. We didn't look to any of those programs for aid for our people to get land, or to reclaim land. Of course at the same time a lot of our people had land, but they had it heavily mortgaged. Knowing farming and knowing nothing else to do but farming, they continued to do what they knew—at the same time wondering why they were failing every year. Of course we all knew the reason was the structures that helped farmers stay farmers weren't geared to help *small* farmers to stay farmers, or to hold land, or to reclaim land.

Actually, during the same time, black *and* white farmers were losing their land. But my knowledge was of the black farmers, the small black farmers principally, losing their land. It wasn't just crop failure or a failure to get financing that was the cause—it was a calculated attempt to *take* land from these farmers. In many cases, we found people paying taxes on people's land and trying to gain land by adverse possession, and other methods: getting people that can't read and write to put their X here and there, and taking that land; getting people to become involved in some get-rich-quick scheme, and losing land *that* way. Through the years we have documented many of these instances where well-known figures have taken land from our people. Those instances are what led us to think in terms of how we could sustain ourselves, sustain people who were being kicked off their plantations. In our area there are large numbers of plantations. Absentee landlords in Michigan, New York, California; large companies that own large tracts of land; and now there's a big influx of foreign land-ownership.

*QUESTION:* Why were people kicked off the plantation?

*CHARLES SHERROD:* Well, technology for the most part. Large machines. Monster tractors come into our area and do 500 acres a day. So no need for small tractors and tractor-drivers to work. The big cultivators and pesticides and herbicides we have—there's no need for pulling weeds and that sort of hand cultivation.

## LONG-RANGE GOALS AND PRESENT NEEDS

*QUESTION:* What were your plans when you founded New Communities? What were the founding principles of the organization?

*CHARLES SHERROD:* One, to hold land. Two, to become self-sustaining, to have this land as a base from which we can allow small farmers some stability of their market. For production.

Dawn Makarios

*Combining the soybeans at New Communities CLT.*

Dawn Makarios

For information. For transportation facilities. The economics of buying together, for example, to bring down the price of seed, fertilizer, and these other things that people need to farm with. Utilization of a large tractor by a larger number of farmers to accelerate the efficiency of the farm unit. These kinds of ideas we had in mind.

*QUESTION:* Have these changed over the course of time?

*CHARLES SHERROD:* No, they're still here with us. Meanwhile, the overriding priority is holding onto this large piece of land. And nobody's come to our aid to help us to finance this land in such a way that we can put part of the money that we make into promotion and development of the land. We haven't been able to *do* any development. We haven't been able to pay any consultants to do any planning. We can't get the fellows in government to help us. We can't get grants—I don't know where we'd get the grants from now to do planning and development. We got the people, we got contacts all over south Georgia, people who'd be willing to live on this land, people who'd be willing to hook up with our kind of idea—'cause it's good economics to them. We got the facilities here that a good number of farmers could use. But we are pressured to talk about *survival,* and holding onto the land. Maybe our children will be talking about how they want to develop or divide the land or how they want to lease it—this part for farming, that part for industry, that part for something else. That sort of thing may be done by our children. But unless someone comes out of the woodwork it looks like we're going to be dealing with holding onto it and paying for it.

*QUESTION:* If someone did come out of the woodwork—if you had the money—what kind of housing would you like to see built?

*CHARLES SHERROD:* We've always wanted to build a large number of houses all at once, not one at a time. Part of the reason for not building just one here and there is that we were scared we'd put the stuff in the wrong place. But if we have some feeling that we're going to put houses in the same general area and if we get a big grant from somewhere, or some big financing to do a wastewater facility, then we could do 15 or 20 houses. Those kinds of things are not easily financed by an organization like ours. We have to get some help on that.

*QUESTION:* But you're thinking now of trying to build a house or two every year?

*CHARLES SHERROD:* Yeah, we gradually build that up, then we'll go after a large lump of money to tie them all together with one water source, one line for sewage, and one line for wastewater. We have those kinds of things in mind. But we still want to go into a *planned* housing development. We don't want to have it be just out here, out there, and out there.

*QUESTION:* You've had to sell 1,348 of your original 5,735 acres. What forced you to sell it?

*CHARLES SHERROD:* We had to sell it to hold onto what we had. We had an annual debt service of $203,000 and we were making about $100,000 clear on our farming, which was our only income. We had to raise the rest of the money every year. Some years I'd have to raise the total million dollars to refinance. Now we have to raise a debt service of about $150,000.

*QUESTION:* Who did you sell the land to?

*CHARLES SHERROD:* Private buyers. We held off as long as we could. People who were financing us were understanding—they thought they had our interest at heart—but they were also forcing us to sell so that they could get part of their money. They saw a great business opportunity to sell for $600 an acre land that we bought for $250 an acre. But we weren't interested in making money off the land in that way. We wanted to hold onto it. What people could have done, they could have cleared 1,348 acres for us. We could have clear-cut it, given them all the money for the trees and so forth. On top of that, in the next four years, we could have brought the land in production up to a sufficient level to satisfy them.

## THE COMMUNITY AND THE FARM

*QUESTION:* Are any people living on the land now?

*CHARLES SHERROD:* Just a few houses, five houses. The people aren't leasing, not legally. People who live on the land don't have to pay rent. They keep the houses up. The houses were already here.

*QUESTION:* And the people are also part of the labor force for New Communities?

*CHARLES SHERROD:* Yeah, for the most part. Everybody's not. Somebody's husband may be working and the wife not, or the wife may be working and the husband not. If you want to be part of New Communities, you can be. If you don't choose to be then you don't have to be, even though you're on the land.

*QUESTION:* Are you employing people from outside communities?

*CHARLES SHERROD:* Everywhere. There's no such thing as *outside* to us. We're not an *inside* community as such. We *are* a community, but we are not a concrete community.

*QUESTION:* How many people actually receive a wage from New Communities?

*CHARLES SHERROD:* About 14—that's full-time. In the summer we might have 25 or 30, kids, adults. When the grapes ripen there might be 20 or 30 people just at that.

*QUESTION:* How are your farm operations organized? How are decisions made on a day-by-day basis?

*CHARLES SHERROD:* It is a controversy among us as to whether or not we should have a farm manager with all the powers that a traditional farm manager has. So far, our creative approach has won out. We have a meeting with the farm committee and decide how many acres of this we're going to plant. Then the staff gets together

as a team during the week, apart from the farm committee, and speaks to the specifics for the week. Then, on Monday, when you're ready to go at it, our team leader—that's Sam Young—has the last word; he'll tell you to do this and you to do that. It may be what we said in the meeting and it may not be because, for instance, if it rains and we forgot to say in the meeting that if it rains we'll do such and such a thing, it may be different.

*QUESTION:* With your need to get as much value out of the land as possible in order to retire the debt, have you been forced to do things to the land or do farming in a way that you'd prefer not to?

*CHARLES SHERROD:* Well, there's not many other ways we can do farming. It's true, though, we wouldn't be planting certain crops right behind one another. We *are* forced, for example, to plant soybeans behind soybeans over and over—just because we have to make as much money as we can. We can't rotate with corn because corn is just too expensive a crop. We don't plant any more corn than we have to to feed our hogs.

*QUESTION:* You have a pretty sophisticated farming operation going here—a couple of hundred head of cattle, a few hundred hogs, 800 acres of soybeans, corn, grapes. Where do you get the technical know-how to put it all together?

*CHARLES SHERROD:* When we started out I didn't even know the difference between grass and hay. But we've learned. We've had people come in that knew about farming and technology. But in the long run it's cheaper to home-grow technology. You know you're going to need expertise; you know you're going to need it from now on. If you are an organization that plans to exist from now on, then you need to home-grow that expertise as much as possible, not rely on people outside. They say you've got to get a surveyor; then your architect's got to come in and he says you got to do this. A lot of that is just bull-jive. You can't tell me that with all the blueprints they've drawn up in this country, with all the kinds of buildings, you've got to pay somebody when all you've got to do is change this and add something here and put it up yourself. If you home-grow these guys, you can save that money a hundred times as you need that expertise again and again.

*QUESTION:* But it sounds like someone like Sam Young already had some skills when he came to you.

*CHARLES SHERROD:* He grew up on a farm. His father was a farmer and *his* father was a farmer. So he knows farming. And his whole family was in the movement. So he started working with us, all through the 1960s. He was on my staff. and when we went into the New Communities project he just worked with it. He also prints. He went to school in printing, two years. He's real smart.

Did I ever tell you about Boll Weevil? This guy was over in Calhoun County. I was invited over there to help with school desegregation. I kept hearing every day about Boll Weevil, Boll Weevil. He'd been working for this white lady, working on her farm. We hired him. We found out he'd never been to school, but he could fix diesel motors, special equipment motors, transmissions, alternators, anything. Boll Weevil! He's got about 36 or 35 children, got about 13 living with him now. I think the first house we're going to build is

Dawn Makarios

*Marge—deputy sheriff, storekeeper, midwife, taxi driver, and keeper of the old ways.*

Dawn Makarios

*Boll Weevil.*

going to be for him. He's got a large family. He lives in that block house there now.

Then there's Marge. She's a midwife, she's a taxi driver, she cures our meat, she makes soap—all those old ways of doing things that people knew to make ends meet. She knows leaves for various teas. All the old ways. She drives for over an hour a day to come here. She's also got a job as a deputy sheriff.

*QUESTION:* It sounds as if most of the folks who actually live on the land are there because of their commitment—beyond just a paycheck.

*CHARLES SHERROD:* Yeah. They understand what we're working for. They understand that it's not just them that's going to prosper from the land. It's going to affect thousands of people if we're successful.

# THE LARGER COMMUNITY; THE FUTURE

*QUESTION:* What kind of training have you been able to do for people who either work here on the land trust or who are from the wider community?

*CHARLES SHERROD:* First of all, we had to learn a lot of things ourselves. The things that we have learned, we've put to use. And by demonstration we've shown people what we know, and what we don't. So based on that, at various times in the past 10 or 11 years we've had seminars, workshops. We've talked about the various kinds of cooperatives that could be developed if people would get together. We've shown and talked about various federal guidelines that were current. And we've helped people hold onto some of their equipment. We've made small loans to various farmers where we could help them. We have sent some young people to school—through our contacts, and we have given some money at various times.

*QUESTION:* Will these students come back and work at New Communities?

*CHARLES SHERROD:* That's what we ask. Not many of them have come back, to be quite honest. But it's not too late, you know. For example, one student in Albany is a lawyer. We sent him to college, and helped him some in grad school. When he came back he didn't come and work with us in the way that we had asked him to—a year or two for free—but at the same time, we still have him. He's here; he's in the area. We can go to him and ask him this and ask him that. He is accessible to the people. So, while he didn't come back to us as an organization, he *did* come back home. That's good enough as far as I'm concerned. And there are other people. In our society, when a woman marries she goes with her husband, so we can look at some of our students we've lost by that. But they are in community-related, upgrading projects, so although we don't have them at *our* disposal, they *are* at the disposal of other poor people somewhere in the country.

*QUESTION:* How does the white establishment in this area regard New Communities?

*CHARLES SHERROD:* They're not opposing us now. There *was* a time when they *did* oppose us. They'd burn, and they'd fire at us; they threw one or two of us in jail. But at this point, they have accepted us. They even ask for our judgment on certain things. The white farmers lease cropland from us, year by year. People come and fish on our land, for a minimum fee—white people.

*QUESTION:* If you had it to do over again, do you think you would start out with as much land as you did or do you think you'd start out with a little less?

*CHARLES SHERROD:* No, I'd start out with as much as I could start out with. See, I've heard those arguments too. But, well, I say it like this: How many groups in the country have as much land as we have? See? Chances are we wouldn't have had it either if we hadn't been lucky to have a certain group of people together at one time, a certain kind of people together at one time.

*QUESTION:* Other people around the South, other organizations haven't tried to organize community land trusts. Why?

*CHARLES SHERROD:* Land costs money. It's something our folk don't have. If they did have, they'd buy land for themselves. They'd buy a car for themselves; they'd build a house for themselves. So also there's got to be political commitment, a deep philosophical underpinning, to move toward these kinds of goals, given our upbringing. There's got to be a commitment to the movement, a broader movement for a better life in our country.

*QUESTION:* Have you talked with some of the black farmers in the area about putting *their* land into trust?

*CHARLES SHERROD:* Not really, not legally. That'll come later. I've talked with some farmers, some people who have land, about willing their land to us when they die—instead of letting it go to certain individuals who really have no interest in it but to sell it and move to New York. These happen to be their children, so it's a hard thing to get over to somebody. But there *are* some people who, when I've asked, find it easier to understand and identify with the idea.

*QUESTION:* Is there still resistance to the idea of *leasing,* rather than owning land?

*CHARLES SHERROD:* Not resistance—why should I resist if nobody's imposing it on me? But if you try to sell that idea—the idea of personal ownership is more intriguing because we've grown up in a kind of greedy society. So you've got to overcome 20, 30, or 40 years of that kind of indoctrination. That's why anybody making the kind of moves we're making has to be *committed* to another way of life. Because we are continually shown the glittering of the individual approach, individual ownership, individual rising from rags to riches. *That* is success in our society. We have to write a *new* way of success, new criteria for success in our society.

*QUESTION:* And this is what you're trying to do with New Communities?

*CHARLES SHERROD:* This is what I'm trying to do with my children and my other contacts and people who are part of New Communities.

*

Dawn Makarios

*Leaving to disc the land at New Communities.*

CHAPTER 4

# Community Land Association Clairfield, Tennessee

Like New Communities, the Community Land Association in northeastern Tennessee has been concerned with meeting the needs of a rural community where absentee landownership has kept many local people without land and without economic opportunities. In its origin and development, however, the Community Land Association contrasts sharply with New Communities. Rather than beginning with a single large acquisition, it has evolved slowly out of an extended period of community development activity in the Clairfield vicinity.

The person who introduced the CLT idea in Clairfield, Marie Cirillo, had been doing community development work in the area for more than a decade before the land trust was started. When it was eventually established in 1978, there was no preexisting agenda. The first actions were to acquire a 17-acre piece of hilly undeveloped land, at no cost, from another nonprofit institution, and then to bring together some of the people who lived near the land to consider how it might be used.

The Community Land Association has now progressed to the point where it may have a very significant impact on the community, but we are presenting its story here not only because of its recent accomplishments. The story provides a striking view of the ways in which absentee landownership affects an Appalachian community. It also offers a very good example of the kind of patient, persistent community organizing that is essential to the success of a community land trust in a situation like this one—and in most situations.

Clairfield is a small community near the Kentucky border in northeastern Tennessee. It lies at the center of a mountain valley that includes numerous other small communities scattered throughout an area of some four hundred square miles. The valley is isolated by mountain ranges and by an interstate highway that cuts across natural routes of travel. This isolation, together with the fact that the valley lies partly in Kentucky and includes parts of four counties, has made it very difficult to attract and coordinate government assistance for local services and development.

The economy of the area has been based almost entirely on coal mining, but today the deep mines that once provided jobs for local people have been replaced by strip mines, which provide very few jobs. Migration out of the area has been extremely high. For those who remain, the sources of income are few: a few jobs in strip-mining, a few public service jobs, a few small groceries and gas stations, welfare, and black-lung benefits.

It was the high rate of out-migration that first brought Marie Cirillo to the area. In 1949, Marie had joined the Glenmary Home Mission Sisters, a newly formed group of Catholic sisters organized to work in the rural South. During the 50s and early 60s she worked in southern Ohio, Kentucky, Virginia, and West Virginia. Then in the 60s she moved to uptown Chicago, where she worked in a neighborhood consisting mainly of white migrants from the South, particularly from Appalachia. By the time she returned to the southern mountains she had left the sisterhood, but the Catholic diocese of Nashville agreed to provide some financial support for her to do community development work in the Appalachian region of east Tennessee.

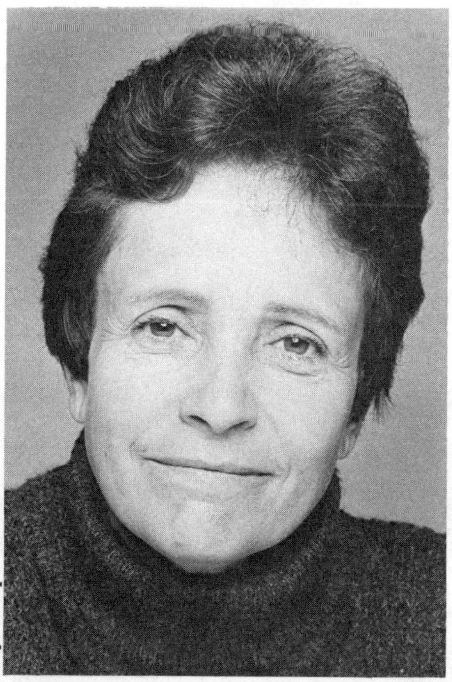
Roy Gumpel

*Marie Cirillo.*

*

*MARIE CIRILLO:* After four years of living in uptown Chicago and seeing how many of the people were really not satisfied living in the city, I became more curious about why people couldn't live in Appalachia. So in 1967, I moved back. I wanted to find a community that was suffering from the problems, and when I started looking around, the postmistress here, who was then in her early fifties and had been postmistress ever since she was 19 years old, told how this community once had 12,000 people—and at that moment, in 1967, the population was 1,200. I thought this is indeed a place that has suffered from out-migration.

It was obvious that the business was coal. No one had jobs but coal. They talked about the collapse of the mines, and they had stories of John L. Lewis and union organizing in the deep mines and the coal camps. It was the coal industry that I figured had something to do with the out-migration. And I tell you, when I settled in here, I was just like a stubborn mule, I made up my mind that I wasn't going to leave here until I found out what was wrong.

I also came with an attitude that government wasn't going to give any input. And even though I was employed by the Catholic Church, the Catholic Church in this area was very small so I knew there was no way the Catholic Church was going to put any major input into this area. I realized that we'd get nothing done unless we found something that the people wanted to do enough to roll up their sleeves and sweat a little to get the job done.

*

Dorothy Metzler, a board member of the Community Land Association, has lived in the valley for "about 35 or 40 years, in and out," as she says. Her husband was a miner, and the family "followed his jobs."

*

*DOROTHY METZLER:* In 1956 we went to Ohio when it got bad down here. I had the five kids then. So we went north and stayed up there a while. My husband worked in factories. But it's just as bad. When you leave and go with your whole family, you can't find nowhere to live. We lived for three months in a little three-room house that wouldn't be big enough for two people. And you don't have any money up there, no more than we would have if we'd stayed down here and just piddled around.

We stayed up there, I don't know, a long time. Then I brought the children and came home, and my husband followed us. We came back without a job, so it was rough, really. We'd sold our cows, pigs, chickens, and everything we had, when we went up there. We had to get money to go up, and when we came back we didn't have anything, and it was rough starting over again. But anyhow, we made it.

People who are raised in the mountains, I don't know—there's no place like the land. You just don't like to live in the cities. You couldn't give me a city, if I had to live in it, and I think most mountain people feel that way. They get disgusted, discouraged, whatever, and they think, well if we go somewhere then we'll have more money than we have here. But when you get there you

Robert O'Keefe

*Dorothy Metzler at home, with Patsy Brown.*

find that it's not true, because you got to spend money to survive anywhere you are. And you don't make that much money. When you leave, you're better off to have stayed home in the first place. I think everyone who's been brought up on this land can survive in these mountains without very much money. They wouldn't even have to depend too much on the coal companies if they had enough land to survive on. Because you can take six or eight acres of land and you won't have to go to the grocery for anything except sugar and coffee.

*

## LAND AS AN UNDERLYING PROBLEM

In the years following Marie's coming to Clairfield, the people of the valley organized the Model Valley Development Council to promote community organizing and community development activities. As they explored a variety of possible projects—clinics, local crafts, new industry, and day care for children—they found themselves repeatedly facing the same problem: the difficulty of acquiring land for their purposes.

Four major corporations owned over 40,000 acres in the valley, including about 80 percent of the Clairfield community. These lands were readily leased to strip miners, but they were not made available to organizations interested in promoting community development.

*

*MARIE CIRILLO:* Well, it was interesting. The first clinic was here in Clairfield. At the time there was a community action agency, and they had negotiated with the big land company for an old abandoned school. They remodeled that building and used it for the clinic and as a community action center. But in a year or so, the people became very disenchanted with the community action program. They had gotten enough help and were feeling good enough about their successes that they wanted to build their own clinic. This was the first inkling of the problem, because the people started looking around for a half acre of land and couldn't find any land.

Then the development council wanted to get some industry started. We formed a community development corporation, and we worked for several years figuring out how to set up our own business. And once again, we had to go looking for land—and it took months and months before we could find a piece of land. None of the companies would sell us any land. At one point, the only thing the American Association [the largest landowner in the valley at that time] offered us was a big slag pile, and they said we could have a six-year lease if we would clean up the mess. And there was no way we'd clean up that mess and there was no way we'd invest in a factory when we only had a six-year lease.

At any rate, the community development corporation finally got hold of a 30-acre piece of mountain land from an elderly lady whose son was on the board. The clinic people asked for a half acre, and the clinic was the first thing that went up. Then we got the factory up [a factory for making wooden pallets] and we kept it going for three years before going bankrupt. We had 15 people working there. They were young married men, and you knew if they didn't have that they'd either be on welfare or making the trek up to the city. So we felt bad when we went bankrupt. One of the major reasons we went bankrupt is that the land companies would not allow us access to any of their timber. That told me something else about an industry like mining that really can't deal with any competitive industry.

A little later, a woman wanted to organize child care, and she went through the same song and dance trying to find a piece of land. What she got was maybe three-quarters of an acre, from Texas Instruments, with a five-year lease. So again it meant that there was no way she could invest in her own building. She had to get one of these mobile units and pay rent with an option to buy. Then it got burned down by some strip miner one night. The first three years that I was here—with the lean-tos and garages and churches that we would find to operate in—seven places got burned down. And anybody that knows anything about Appalachia knows that that's a traditional way of getting rid of the unwanted.

Anyway, it was pretty early in the game, probably about the third year I was here, that I began to get this sense that the reason nothing can happen in this community—and probably the reason that nothing can happen in Appalachia—was because of the land problem. It was a few years after that when a reporter in West Virginia did a study which showed that 75 percent of the whole state was owned by outside corporations.

That really was weird to me, knowing that these companies own that much land and if you tried developing industry, or housing, even as simple a thing as a clinic, that they couldn't even let loose of a half acre. So I thought, there must be a lot of reasons why companies aren't about to let anything go that would help community development. And I guess I came to understand that strip-mining is so environmentally damaging—and they need so few workers—that the more people that are around, the more people are going to complain. They just didn't need the likes of anybody living in the area. So I really got hung up on this landownership issue. It has obsessed me for years.

*

Dorothy Metzler comments on landownership and land taxes.

*

*DOROTHY METZLER:* Nobody has the rights to land, no one person more than another one. It was made for man, and man covers a lot of territory. Really though, here, all of this land—this valley and all these mountains through here—was never bought from nobody. They just came here and taken over.

They liked to get somebody drunk and get him to sign a paper. It was pretty common. And some of them traded their land for a rifle. My grandfather did that. Or maybe somebody gets behind a couple of years worth of land taxes and they don't know that the land company's paid their land taxes up. And then if they don't go and pay their taxes, then the land ain't theirs. There ain't a thing they can do.

The land companies don't pay their land taxes on all their land. Oh, they pay some. They have to pay some. But they don't pay taxes on all the land they claim they own. And they don't *own* all the land they claim they own. But they don't pay, not too much more taxes than a lot of us pay. Because we just don't have anybody who would care enough to say anything about it and they just get by with it. I guess a lot of people is afraid if they kick up a fuss they won't have no job. You got to keep your mouth shut. And when it comes to keeping your mouth shut or letting your kids go hungry, I guess most people going to keep their mouth shut.

*

## FORMATION OF REGIONAL AND COMMUNITY LAND TRUSTS

As Marie became more aware of the land problem as the root of many other social problems, she found that a number of her former Glenmary Sisters were experiencing the same thing. One of the sisters happened to meet Bob Swann, and she later spread the word that land trusts might be one answer to the land problem. In 1970 a group of Appalachian activists, Marie among them, collected enough money to bring Swann to Knoxville for a workshop on land trusts. However, it was not until seven years later that the time seemed right to promote the idea in the region.

*

*MARIE CIRILLO:* As an organizer I don't do an awful lot of initiating. I try to get a sense from the people, and once I think there's enough folks with it, then I project this idea and we can rally around it. In 1977, we had terrible floods throughout central Appalachia, and people got together in Mingo County and were trying to think of what to do, and this was really a turning point in the mentality of organizers all over Appalachia, because at that point—while they were blaming some of the flooding on the fact that there is so much strip-mining—they also started talking about the problem of land. There are few enough homes, few enough house sites, but when half of those homes got washed away, and people couldn't get loans to rebuild because their land was on a floodplain, and they started scrambling around for more land, and there wasn't any land—this was a moment when people from all over the region could get together and say there is a problem here. So when I came home from that first meeting after the floods, I just thought, this is the time to get the land trust started. What I did then was go to some of my friends in West Virginia, Kentucky, Virginia, and Tennessee, and I said, "What would you think about us forming a regional land trust?"

*

The regional trust was incorporated in Tennessee as the Regional Land Trust for Appalachian Communities. It had two basic purposes: to promote the formation of community land trusts and to achieve the kind of expertise and strength that would allow it to deal with large landowners and public agencies. Its policy was not to develop the land it acquired but to make it available to community land trusts as they were formed. One of its first acquisitions was a 46-acre piece of land in Rose's Creek Hollow near Clairfield.

About the same time, Marie initiated an effort to acquire a 17-acre piece of land farther up Rose's Creek and to establish a local trust to hold it. Here she describes that effort.

*

*MARIE CIRILLO:* This was a piece of land in Rose's Creek Hollow that was settled by the Metzler family, but they had sold that 17 acres to the folk school—another nonprofit group we'd formed here—and the family moved further up the mountain. Well, after two years everything at the folk school got burned down, and the fellow that ran it got discouraged and went off, Earlene Duce. That land sat for something like seven years, doing nothing, and I kept thinking, we've got to get this land back—how do we do it? Legally I knew that if a nonprofit group ceases to be, the assets are supposed to be turned over to another nonprofit group. Then I found out that if there's no corporation functioning, the original incorporators are the people legally responsible. Well, those three people were Dorothy Metzler, Earlene Duce, and another woman up the mountain, Bonnie King. I spent a good bit of time with Dorothy Metzler, explaining what a land trust was. And I talked to Bonnie and she had no problems with the trust. Then I said to Dorothy, if Earlene would be willing, would you be willing for this to shift hands? I felt very sensitive about this, because she had lived there and she had turned it over, and now her children were all grown and married and I'm sure they could have used more land. Well, she said yes. I got in touch with Early, and finally we did get the land turned over to the trust.

The next thing we did was pass the word around in the community, that this land was now in the hands of the land trust, and we explained what a trust is. Then we had a community meeting down here at my house. We invited everyone up Rose's Creek. [About 65 families live in Rose's Creek Hollow.] We said if you feel you need a little extra land, or if you have any teenagers that you think will be needing land, you might come, and have them come down. About six people attended, and we had some of the people from the Community Design Center who listened. [The East Tennessee Community Design Center is a group of public interest architects and engineers, located in Knoxville.] It was an interesting group, and they talked about their needs, and the tightness of land, and the company land, and all the stripped land. It was just a good dialogue. And it was

*A view of the CLA's 17 acres, scarred by strip-mining.*

wonderful, because it was a first opportunity to call community people together where the only thing we would talk about was land.

At the second meeting, the Community Design people brought back a map of that land and presented a plan of where they might put the houses—we figure there are four good house sites—and where the garden, and the roads, and how to least tear up the land. Just dealing with those things together, with community people and the architects and engineers, was a wonderful learning experience.

It was fascinating to me that we were coming up with a whole different agenda than anything I had ever dealt with in this community before, because the agenda before was how to get child care *service,* how to get health *service,* but now they were talking about cows and pigs and corn and houses and woodwork and timber for fuel. They were talking about another whole set of things, and you realize that you can't talk about those things unless you have land. A community in Appalachia can't even dream about things, other than a welfare system, unless they have land.

In fact, as an organizer in the mountains, I put very little value on organizing the clinics, for instance, because once the professionals get in, the community people are reduced to nothing but janitors for the building. There is quite a mystique around the professionalism of doctors and lawyers. I mean, if a doctor says this is the kind of pill, nobody would ever say, "No, this isn't the kind of pill." But if a *surveyor* says that's where the mark is, the family will say, "No, it's not, it's over here."

When you organize around land, there's no mystique. People have eked their lives off the land, and they know not only what's on top of the soil, but what's under it. They know what stones are good for what; they know where there's spring water. Even professional people are dependent on their knowledge. So when they started this relationship, between the architects and engineers and the local people, it was a good, open dialogue. Then when the professionals came back and explained certain things, it gave it a new dimension. Sure, they knew that place was swampy and this place was steep—but just to have laid it out so we could start a process of planning was sort of a new experience. But nobody had any problem relating to it or participating in it.

*QUESTION:* How was the CLT idea itself accepted?

*MARIE CIRILLO:* I don't think there's any way you could go into a strange community and talk people into that. In a sense, I paid my dues here before introducing the concept. I think after 10 or 12 years, enough people had tested me out and felt that they could trust me, so that when I raised the question of a trust, they were at least open. Some of them—like Lester that came in a few minutes ago—didn't like the idea at first. Lester thought, well I'd rather have my own land. But we have worked together and I've shared some of the major issues of land, and he is now open to the idea of a trust. I don't think we would get that idea across in Appalachia unless there was first a trust level with the person who's telling you about it.

## PLANNING AND RESOURCE MANAGEMENT

*MARIE CIRILLO:* We have used the Community Design Center's plan to the degree that we put the road where they said, and when we look for house sites we'll go to those spots they suggested. There's a local man right up the road who has a dozer, so we asked him to put in the road. The land trust had $2,000 it had gotten from the church last year, and they spent $600 of that on the survey, and then they spent about $500 on that dozing job. We didn't do the dozing job as completely as the Community Design Center suggested. They planned a big circle at the very end for cars to turn around in, and it would have leveled out that land for housing. We were hoping at the time that we might have gotten more money and could do it right. But we just felt that it was important to cut the road through so people could at least see where the homesites were.

The Community Design Center identified two acres of level land as a garden area. In the fall and wintertime, the men say that's a wonderful place to target shoot, and the last time we had a meeting here, I asked Lonnie if he thought it could be used for gardening in the summer and for sporting events in the winter. He didn't think so; he thought gardening would make the ground too muddy. So that will be interesting. Already, on the only flat piece we have there are conflicting interests for the use of that land; and how we resolve that will say a lot about how we're going to be able to resolve conflicts over land use in the future.

*

In the spring of 1981, the Community Land Association did establish a community gardening program, utilizing the piece of land Marie has mentioned. A VISTA position was awarded to the trust for someone to oversee the management of resources on its land, and on April 1, Harold Osborne, a local farmer and member of the CLA board, went to work in this position.

In 1981, a one-quarter-acre vegetable garden was planted, tended, and harvested by Harold and several local volunteers. The initial plan was to sell the vegetables in some sort of market stand. However, this proved unnecessary since Rose's Creek families who were unable to have gardens of their own purchased all of the vegetables—and would have purchased more. A larger garden is planned for 1982. The group would like to plant 5 acres—some on the 17-acre piece and some on the 46-acre piece—if the money necessary to develop this much garden land can be raised.

Currently a root cellar for storing garden produce is under construction on the 17 acres. A session on growing herbs and possibly establishing an herb growers co-op has been sponsored. A solar food dryer has been constructed. Generally the gardening program was the focus

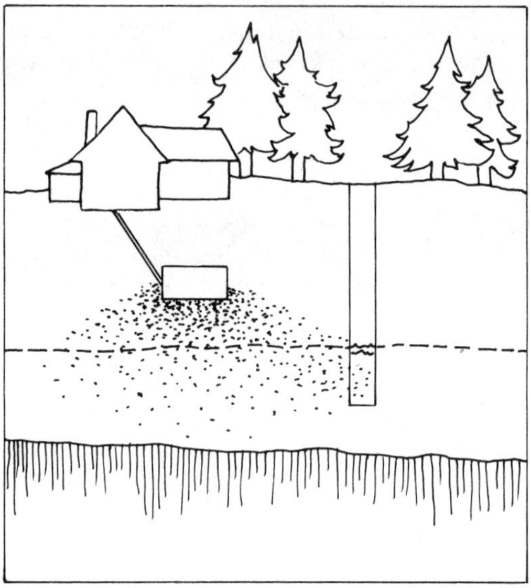

*Excerpt from "Land Use Guide," prepared by the CLA with help from the Tennessee Valley Authority. This guide may be cited in lease agreements as the CLA's standard for appropriate land use.*

of a good deal of interest and activity in 1981.

Through another resource management project, firewood has been culled from trust lands and distributed to low-income people, particularly to elderly people who are unable to cut wood for themselves.

## HOUSING DEVELOPMENT AND POTENTIAL LEASEHOLDERS

The Community Land Association members were eager to lease portions of their 17-acre holding to people who would build homes on them. They also wanted to plan and lease homesites on the 46 acres available to the local trust through the regional land trust. They are now closer to realizing both of these goals than they were in the spring of 1981 when the following remarks by Marie Cirillo were recorded. Because it seems useful to emphasize some of the problems that a CLT may face in its early stages, we are including these remarks before describing later developments.

*

*MARIE CIRILLO:* At one point we had two families interested in leasing land to build on. One man was so interested, he started putting the footings in for his house, and then he called us up one day and said they had found a house closer to LaFollette and since his wife had a job in LaFollette and his son was going to school down there it just made more sense to settle there. But we weren't sure if they bugged out on us because it was looking too complicated. We didn't have a paper ready for them to sign. We were still trying to work out the details of the lease agreements and make sure everything about the land trust was clearly explained.

I think we all have a feeling at this point that we're going to have to get some money to build some houses and then make those houses available to people to rent with the option to buy, because we can't see many people going up there and starting to build their own house. Every once in a while, in my weaker moments, I'd give a thought to a trailer. You know everybody hates them in principle, but somehow they have been the only viable solution. People get trailers because they don't have time to fool with negotiating for a house. It's difficult in an area like this because you can't just call up your local construction company and get a house put up in three months—you have to create the construction company. If you're busy and if you don't know how to do that you just go buy a trailer. Then, if it's on permanent land, people tend to stabilize it and before you know it there's a porch and an added room on the back. It's not the best thing in the world, but if you keep waiting for the best you never get anything.

But I think the route we're going to concentrate on is model houses—warm, dry, low-cost houses. The simplest thing would be if we had a model house that the community could talk about. When we cut the road it created a little bit of excitement, and when we thought these families were going to build, everybody knew about it—and then they saw it didn't happen. Well, I've been here 15 years and eventually things do happen, and actually when they don't happen too fast it's better in this community since you don't raise a lot of suspicions.

*

In the fall of 1981, more has happened. Plans have been made to build 5 houses on the 17 acres and/or the 46 acres available from the

Robert O'Keefe

*Patsy Brown (left) and Carol Osborne, in the community garden.*

Mike Brown

*Harold Osborne digging potatoes in the community garden.*

regional trust. This is the first phase of a long-range plan calling for a total of 15 houses. The houses will be small, economical, conventional structures which owners can add on to at a later time if they wish.

Current plans are to utilize a basic design that originated with the Warm and Dry Housing Project of the Federation of Appalachian Housing Enterprises, Inc., a federation of non-profit organizations that are involved in providing affordable housing for people in the Appalachian region. The Warm and Dry Housing Project grew out of a particular concern with rapidly rising construction costs, the cutting back of federal subsidies, and the fact that most conventional housing, even with federal subsidies, was not affordable for low-income people. Part of the problem has been that the Minimum Property Standards (MPS) that are applied by the Farmers Home Administration and the Department of Housing and Urban Development in deciding whether to finance low-income housing do not allow for very small basic houses. In other words, to qualify for low-interest FmHA loans, low-income people must build a more elaborate house than they can afford. A long-range goal of the Warm and Dry Project is therefore to demonstrate the practicality of building small "starter houses"—in an effort eventually to get the MPS amended to allow housing on this model to receive government financing.

The plans to build such houses on land trust land also involve a local association known as the Mountain Women's Exchange, an association of organizations in the Clairfield community which includes, among other groups, the land trust itself and the Home Makers, an organization that offers training in house construction and repairs. The Home Makers will provide on-site supervision and low-cost labor—to be supplemented by other local volunteer labor—for the house construction project. It is expected that prospective leaseholder/homeowners will also be asked to contribute some labor on their own houses.

A financial plan has been developed to cover the total cost of the five houses. Capital is being sought primarily from several religious institutions. As of this writing, a grant for $12,000 and a loan for $20,000 have been received, contingent upon the rest of the financing being secured. Total cost of the five houses, including site development and other necessary expenses, is estimated at $97,551. Monthly mortgage payments under this plan would average $110 per family for 30 years.

Mike Brown, who has worked for the Community Land Association in a staff position since the spring of 1980, comments below on the housing project.

*

*QUESTION:* Has any decision been made on where to locate the houses—on the 17-acre parcel or the 46-acre parcel?

*MIKE BROWN:* A final decision hasn't been made on that. I anticipate that there probably will be houses built on both parcels. It would seem to make sense to utilize the 17-acre parcel because of some of the site work that has been done already. One of the drawbacks of that parcel is that it's isolated about three miles back off the main road. We have now organized a utility district in this area, and there will be a public water supply available in the valley probably by next fall, but it will not go up the road that far, so one of the problems for any housing up there is how to deal with water. The public water will come up as far as the 46-acre site, so the houses built there will presumably have public water.

*QUESTION:* The 46-acre parcel still belongs to the regional trust. If houses are built on it, would it be turned over to the local trust at that point?

*MIKE BROWN:* Yes. In preliminary discussions with Marie and some of the other members of the regional board, they seemed to feel that once we've developed the plans for it the land will be turned over—either completely or at least the parts that are developed.

*QUESTION:* Do you have leaseholder/homeowners lined up for these houses?

*MIKE BROWN:* It's a process that we're involved in right now. Our strategy has all developed within the past couple of months, so we do not have five families lined up to move into the houses, but we've set it as a priority for ourselves to continue the process of looking for local families—not only so that we can be secure in knowing who the families will be but so that they can have a part in actually doing it.

We participated in a large-scale survey of housing needs in the area—surveyed some four hundred families for their current housing position, as well as their preferences and their ability to pay: their income, their monthly housing costs now, etc.—and this has given us some clues as to families that we can go back to now that something specific is developing. Also, we've got just a really fine group of local people involved in directing this effort—the local board themselves—who have some very natural connections, through kin, through friends, and they know any number of people who are in the situation of needing affordable housing.

*QUESTION:* So you feel there will be a good deal of interest?

*MIKE BROWN:* Oh, undoubtedly. There just doesn't seem to be any question at all on the part of the board that once something specific for new single-family housing is made available there will be any difficulty in getting families to live in them. Our housing situation is that critical.

*QUESTION:* You have a long-range plan for 15 houses. Is that a firm plan for the land trust itself to develop that many houses?

*MIKE BROWN:* It's firm in terms of our commitment to it. We've not developed the specifics of how to do that. Our belief is that if we can get the process rolling we can begin to tap into sources of permanent financing that are necessary to build more houses.

One of the things that we've discussed is that at some point there will probably be a committee within the land trust board itself that will deal specifically with housing. The board doesn't want to become so consumed with the business of housing that they lose sight of the other issues that it's necessary to deal with as a community land trust—locating more land, negotiating with land companies, working on gardening and small farming possibilities—so I suspect over the course of time we'll identify a couple of board members who are currently playing a real active role in developing the plan for the initial five houses, who then can work with perhaps some other community people on developing a plan for the other houses, so that the rest of the group can begin to look at the other concerns of the trust. We haven't wanted the land trust to evolve into a local housing development corporation, but initially, for the first houses, the land trust will play a role as developer. We will probably contract out the construction of the houses to the Mountain Women's Exchange, the nonprofit group that sponsors the Home Makers.

## MARIE CIRILLO: OVERVIEWS

*QUESTION:* It seems important to emphasize the difference between community land trusts and what are sometimes called enclaves. How do you see this difference in Appalachia?

*MARIE CIRILLO:* There are many people who come to settle in Appalachia because of some affinity to the land, and they find a few more people who are anti-nuke and against all this environmental destruction and want to care for the earth. The land trust idea is very attractive to them. They'll commit themselves to work together, and once they find 50 or 60 acres, they'll buy it and put it in trust. They call it a trust, anyway, but it's better described as an enclave. It's one piece of land, and five or six people. It becomes noticeable to the community, and they're looked on maybe as odd or different or they're talked about as a commune.

But I don't think that it should just be a select group of people who get a little piece of land in a community and, once they take care of themselves, forget the larger problem. I think as the Regional Trust tries to encourage groups to form community land trusts, it's going to have to be to the broad interest of the community.

*QUESTION:* You mentioned that after the floods in 1977 there seemed to be a common consciousness of the land problem in Appalachia. Have other efforts developed out of that consciousness?

*MARIE CIRILLO:* I came home from that meeting committed to deal with a community land trust. There were others who were committed to getting the facts on landownership and land taxes. There were also people who were working on nonprofit housing, and they had come up with so many problems with land for housing that they decided that what they needed was to have a bank, where money could be accessible to community groups to buy land. So we've had, within the region, these three things going at the same time—the land trust, the land bank, and the land study. The land study, for a while, was off on its own a little bit, but now that the study is done they're starting to talk about strategy. So we're concerned about the economics, we're concerned about the facts, and possible tax reform, and the concept of trust—and if we can keep those three groups interacting in a healthy way, and if each one of them can get a certain constituency in the region, then we have something mounting that could lead to something.

*QUESTION:* Would you comment on the role that religious organizations can play in dealing with the problems in Appalachia?

*MARIE CIRILLO:* Every church feels some obligation to do something in terms of social justice. Some do more than others. Churches tend to get more involved where they have a lot of people, where they collect the money. A big parish will collect money and send it overseas, but it's hard for Americans to think of Appalachia as a third world, a mission. Appalachia has its problems, and it has pretty clear ideas about solutions, and I think if the church got involved and were supportive of some of the activities, they would be well rewarded for their involvement. But I basically feel much stronger about the responsibility of government. I really get angry when government doesn't do what it should be doing in an area like this. I feel that one of the most sacred obligations of government is to protect the lands for the citizens, and when I don't see government doing that, I get most upset about them. So I guess if I were going to strike out at any institution that's not doing right, it would be the government.

*QUESTION:* Do you see any risk that the land trust might eventually become too independent from the community—lose the community involvement that it has?

*MARIE CIRILLO:* I think the only way to protect the corporation from internal deterioration is for the public to be able to get to it and shake it up. I think if we start out right, and do enough good to start with, the community will appreciate that. It's sort of like TVA [Tennessee Valley Authority]: In the early days it was set up so that a board of three men had total control. When they were doing good things, everybody thought it was wonderful and didn't mind that control; but as soon as things started turning sour and people were getting disturbed, they wanted to get at TVA, and there was no way they *could* get at them. So I think we should build into our organization some way that citizens can get at us. And I think if the community ends up being bad, and wants to get at us for the wrong purposes—well, that's got to be. It's risky because at this point community people could be harassed by the absentee companies to do certain things, like they've done in the past. Oppression is pretty real in Appalachia. So it's risky, but nothing else has worked. To me this seems like the best thing to take a risk on—and taking the risk is better than just watching things continue the way they are. So I guess even if there were certain things that I'd worry about, I still see it better to try than to live as a nation of people alienated from our land and cut off from our roots.

*

CHAPTER 5

# Covenant Community Land Trust and HOME Co-op Hancock County, Maine

The case of Covenant CLT is similar in a number of ways to that of the Community Land Association in Clairfield, Tennessee, described in the preceding chapter. Both organizations are in rural areas where people who once drew their livelihood from the land now have very limited access to land and very few economic opportunities. Both grew out of local efforts to provide employment and basic human services for low-income people. Both have concerned themselves with providing appropriate, affordable housing and have encouraged self-sufficiency in food and fuel production.

In other ways, however, Covenant CLT is unique. It is distinctive in its close relationship to the other programs of its parent organization, HOME Co-op (Homeworkers Organized for More Employment), which is itself a unique institution. Covenant CLT and HOME Co-op together are notable for the intense commitment of the people who have developed them, for their success in attracting large numbers of volunteers from outside the area, and for the tangible results they have produced from limited financial resources. HOME's dedication to helping people who are struggling to subsist on the fringes of modern society has given it a strong identity, and a sense of community that is quite separate from the established governmental, social, and religious structures in the county.

One significant issue that has emerged from this independent commitment is the question of whether the CLT should utilize government programs—particularly those of the Farmers Home Administration—in providing low-income housing, or whether it should do things its own way and look elsewhere for financial support. Both approaches have been tried. The resulting experience has involved both frustration and real accomplishments and should be of interest to anyone concerned with housing problems. This is the story of a very active organization. Its record is worth examination.

Hancock County lies along the east side of Penobscott Bay. It is an area of economic contrasts. Most of the land along the coast is owned by affluent people—and in some cases extremely wealthy people—or else by speculators or developers who will eventually sell it to such people. Most of the inland part of the county is roadless, wooded land, owned by several large paper companies. A large majority of the permanent population live in extreme poverty. It has been estimated that 91 percent of the population could not qualify for bank mortgages. Sister Lucy Poulin, founder of HOME Co-op, comments on the economic situation.

*

*LUCY POULIN:* We have two major employers—the St. Regis Paper Company and the Jackson Lab. The Jackson Lab is highly specialized, and the St. Regis Company employs, at a very good wage, about 800 to 1,000 workers. Then there's a whole class of people who rake blueberries, dig clams, or they do domestic labor for the wealthy. They are people who at one time were part of farm families—and those farm families no longer exist—and that's the group of people that we work with. It's our understanding they represent about one third of the population of the county, which is about 40,000 people.

*QUESTION:* What sort of farms used to be here?

*LUCY POULIN:* Well, it would be like my mother's farm—I grew up about an hour and a half from here. They were a diversified farm. Like on our farm, there was a potato patch, apple orchard, and the cider mill. They had cows and pigs. And I know a couple of farms here were goats and sheep. They wooded some. They usually made their own lumber. There were many small sawmills. The marketing was very decentralized, which may have been one of the major differences. One of the things we have observed is that government policy centralized the marketing and controlled access to capital. And there was the onslaught of the tractors. Tractors just cannot farm those old farms with their steep hillsides.

*

Sister Lucy came to Hancock County in 1968 and, with several other Carmelite nuns, established a hermitage in the town of Orland on U.S. Route 2. The nuns supported themselves at the hermitage by sewing shoes for a Bangor shoe company, which provided similar employment for a number of other women in the area—until, in 1970, the company closed. Below, Lucy tells how this situation led to the founding of HOME Co-op, and how this effort led to other efforts on behalf of local people—including, finally, the creation of a community land trust.

Kerry Mackin

*Sister Lucy Poulin.*

*

*LUCY POULIN:* We had about 30 local women sewing shoes in the area, and what happened was, because of the lack of protective tariffs, the shoe business was cut out, which cut off our income. So the craft cooperative emerged out of the need for home work. For us, that meant the freedom to stay in the home, and for a lot of other women it meant the same freedom—women who were housebound with children and such. And so we decided, why don't we make the crafts and sell them? We bought the little farmhouse, which is now the office, and just opened the doors and filled it with crafts from the same women who had been sewing shoes. We sold on consignment. We were told it was impossible, but for us it has worked out well. [In its fiscal year ending in 1981, HOME had sales of $172,432 and distributed $107,910 to its crafters.]

What happened was that everything grew rapidly based on people's needs. We got to know the people better through selling the handcrafts. Every time the checks went out more people came to us. We began to observe that people couldn't read; we began to observe that people were being told that if they burned wood they couldn't get insurance; and we began to observe the problems of social security with people who lack the ability to check it out. It was just part of what we now understand is our stratified class system. The poor are totally out of touch with all institutions, including the church and social workers.

So we started a school where we stress reading and writing, and also other things—like this week we're having something on draft horse husbandry, which is of great interest to me; last week we had sheep. And we get into gardening and wood harvesting and forest management and so on. And then the day care center started in the school, because the mothers who came to school were housebound and we began to understand that a woman who was out on a back road with children and didn't have a car or telephone was extremely socially isolated. So she could come to school and bring her children. And then we discovered that the children sometimes had nutritional and health problems. And so the deeper we got into it the more needs we saw, and everything that the co-op does has emerged out of a really very obvious need that the people have had.

One of the classic examples is Project Woodstove. We truly found an elderly woman who had adjusted her life by cutting off her phone, among other things, and was burning charcoal briquets because she could get them in the grocery store and she could handle it. Sometimes the elderly physically can't handle the wood. So we have a program where we cut and split and deliver wood, and check their stoves, put the wood in

*HOME Co-op's buildings on Route 1 in Orland.*

Kerry Mackin

their woodsheds—and discover that they need other things too. And so now we have several elderly where we have friends to help them—members of the co-op community have friends who they visit and shop with.

And then at the same time the craft programs developed out of a need to produce better crafts and to teach crafts. Then the hospitality house emerged out of another need. We just could not provide space for hospitality for people, whether it was visitors and volunteers or people who had needs—and we all *do.* People come here who are highly skilled to help—their needs are often as great as those we normally help. So we have a hospitality house down in Bucksport. The main residents have been women and children who have been abused, but we have had other people who just happen to have no place to stay.

*QUESTION:* How many members does HOME Co-op have?

*LUCY POULIN:* Well, we have maybe 1,500 people who would fit into broad categories of membership, and in our organization participation is membership—if you're a volunteer, if you're an elderly person getting firewood, if you go to the school, or if you're a crafter, or sell produce. It's a very broad base. But the figures are misleading, because if people associate that with the clear conceptual sense of the cooperative it doesn't fit.

*QUESTION:* What led you to think about a community land trust?

*LUCY POULIN:* Well, as the co-op has grown out of the needs people have had over the years, it came to people's minds that one of the most serious needs was housing. We began to understand that houses and space affected so much in the family. If you have four kids and two parents in a little, teeny trailer, the potential for violence just rises radically. We now have two or three years experience, and realize it's a major thing to build houses—it's no easy task—so it's a major operation that we've taken on. But it's also the most critical thing to families to have this space.

*

## CREATION OF THE COVENANT COMMUNITY LAND TRUST

Dick Tracy is the HOME staff person who oversaw the founding of the Covenant Community Land Trust and acted as its coordinator through its first several years. Originally from New Jersey, he and his wife Cathy and their children now have their own homestead outside of Bucksport. Cathy, an experienced social worker, directs HOME's outreach program, dealing with the most immediate and pressing needs of individuals in the area. Dick, before the creation of the land trust, was involved with HOME's Down HOME Farming Program, which promotes self-sufficiency by such means as supplying hay and grain at cost to its members, and by educating its members in various phases of small-scale farming. Also, with the help of Heifer Project International, it is able to provide quality farm animals to members at no cost, receiving back from each the first female offspring, which can then be donated to another member.

Self Help Family Farms (distinct from Down HOME Farming) is the name HOME has given to its effort to settle low-income families, as leaseholders and homeowners, on land where they can enjoy a degree of self-sufficiency. The Covenant Community Land Trust is the actual landholding institution at the center of this effort.

*

*DICK TRACY:* In the beginning I was asked by Lucy to serve as an advisor on the agricultural aspect of the project. Then we got a CETA slot for a project coordinator. I thought maybe I could do something as coordinator to get it to move a little, so I took the CETA job. That's when I became fully involved in it.

I had done the animal program for a while, so I knew some of the people who were involved, and of course my wife knows quite a few people, so we were able to give the land trust an impetus because of our contact with the people and because I had the experience to get organizational work done. Hopefully it will carry on by itself with the people that are involved in it.

*QUESTION:* What advantages do you see in the CLT idea for this area?

*DICK TRACY:* We saw in the philosophical concept of the land trust a vehicle to help low-income people. A low-income person cannot afford to buy a piece of land. But several of them together—pooling their resources, and with a little bit of help from people like ourselves who've had some experience in raising money—could get the land, and then we could *hold* the land. Part of our experience with low-income people: We would get a very good goat for a person, say, but once they had paid back the first female offspring they would turn around and sell the goat and buy two or three scrub goats, because it was attractive to them to have more quantity than quality. The concept of the land trust is, of course, that the land does not get sold. If the people go in with that concept from the beginning, they cannot be tempted to turn around and sell the land and put themselves right back where they started.

So we go in with the straightforward and say, "The land will never be sold, it will be available, you can leave it to your children, it is the same thing as ownership, except you cannot sell it. The house is yours, you can sell it, but you must sell it back to us at what it cost. There's no profit-making. That's what we are trying to get away from." They can get their equity back, but no profit, because we have seen that housing costs have gone up to the point where they are pricing poor people out of housing. Because everybody's got to get his bucks. Interest rates make it impossible. For example, I know someone who has about 25 acres, paid $8,000 for it and borrowed the money from the bank, and by the time he ends up he's got to pay $12,000. Now when that person goes to sell the land, he has to get at least $12,000 to break even. And maybe he wants to make a couple of bucks, so maybe he's going to sell it for $14,000 or $15,000. This whole problem keeps pushing it out of sight for poor people.

*QUESTION:* Once you were organized, what was your first project?

*DICK TRACY:* When we started out we thought we were going to do a real bang-up-whizz job of it; we were going to supply all sorts of housing. The word got out and we had these 20 applicants in looking for housing. But we could not come through for these people because of the resistance we ran into on the local level. That's going to be three years ago. We were incorporated in June of 1978.

See, we were going with government funding, and the government insisted on large numbers of units. In fact, the name Self Help Family Farm comes from the Farmers Home Administration, Self-Help TA 625 grant. We had 700 acres of land in Penobscot under option. The owner was going to finance it, and we had a suitable 50-acre parcel for about 12 to 18 units, so we went to the local planning board to get an application. Their attitude was negative. I went back the second time; they were a little bit more friendly, and I said we're still going for it, and I showed them a plan that we had drawn. Next thing I knew they had declared an 18-month moratorium on subdivisions. We lost the money we had put down for the option on the land. We had all those 20 applicants, you see, and we couldn't build any houses. We had the financing arranged; we had the 625 grant all approved except for the rigamarole with the planning board. I think one of the problems we ran into when we went to Penobscot was we had to do 6 buildings, and to put the application in we had to say 18 buildings over a three-year span—and that's all in one community. They didn't like that. I think part of our problem from the very beginning was that we were going after the government money.

So at that point we backed off and went low key. Because it's very difficult to hold up hope for any poor person to get land and decent housing, and not be able to come through for them. I think if we knew then what we know now, we'd do what we're doing now, which is to buy a piece of ground and never mind the government funding, because the government insists on putting a maximum number of units on a minimum amount of land, which is not our concept. We're buying land and we're putting the allowable amount of housing on it without going through the local subdivision process, because then the local governments cannot interfere and prevent us from doing it. Because we know that they are not sympathetic to the poor; they don't want the poor moving into their communities, although they *are there.* And I guess we are trying to disperse the operations in the different towns.

## THE FIRST HOUSE AND THE FARMERS HOME ADMINISTRATION

*DICK TRACY:* That first year [1978] we did start Connie Burgess's house. We thought everything was rosy, and we started Connie's house on two acres of land, and we had a conditional commitment for a mortgage from Farmers Home—and then they cancelled it. And we've been fighting them ever since.

*

Negotiations with the Farmers Home Administration (FmHA) lasted for more than two years and were extremely complicated. Connie Burgess was a single mother living with her three teenaged sons in an inadequate rental apartment in Bucksport. She had been involved with HOME for several years, and now, in 1978, was pursuing a college degree in human services. The house was designed by Housing People, Inc., of Ellsworth, Maine, as a small, energy-efficient dwelling that could be built utilizing local material and volunteer labor as well as the labor of Connie Burgess and her sons.

The efforts to secure FmHA financing that would allow Connie Burgess to own this house involved three basic questions: (1) whether her finances would qualify her for an FmHA 502 Rural Housing Loan, (2) whether FmHA would approve a mortgage for a house on land leased from a CLT, and (3) whether this house on this site would meet FmHA's standards. Concerning the first question, Connie was initially refused on the basis that her income was too low, but she and Dick Tracy persisted and eventually discovered that a change in regulations now allowed an applicant to qualify if she had been paying as much for housing as the new housing would cost her each month. On this basis she was finally approved. The question of financing a house on leased land was also finally resolved, after a number of meetings between Chuck Matthei, of the Institute for Community Economics, and FmHA officials in Washington. This cleared the way for FmHA financing not only for houses on Covenant CLT's land but for houses on CLT land throughout the country.

The house itself, however, was never approved. At issue were the quality of the amateur workmanship and the design and siting of the house. An earth-sheltered passive solar design, the house was set on level ground facing south, away from the road, with an earth berm raised against its north wall. State FmHA officials believed that this unconventional aspect, combined with amateur workmanship, compromised the marketability of the house, though there was no question but what the Burgess family and other potential CLT leaseholders found it desirable.

While these issues were being debated, the house was finished and the Burgess family moved in. Unable to secure permanent financing, however, the CLT was forced to continue short-term financing at relatively high interest, which created a serious drain on its resources. By the summer of 1981 when these interviews took place, Connie was enrolled in graduate school; her sons were growing up. The house had met their needs for a time, but it was not to be their permanent home. Covenant CLT, which has now built four other houses, plans to sell the Burgess house. Connie Burgess, however, has made a real contribution to the CLT effort.

*

*CONNIE BURGESS:* The process has been on and off and we've been up and down. If I didn't feel strongly about the land trust concept I don't think I could have taken it. Most of our land here is being bought up by people from out of state or people that really can afford it. And there are a lot of people left that are not going to have any land. So I think that this is the only chance for low-income people, for one thing. For another thing, I feel that land is entrusted to people and that it should be used by everyone, and taken care of, and that no one person should have it so a lot of people can't use it. And I feel that means take care of the land. And the land trust is a way of doing that.

I guess if I was sorry at all, it's because of the uncertainty with my kids—wondering, if this doesn't go through what is going to happen? It is a precedent-setting case, which has made this unusually long, but I think maybe now a pathway has been made for some in the future. So it's not all for nought.

*

## MORE-RECENT HOUSES

In 1980 two more houses were built, on a piece of land near Bucksport, for Jack and Melody Hovey and their children and for Mary Giordano and her children. Both were built from the same basic plans—a fairly conventional 1½-story design, well insulated and incorporating a solar greenhouse.

Kerry Mackin

*The Burgess house.*

Barbara Harce

*The Hovey house.*

*

*DICK TRACY:* FmHA has seen pictures of the new houses. They are much more comfortable with them. Also their funding is getting cut, and we are saying, in effect, that we can provide three houses for the price of one—because prices of houses that they are financing now are $50,000 to $60,000, and for those two houses up there, our total price was $18,000 apiece. And that's with eight or nine acres of land with each one. Our problem is: Will our people qualify for those mortgages? The second possibility—and this is the one we are concentrating on—is our own revolving loan fund. A foundation in France sent us $10,000. We have that tied up in those two houses. Then we've had other donations totaling about $4,000. We have a commitment which we hope will come through, for $36,000 at little or no interest, which will finance those two houses on a long-term basis. [This loan did come through and mortgages were thus arranged.]

*

Jack and Melody Hovey, leaseholder/homeowners, describe their experience.

*

*QUESTION:* Before you had this house, were you renting?

*MELODY HOVEY:* Yeah, $175 per month.

*JACK HOVEY:* This year it would have taken $2,000 to heat it.

*QUESTION:* How do people in the community feel about the house being built here on community land trust land?

*JACK HOVEY:* The only real opposition was the [Bucksport] Planning Board. The first plan we had when I came was for eight houses up here. And the planning board turned them down. [If more than two houses are to be built on a single piece of land, subdivision approval must be granted by the local planning board.]

Now that we're here, the people who live around us are good neighbors—they mind their business and we mind our business. If you needed them in an emergency, I imagine they'd be down here. The main thing is that people who own their land are very close to it. They don't want to let go of it. And they don't want people from outside coming in.

Barbara Hance

*Yvette Hovey, at home.*

*MELODY HOVEY:* We found out later the main reason this one guy was really upset. His little boy came down, and we got to talking—a real cute little kid—and he said, "Suppose back there's going to be your pasture." I said it was. "Oh." He looked down. "They still cutting wood over there?" I said, "Yes, what's wrong?" He said, "Well, we walk back in the woods all the time, look things over and check things out. Once you put your pasture up we won't be able to get in it." So I said, "When I put my pasture up I'll bring you over and I'll show you where to trap, and where you can ride your three-wheelers. We'll try to leave a path there." "You'll do that?" I said, "Sure, you can go up there any time you want. In the winter they quit cutting 2:00 or 2:30." "They wouldn't mind?" I said no. That's what was bothering him. They ride all back there.

*

## ONGOING CONSTRUCTION

Covenant CLT owns 60 acres on the shore of Patton Pond in the town of Orland. The land is separated into two pieces by a road, so a total of four houses can be built without going through subdivision procedures. Of the two houses completed in 1981, one is essentially the same in design as the two completed the previous year, in Bucksport; the other is a distinctive octagonal house built for and by Paul Gorski and his family. Paul is one of HOME/Covenant CLT's two building supervisors. The other is Phil Grey. Between them they direct the work of the many volunteers. It is common for HOME/Covenant CLT to have as many as 30 volunteer workers at a given time during the summer months. Leaseholder/homeowners are normally expected to put in 700 hours of labor on their own houses.

*

*PHIL GREY:* We get people from all over. We had Claire and her son from Texas, Betsy's from Pennsylvania, Jack here was up last year, too. And

Kerry Mackin

*Construction supervisor Phil Grey.*

we've had them from Denmark, England, Mexico. You can do quite a bit of traveling—you don't even have to go anywhere.

*PAUL GORSKI:* I know everything about these houses—who put in what nail, what board, inside and out for all four houses. The Sisters of Mercy put these rafters together. And there was one nun—she was in her eighties and she had a bad hand—but we got her working, marking shingles. She felt good, she was contributing. You can walk in other new buildings and you feel cold, you walk in here, even when it's just a shell, and you feel warmth. Jack's house, I go upstairs and I feel like the walls are hugging me.

The families [leaseholders] get together once a month to discuss things. I mean, how can you do something if you don't know what it is? You want to know where you stand. This is different—you own the home but not the land, so you want to know what's going to happen. I want to see it running as a land trust, not just houses.

Kerry Mackin

*Paul Gorski and his children, at their new house at Patton Pond.*

I hate to see families breaking up, kids not knowing their grandparents. What we want to do is build a unit for elderly people on each unit of land. Elderly, they need kids, so they can dream back to when they were kids. And kids need old people. You can't go separating everybody, a herd of elderly here, a herd of kids there. Life isn't based that way. It's all of us together—that's how you'll really make it work.

*

Sister Lucy comments further on the new houses and leaseholders.

*

*QUESTION:* You have a small sawmill of your own now. How much of your own lumber are you using in these new houses?

*LUCY POULIN:* Paul's house has all the underpinnings from our sawmill, and in Mark's house all the 6 × 6s and a lot of the 2 × 8s. The more we do that, the more we can just continue to build. The problem is that the wells, the septics, and the road work you have to pay cash for. We had enough cash. We got a small grant from the Sisters of Mercy and we put that in the construction fund, and when these houses are mortgaged, we'll pay that money back into the fund and we can build some more houses with it.

*QUESTION:* You've been remarkably successful in getting work done with volunteers. Is there a secret to it?

*LUCY POULIN:* Our secret would have to be our supervisors, Phil Grey and Paul Gorski. But another reason that the volunteers work well here is that they are not adjuncts to a project; they *are* the project. We don't have layers of administrative

Mary Beth Lewis

*Volunteers at work on the Patton Pond land.*

level people, whether its house building or working at the co-op. They head up projects, with other volunteers. That seems to work well for us.

*QUESTION:* When you are ready to build a house, or help someone build a house, how do you choose among the applicants?

*LUCY POULIN:* That's a critical problem. We're talking about people who have between $300 and $500 a month. We have some who earn $10,000 a year—we haven't yet considered that community of people, but if they have four or five kids they're very needy. What's happened, in fact, is that we built five houses and there's maybe a hundred people who know about it or families that want houses right now. There's no way that we can meet that need or keep up with that need. So what's happened is that as land has become available in a certain area, the question has taken care of itself. We have a family right now in Ellsworth that's critical. I don't know if they'll make it through the winter. They have four children. But they need to live in Ellsworth, and we don't have land in Ellsworth yet. We maybe could have built a home for them on the Patton Pond land, but that would mean their children would lose all the support they're getting through human services in Ellsworth, and the children need [that] to just survive. So some of the questions are taken care of that way—we have to choose families in terms of where they want to live. Then there's a list, and it's a first-come, first-served basis. And people have dropped off the top of the list because it's a highly mobile community—families break up, or they move to different towns and move in with people and such.

*QUESTION:* Have you had to disqualify people because they couldn't handle the financing at all?

*LUCY POULIN:* We haven't dealt rationally with that problem. Most of them are paying rents. They are somehow surviving in housing that costs as much as ours but is terribly unfit, paying rents of $150 a month. So we're going on that. And I don't think people are going to fail each other on the money, or it will be brought out as a problem. We've talked about maybe getting a little fund for that.

## MORE THAN HOUSES

*LUCY POULIN:* We didn't want to just build houses because we realized that the community that forms is as critical as building houses. We don't want to just say we built 5 houses or 30 houses. We would like to see that cooperation and sharing grow among us, the families and ourselves. On the Patton Pond land they're going to have a community dock, a place where members of the land trust and the community can fish and swim and have barbecues.

We also, in terms of housing, have seen enough people who have just the house, and we knew that that wasn't the solution. The people needed to have access to food and fuel. Houses needed to be energy efficient. So when we build a house, it's complete. We do the greenhouse. And access to firewood. We're trying to vertically integrate the farm and forest products, because the people need the houses, the community, the food, the fuel; they need work, jobs where they're treated as human beings. We've been able to create a few jobs yarding the wood, and we have a young man who wants to run the sawmill. We will have a sawmill and a shingle mill and more of the craft work that would support, which will help a lot of families to support themselves.

Each family has about ten acres in their leasehold, but they don't hold the wood rights. They hold all the agricultural rights, and the right to have enough wood for their heat every year, but they can't go cut a bunch of trees down. What we do with woodlots is every year we thin them, and besides getting firewood we take any good logs to our little sawmill.

We're trying to do more with intensive gardening. That is a very accepted concept among our farm families. We had maybe four seminars on it last fall and we'll continue it in our learning center. That's a way to raise food when you have a minimum amount of land—with raised beds, greenhouses, and organic matter. If they want livestock, they can negotiate for larger tracts among the families themselves. Out at Jack Hovey's and Mary's, Jack owns cattle, so I think he's arranged to use Mary's land, and it's fine with her because she has no desire to have livestock. So that's something they've arranged among themselves as leaseholders.

*QUESTION:* How many houses would you like to be able to build?

*LUCY POULIN:* We think six per year would be maximum, figuring on how many families you can relate to with some quality in the relationships. I think we all feel that if we could build that many and families could live there—own their homes, raise food, have firewood—that that freedom would be a great blessing to them. A beautiful place for children to grow, a community where they would really feel that sharing and cooperation which we all feel, and they feel, is absolutely essential to survival. We've got to learn to help each other and share.

*QUESTION:* When you speak of community you speak of the HOME community, not the larger community?

*LUCY POULIN:* The HOME community. These people didn't have any relationship with the larger community. We're not talking about people who are accepted; we're talking about people who never have been accepted or had value in the community. And we're prejudiced in favor of those people—that's the community of people that we want as our community. And we're sticking with that. We don't care, I for one don't care, what the larger community thinks. They're part of the problem.

*QUESTION:* Are there plans to turn over any of the co-op's land to the land trust?

*LUCY POULIN:* It's been mentioned several times that it would make sense to have the co-op's 23 acres in the land trust. But right now that's a question that we're not worrying about. Maybe people with longer-term thinking would. If someone came with that kind of gift, they'd be saying, let's do this for the future. But we're not strong on that kind of people at this point. Maybe it will show up later, I don't know.

*QUESTION:* Marie Cirillo in Tennessee, who is doing some of the same kinds of things that you are, has told us that the problems in Appalachia are so extreme that unless the government takes responsibility for doing something, the situation can't really change. Do you feel that the same thing is true in this area?

*LUCY POULIN:* Well, I think that is a very complex question. One part of me would say we have always gone to the government, whether it was work programs during the Depression or what. The only organization large enough and broad enough with capital enough and resources is the government. I question that as a solution now, but that in no sense lessens the energy I think we should put into getting the government to do the things that it should and can do well—which would be making capital available. I think that the programs of the 60s and 70s failed miserably in really altering the lives of the poor. If you put the power in the hands of the government, if that is your only solution, you give total control to an institution that is amoral, without values. In that sense I disagree, but I do think they should make capital available, loan money. I also would say that I feel, if it was the responsibility of any group, it would be that of the Christian churches, because that's their call to being.

*QUESTION:* What advice would you give to others who might be starting community land trusts?

*LUCY POULIN:* Hard work, hard work, hard work. Working, not talking. I think that the kind of people that are going to buy your book are

*Sister Lucy, working.*

middle-class people. They have the words, they read, they know all the new ideas. They go to meetings where everybody wants to do land trusts, but they *haven't* for 20 years—they've been talking about it for that long. If they'd gone to work, I think that divisions that might arise in ideology would have become kind of lost in the task at hand—which is to build a home, buy the land. I would encourage people to *do* it.

*

## CHAPTER 6

# Columbia Heights Washington, D.C.

The Columbia Heights story is a story of an old urban neighborhood, now a low-income black neighborhood, beset by extreme housing problems. The community has been the scene of what has been called the first urban community land trust—the Columbia Heights Community Ownership Project, an ambitious effort initiated in 1976 by a small group of extremely dedicated, hard-working people. This organization has not succeeded as a permanent trust and is now in the process of turning over its remaining properties to other appropriate organizations. Several problems proved insurmountable, including rampant real estate speculation, the lack of established community organizations, and the lack of any guiding precedents for urban CLTs. The time was not ripe for a CLT in Columbia Heights. Still, the effort was very effective in calling attention to the city's housing problems and in sowing the seeds for later community action—including the creation of well-organized and effective tenants organizations.

Now, as community control increases, and as the prospects for significant local ownership improve, there is again talk of a land trust as a means of consolidating the community's control of its housing for the long run. If a new CLT does eventually develop, it will develop out of this well-rooted neighborhood effort, and out of the community's own recognition of what it could gain through a land trust.

Clearly, there is much to be learned from Columbia Heights—both about the nature of urban housing problems and about the opportunities, the risks, and the problems that face a CLT in such a community.

Columbia Heights is an area of approximately 20 blocks in northwest Washington. A hundred years ago it was a fashionable hilltop neighborhood, the home of Supreme Court justices, senators, and cabinet members. It was once proposed that the White House be built here.

In the 1950s and early 60s rural blacks moved into the neighborhood in large numbers, as the middle-class whites who had been living there moved out to the suburbs. In 1968, following the assassination of Martin Luther King, riots erupted along Fourteenth Street, the central business street of the neighborhood. Two hundred businesses were burned; the business district was totally destroyed and has never been restored. In the 1970s, prosperous suburban whites began to move back into the city, rapidly gentrifying other Washington neighborhoods, but Columbia Heights was slow to change, in part because of the devastation wreaked by the 1968 riots.

Perk Perkins, who has worked with the Columbia Heights housing situation since 1975, as a member of the ecumenical religious community known as Sojourners, describes the community as he has known it.

*

*PERK PERKINS:* I'd say most people I know haven't lived in this neighborhood a long time. The transition from a middle-class white to a lower-income black neighborhood has occurred within the last 20 or 25 years. So for the most part, when you find a low-income person who's lived in this neighborhood for a long time, their long time is maybe 19 years, while most people have lived here more like 2 to 6 years. The president of our neighborhood tenants union, Shirley Hines, was born in Georgetown, which was the first neighborhood in this city to gentrify, back in the late 50s and early 60s. When all the other neighborhoods, everywhere in the country, were becoming poorer, Georgetown was switching from a slum—what was termed a slum, although Shirley would tell you it was a nice, low-income neighborhood—to rich people's places. She was evicted five times within Georgetown. And basically what she says is that this has become her home. People here like the neighborhood; they don't know where they would go if they weren't here. You know there's not a lot of choice, and they feel that the question is this neighborhood or the streets—and in some senses, for many people, it really literally is that.

*

Ed Spivey

*Perk Perkins.*

## FOUNDING OF THE COLUMBIA HEIGHTS COMMUNITY OWNERSHIP PROJECT

By the mid-1970s the housing situation in Columbia Heights had become particularly grim. The old housing stock was badly deteriorated and overcrowded. The gentry were not moving into the neighborhood, but urban renewal and gentrification were in the wind. Speculators were buying up property. More and more evicted families were joining the already large numbers of totally homeless people on the streets of Washington. This was the situation in the winter of 1975-76—one of the coldest winters in Washington's recent history.

It was at this time that the Community for Creative Nonviolence (CCNV) became involved in the Columbia Heights housing situation. CCNV was a community of five households that had organized nonviolent protests against the war in Vietnam and social injustice in this country, and had provided relief for needy people in Washington. Each household provided service for these people—a soup kitchen, a free medical clinic, an emergency shelter, etc.

One household had settled in Columbia Heights, and in 1976, their current lease about to expire, they began looking for a house to buy in the neighborhood. The difficulty they had in finding a house led to a weekly discussion group on the neighborhood's housing problems.

Cathy St. Clair, who worked with CCNV and the land trust, explains what the group learned.

*

*CATHY ST. CLAIR:* They started doing research on different parts of the neighborhood and discovered that 89 percent of the neighborhood was owned by absentee landlords, that one-third of those buildings were owned by the city, and that most of those buildings that the city owned were abandoned. The city had either claimed these buildings through eminent domain because it was an urban renewal area or had seized them for back taxes because previous owners had just left the buildings after the riots and never bothered to do anything with them.

Most of the buildings in the neighborhood were large row houses that had been converted into apartments or were rented by the room. Perhaps one-quarter of the buildings in the neighborhood were large, multifamily dwellings. Evictions were beginning to increase in the neighborhood, and in the city in general. Over 2,000 families were evicted during 1976, and the city only had two shelters, with a combined capacity of 40 people—which was just a drop in the bucket when there were 2,000 families who were on the streets. So one of the immediate needs was for emergency shelter for evicted families. At the same time, Columbia Heights obviously was going to be the next area for real estate speculators. The pattern had already been established in other neighborhoods—Georgetown 15 years before that, Mt. Pleasant, Adams Morgan—and the real estate developers were slowly moving east toward Columbia Heights. The effects of speculation were very drastic for the people who lived in those neighborhoods. The pattern was that landlords would evict their tenants, put their buildings up for sale, and the new owner would do a minimal amount of renovation and put it back on the market with a high price. And then speculation would cause prices to jump. A building that might have been bought for $20,000 would eventually wind up on the market for $100,000. Then over a period of a year the next property tax assessment would double, or triple sometimes, and then the taxes would rise, the rents would rise, and more evictions would take place because people weren't able to keep up with the rent increases.

With the makeup of the Columbia Heights neighborhood, it was clear that many of the residents were going to be forced to move out as soon as speculation did begin to occur there, so the need was not only to find an immediate solution for the people who were being evicted but to find a long-term solution that would prevent people from being displaced. In the discussion a lot of different options were proposed, but the land trust seemed like the best possible solution. The community ownership that occurs through the land trust would eliminate the possibility of displacement in the future. It would give permanent control of the

Mary Reiser

*Cathy St. Clair.*

neighborhood to the people who lived there. It would also build cooperation between people in the neighborhood to try to solve other problems—food clubs, work co-ops, and day care centers could all come out of the formation of a land trust.

*

The land trust, the Columbia Heights Community Ownership Project (CHCOP), was founded in 1976. Its primary goal was to acquire housing that would be leased to neighborhood families. Its first project, however, involved a different goal, as Cathy St. Clair explains.

*

*CATHY ST. CLAIR:* About the time the discussion group had finished developing its plans, the city, in a very timely move as far as we were concerned, invited people to suggest what could be done with the abandoned buildings that the city owned. So the group located a 33-room building on Fairmont Street that had been abandoned for about ten years and so needed a lot of renovation but would serve as an emergency shelter for evicted families. They proposed to the city that ownership of the building be transferred to the land trust and that the building would be renovated and staffed by CCNV at their own expense as an emergency shelter. The city wasn't too pleased with this offer. They were afraid that a precedent would be set for other groups in the city to demand the same opportunity. So a year-long campaign ensued—which got the support of hundreds of community organizations and church leaders and neighborhood residents. In August of 1976 the negotiations still had gotten nowhere. Discussions would stop with the city and then start up again, but in August they had pretty much come to a standstill—so civil disobedience was begun to dramatize the issue. [CCNV people and others occupied the Fairmont Street building and were arrested.] Due to all the public pressure that was sparked by the civil disobedience the city was forced to reopen negotiation. However, the city does know how to drag its feet and it certainly did it at that point. We informed the city that if they

Washington's raw winter nights have forced hundreds of its homeless to seek whatever meager warmth or shelter is available. For some, this might simply be the heat from a fire burning in a garbage can in a vacant lot, or the rising steam from a street grating. Still others find that a large cardboard box, insulated with newspaper, can provide some temporary relief from the cold.

Scenes such as these are extreme representations of this city's housing crisis. Slightly less visible but just as real are the thousands of families who are evicted from their homes every year, many of them victims of speculation and urban renewal. The assistance offered to these families is wholly inadequate, as the District government operates only two emergency shelter facilities, each with a maximum capacity of 10 moderate size families.

The Community for Creative Non-Violence, which for the past five years has maintained Zacchaeus Free Medical clinic, Soup Kitchen, and Hospitality House, has now undertaken a response to the housing crisis. In April, CCNV proposed to the Department of Housing and Community Development that it place a large, city-owned abandoned building at 1361 Fairmont Street NW into neighborhood land trust. CCNV offered to both rehabilitate the building and operate it as an emergency shelter for evicted families with its own funds and labor. Over 1,000 neighborhood people signed a petition in support of this effort.

Last June, DHCD rejected the proposal, and in August, five CCNV members were arrested during two non-violent attempts to occupy and begin rehabilitation of the proposed shelters. Yet further direct action was postponed in order to facilitate renegotiations. By the end of November, no significant progress had been made, and the city had cancelled one date of decision. CCNV's sense of urgency and impatience grew, as Washington is experiencing one of the coldest winters in over 50 years.

Throughout the past eight months, CCNV has attempted to maintain a spirit of patience, honesty, and non-violence. Much time has been spent writing, calling, and keeping in personal contact with DHCD officials. But time is running out. It is running out on those who must live through another winter with no place to turn. CCNV has therefore notified the Department of Housing that if an acceptable decision is not reached by January 7, the public campaign will be renewed and continued until resolution.

If necessary, on Friday four persons will set up cardboard boxes in front of city hall, to live there until the campaign is ended. This will be an attempt to make visible and concrete what has become invisible and abstract—to portray the life that many are forced to live. If there are no arrests, support from around the city and elsewhere will be mobilized. If arrested, people will plead guilty, refuse bail, fines, and special privileges, and will return "home" to their cardboard boxes upon release.

CCNV has been informed that a DHCD recommendation is forthcoming before the January 7 deadline. It is hoped that this decision will be one which best serves those in need, and will resolve the conflict without confrontation.

Anyone interested in helping in this project can do so by writing or calling city government officials to express support for the proposal.

Contact either:

Lorenzo Jacobs
Director, DHCD
1325 G St. NW Room 959
Washington DC 20005
724-8721

or

Walter Washington, mayor
District Building
14th and E Sts. NW
Washington, DC 20005
628-6000

For more information, contact the Community for Creative Non-Violence, 1345 Euclid Street, NW, Washington, DC, 20009, 667-6407, or Sojourners, 1029 Vermont Avenue, NW, Washington DC, 20005, 737-2780. □

**This is a cardboard box.**

**Some people take home their new refrigerators in them.**

**Others have to live in them.**

*CCNV leaflet.*

didn't come up with a decision by the end of December we would engage in another public protest. [CCNV was prepared to move into cardboard boxes in front of city hall to dramatize the fact that homeless people were living in such boxes in the city.] At the last minute they came to a compromise with us. They would lease the building to CCNV until a year after the building had been renovated and the shelter had been operating, and at that point they would consider transferring ownership of the building to the land trust. We accepted that as a reasonable compromise, trusting that we would be able to work things out later.

*

But things did not work out later. Renovation of the building began in March of 1977. The

CCNV people invested $20,000 (earned through their own manual labor) in the project—as well as a tremendous number of hours of volunteer labor. However, late in the year problems arose around vaguely defined terms in the lease. During the primary election campaign of 1978, the city assured CCNV that these problems would be resolved, but on the day following the primary election, when the incumbent mayoral candidate was defeated, the city demolished the building without warning.

## ACQUISITIONS

While the struggle over the Fairmont Street house was going on, CHCOP did acquire several dwellings, all requiring renovation. The plan was to lease this housing to people who would be able to participate in the renovation, and thus earn sweat equity. Fees were set at 25 percent of the occupant's income. To assure that all leaseholders would develop some equity through these payments, a straight 5 percent of the leaseholder's fee was to be treated as equity regardless of other factors.

Cathy St. Clair tells of the land trust's experience with its first building, which it acquired to provide a home for a family it had been sheltering for several months.

*

*CATHY ST. CLAIR:* About the same time that the campaign for the Fairmont Street building started getting under way, the Brody family—15 of them—were illegally evicted a few blocks away from CCNV. Three of the Brody children had been poisoned by the lead paint in the house, and for that reason, even though the eviction had been illegal, the family could not be moved back into the apartment. The city shelter had no place for them so CCNV offered to house them. The Brody family had been on the public housing list for ten years waiting for a place, and it didn't seem that it was going to be forthcoming. The first building, located at 1302 Euclid Street, was bought for them for $20,000, and plans were made for them to begin renovations of the house with help from people at CCNV. But in the meantime the city suddenly, magically came up with housing for them and threatened the mother of the family that if she didn't move into this house the family would be cut off from welfare and Medicaid benefits.

*

As a result of this threat, the Brody family moved into public housing in another part of the city and eventually gave up its effort to renovate the Euclid building. Knowing that the choice of a family to occupy the first land trust house could have a major effect on the trust's future prospects, CHCOP distributed leaflets throughout the neighborhood to attract applicants. Though previous leafletting campaigns aimed at drawing people to neighborhood meetings to discuss housing problems had received little response, this campaign attracted 86 applicants. All were interviewed and a family was selected on the basis of its size (being right for the house), its need, and its understanding of the

CCNV

*Typical eviction scene in Columbia Heights.*

land trust idea. Unfortunately, after several months of working at renovating the house, two members of the family developed health problems and the family had finally to give up its plans. A third family was then selected and again there was hope for the future, but in this case misunderstandings eventually developed between the family and the trust concerning the lease arrangement.

*

*CATHY ST. CLAIR:* It was very debilitating to the morale of the people working with the trust to have gone through these three experiences with families and to keep struggling to get the place done.

At last the Thompson family—Hazel and Mike Thompson—agreed to do the work on the house at 1302 Euclid Street. They had six kids and were living in a very small two-bedroom apartment and were being threatened with eviction. So the trust worked out very well for them. And even though the trust is now dissolved, the Thompsons now own 1302 Euclid Street.

*

A second building was acquired in October of 1977 as a group home for low-income elderly people. The building appeared to be in relatively good condition but turned out to need a good deal of work, which took a year to complete with volunteer labor. Then six elderly people (who had been paying up to 90 percent of their income for housing) were moved into the house. Management problems proved more difficult than anticipated, and were never solved to the land trust's satisfaction. With the dissolution of the trust, the building was turned over to a nonprofit housing corporation and is therefore available to low-income people.

A third building was acquired from an elderly owner-occupant who was no longer able to maintain it but wanted to continue to live there. When the trust dissolved, the building was returned to his ownership.

## BASIC PROBLEMS FACING THE TRUST

CHCOP had made an unsuccessful attempt to acquire one other building, which had involved the trust in a direct confrontation with speculators. An occupant of a five-unit building that had been purchased by speculators (for $52,000 and immediately put back on the market for more than$80,000) approached the trust with a request for help in resisting the new owner's attempts to threaten the occupants into vacating the building. CHCOP organized an intensive campaign to bring public pressure to bear on the owners. Petitions were circulated, asking the owners to sell the building at no profit to the trust. CCNV and Sojourners people occupied the building at one point to protest the owners' plans. Other forms of public protest were carried out. A great deal of energy was put into the campaign over a six-month period, but finally to no avail. The owners succeeded in forcing some tenants out, moving in some of their own friends and selling the building to them under the terms of an ordinance designed to allow tenants to purchase their own building.

It seems clear that, to resist forces such as these, a CLT—or any community group—must have strong, well-organized support from the community. The lack of an organized base of support was one of the basic problems in Columbia Heights.

*

*CATHY ST. CLAIR:* Before the land trust idea had been developed we leafletted the neighborhood several times, inviting people to a meeting to discuss the housing problem in the neighborhood—and there was no response. I think there was a mixture of problems that caused this lack of response. Columbia Heights had no real grass-roots community organizations functioning at that point. There were two organizations that were supposed to be community organizations. There was a Project Area Committee—by federal law, all urban renewal districts must have Project Area Committees (PACs) to allow community participation in the planning process—and a group called Change Incorporated, a service organization trying to meet different needs in the neighborhood. Basically the people who were involved in one organization were the same people who were involved in the other, and we discovered that the people who did come to our meetings were mostly the same people who worked at the PAC and Change.

When CCNV was trying to get the Fairmont Street building from the city, the people at the PAC were very hostile toward CCNV. I think somehow they felt threatened by this group that was coming in. So already there was somewhat of a bad relationship between CCNV and the PAC, though there were several individuals who did get involved with the trust.

These groups really didn't have the participation of the residents of the community. I talked with people who complained bitterly about many organizations that had gotten started shortly after the riots. These organizations would make a lot of promises, and then eventually they would fall apart—and people had given money to these organizations and supported them and then were ripped off by one or two people in the organization. For example, there was a credit union started about five years before that and someone embezzled the funds from it. So there was already a lot of apprehension and bitterness toward the idea of community organizations.

Another thing was that people were struggling just to make it each day. It was hard to look beyond next month's rent or the medical bills for your kids, in order to see what was really happening in the neighborhood. The speculators crept in and picked their buildings until eventually a whole block would have been transformed. I think it was really hard for people to feel that it was going to have an effect on them.

The land trust was sponsored by a mostly white group, and while that didn't help very much, I'm sure, I honestly think the greatest hindrance was that the land trust was presenting a solution to problems the neighborhood didn't recognize they had. And because of the pressure that the speculators were putting on the neighborhood, there wasn't enough time for a lot of grass-roots organizing to take place.

*

As it became clear that CHCOP could not succeed, the people associated with it did not turn away from the problems. CCNV has continued to publicize the city's critical housing problems, has pressured the city to provide emergency shelter for the homeless, and has continued its own efforts to care for the homeless. The Sojourners people have worked in a different direction. They have been less concerned with publicizing the housing issue but have worked to help neighborhood residents organize their own tenants organizations. Perk Perkins of Sojourners discusses the views that have led this group to take their current approach.

*

*PERK PERKINS:* The land trust was seen as a means of raising the issue. And what I came to understand, and I think what people in the neighborhood have taught me, is that raising the issue is one thing, but once you've raised an issue, doing something is another thing. And whether it's a land trust or it's winning a legislative battle, or it's forcing a landlord to do something, or it's buying a building, what's important beyond the initial raising of the issues is to actually do something about the issue. You need to always question whether justice is being served, but if nothing is really happening because you're applying a real strict standard of what justice is, then you've got problems.

Another problem was that we actually took on the sole management, renovation, and acquisition of property, and really were more a housing development corporation, without the resources to be a housing development corporation, than a land trust, as I look at it now. We also attempted to do something very difficult—provide housing

Ken King

*On Thanksgiving Day, 1981, CCNV members established a symbolic tent city and graveyard in the park facing the White House to publicize the plight of increasing numbers of homeless people. Each marker represents a homeless person who has died on the streets of American cities in recent years.*

with a subsidy, so that the people who were in the housing would only pay 25 percent of their income, when we knew that that would not cover the cost of the house. The original idea was to rely on subsidies from private sources such as churches, but that puts a tremendous responsibility on the trust to come up with all those resources.

## TENANTS ORGANIZATIONS

*PERK PERKINS:* Some of us at Sojourners became disenchanted with the land trust. We felt that it was an idea that had been premature, and we decided that something else needed to happen. People didn't feel that they could deal with the issue of stopping displacement. They were more concerned about not having heat on in their houses, about illegal eviction notices, about illegal rent increases. They weren't ready to talk about displacement. And so we formed a housing ministry of Sojourners, which was basically a group of organizers. It was two organizers at first and now we have a staff of six. The idea was just to organize people in individual buildings and to see what developed. What has developed is a neighborhood tenants union, a coalition of tenants in 27 buildings who are very politically active in the city. They have helped obtain a condominium conversion law that keeps condominiums from displacing people. They've helped get an anti-speculation tax law that keeps landlords from speculating on the property. They've helped implement the tenant First-Right-To-Purchase law. They've also helped to keep rent and eviction control.

The Southern Columbia Heights Tenants Union very soon knew that it needed to deal with development and with purchase, but it did not want to make purchase a goal unless people within a building wanted to make purchase a goal. And usually what makes purchase a goal for people in a building is a few victories—when they've fought back some illegal rent increases, when they've had a rent strike, when they've kept the heat on for the whole winter.

*

One such situation developed in an apartment building at 2618-20-22 Thirteenth Street in the central part of southern Columbia Heights. Beginning in January of 1979, Jim Tamalis, a member of the Sojourners staff, worked with the tenants in this building. He describes the history of the building, from early organizing efforts to the eventual purchase by the tenants.

*

Paul Brubaker

*Jim Tamalis.*

*JIM TAMALIS:* We got involved in the building through a couple of people that lived there that we knew. They received a notice that the Rental Accommodations Office [the agency that implements city rental housing laws] had granted something like a 30 percent rental increase and they were pretty frustrated because they had been having a hard time getting the landlord to provide repairs and services for the building. So those two people that we knew gathered several friends in their building, and we talked about the possibility of developing a tenants association, to demand repairs and services from the landlord.

There were problems with windows not fitting properly, plaster and paint coming down off the walls, doors that weren't working properly. During winter months there were some problems with heat. One elderly man had a good portion of his kitchen ceiling fall down and hit him in the back of the head. And so actually the issue wasn't really the rent increase; the issue was the demand for a rent increase coupled with the hassle that the tenants had been experiencing, trying to get any repairs or services. Well, those tenants were pretty low-income people, and one of the things that was outstanding to me in beginning to work with them was how little confidence they had in themselves, in terms of affecting anything that was going on in the building. Many were elderly, and for most of their lives their experience had been just do what you can to accommodate the poverty and try to survive. Some of the younger people were less convinceable for other reasons. They were just trying to get their lives together and establish themselves and had some concerns about putting the places where they were living in jeopardy.

There was one older woman in particular, Granny Overton, who was respected by everyone in the building and seen as a leader. When she went along with this thing, it gave the organizing work some legitimacy and some respect.

At that first meeting of seven or eight people the idea of organizing to deal with their problems was presented, and they said it was something they wanted to do.

The next step was identification of specific issues to take before the landlord. It was obvious that if we just brought the landlord in and opened the meeting up, people would bring all of their hundreds of complaints and it would be pretty unfocused. The landlord might be able to be pretty manipulative. They came up with a basic set of demands that would benefit most everyone so that people could see that the activity of the tenants association would be beneficial to everyone.

The strategy was to identify four to six things that could be responded to within a month. The first of these demands was to replace the resident manager with somebody better. There were a number of vacant apartments in the building and he was allowing friends of his to come in and drink and sleep in them. People were pretty distressed about that. Another demand was the installation of exterior doors on the building that locked. The three entrances to this three-section building all just flopped open and shut on hinges, and people could come in and out at any time. Granny Overton kept a baseball bat behind her door and

Ed Spivey

*2618-20-22 Thirteenth Street.*

never went out of her apartment without it, no matter what time it was, because she never knew who she was going to run into in the hall. Also the mailboxes in the lobby of the building were in real bad shape. Most of them didn't lock. Many didn't have doors on them. And so people were regularly losing mail, and there was an ongoing hassle of people trying to be home when the mailman came if they were expecting something important—particularly at the beginning of the month when the public assistance or social security checks came by. The last demand was better trash removal. There was constant trash buildup in back of the building, and so there were rats and it was just generally unhealthy.

I think about a third of the tenants were represented at the meeting. The owner was fairly new to the building. He hadn't quite owned it a year. My impression was that he thought he could come out and placate the people who lived there with promises. Because it was an initial meeting, the tenants were fairly pleased and fairly hopeful. The person who was chairing the meeting said, "What we want to do is get back together with you in another month to see whether the things have been done." And that proved to be a really good strategy because as it turned out, there were to be many ongoing meetings, both large and small, with this landlord in order to try to ask him, beg him, coax him, intimidate him into making repairs that he just was not making.

The only one of those four issues that was responded to pretty promptly was the replacement of the resident manager. We chose that issue because we knew that it would be to the best interest of the owner to get rid of the poor employee and replace him with somebody who was more responsible. We really made out like a champ on that one because the new man has turned out to be one of the best things that's ever happened to that building. He's been helpful and a friend of the organizing effort all along, and people in the building have come to like him and appreciate him.

The trash removal didn't really improve and the nonlocking doors and busted up mailboxes continued.

Just about the time that we were trying to figure out what other approaches to take, it just so happened that the owner had court summonses sent out to around a dozen people in the building who were behind in their rent payments. This stirred people up—they had been working for a long time to try to get the landlord to make repairs and now here come these summonses. We used that event as an organizing tool. I spoke to the leadership of the group about beginning a rent strike—about saying not only are these people not paying their rent, but the rest of us who have lived in this building for years and never missed paying one month's rent are no longer going to pay and get nothing in return. With the assent of the leadership, I as the organizer went around and presented the idea to other people.

There was a wide range of response, ranging from, "Yeah, that sounds right and I want to be a part of it," to a great deal of fear—"There's no way I can do that because I don't want to come home and find my stuff out on the street," or "That's not right; if you live someplace you're supposed to pay the man." That sort of attitude. The fear could be dealt with by talking about other people's experiences and the process of the law—knowing that you couldn't just come home and find your things set out, that there were several notices that you would receive about the court process and that, at each point along the way, we could easily step in and stop an eviction if one were ever ordered.

The withheld rent was put in an escrow account. It was important that we be able to show that we were organized to that level and show where the money was. The stance that the tenants were taking was, we are paying our rent, we're just not releasing it to you. About a third of the building received summonses to court, and another third of the building joined the rent withholding action. Later on, a few more people joined to increase that percentage, and a few more just stopped paying rent to anybody. So as it turned out, the tenants association was controlling probably around 90 percent of the rental income.

The landlord's initial response was quite hostile. And people had prepared themselves well enough to not be intimidated by that, and, as a matter of fact, had prepared themselves to turn the situation around on the landlord. The landlord's threat was, "I'll take you to court." They said, "Fine. That's where we want to be, because that's the only place that we feel that we're gonna get a proper hearing, and you're gonna lose." He knew that was true and backed off and became very concerned and asked for a meeting before the court date.

*

The tenants agreed to meet with the owner one hour before those who originally received summonses were scheduled to appear in court. At that time he agreed to make specified repairs on the building during each of the next four months, with one month's rent to be turned over to him when each month's repairs were completed.

Once again he completed only a small part of the agreed-upon repairs, so the tenants continued to withhold most of the rent. Eventually, he decided to escape the situation by selling the property. As previously noted, the District of Columbia has a law giving tenants the first right to purchase. The landlord notified the tenants that he was selling the property and that he had an existing contract with somebody who was willing to buy the property. At this point the price was established and had to be met by the tenants. He was asking $375,000 for the building.

The third party in this case was a developer, who eventually contacted the tenants to find out what was going on in the building. Impressed with the tenants organization, this developer proposed an arrangement whereby he would rehabilitate the building for a fee and the tenants would own the building. The tenants found no advantage in such an arrangement. The developer then backed out and the tenants proceeded to negotiate for a lower price from the owner—who again tried to take them to court for nonpayment of rent, but again backed off when the tenants arranged an inspection that recorded several hundred building code violations. The owner finally agreed to sell for $340,000 and to credit $17,000 in withheld rent toward this price.

In the meantime, the tenants association had incorporated and had secured a loan for $18,500, needed as earnest money, from the Revolving Loan Fund of the Institute for Community Economics.

While these events were taking place, similar situations had begun to develop in other buildings in the neighborhood.

*

*JIM TAMALIS:* In other buildings in the Columbia Heights area, tenants were organizing and putting similar kinds of pressures on their landlords to perform the duties that were required of them by law. In a few other buildings in the neighborhood, we discovered that when tenants really pushed their rights to the limit, landlords were looking for a way out. So a couple of other buildings in the neighborhood are going through a similar purchase process.

Leaders from the individual buildings began meeting to discuss what was going on in their buildings and share experiences—which was really uplifting for a lot who were feeling quite alone in their struggles. A decision was made to form the Southern Columbia Heights Tenants Union [SCHTU]. Then we began to discuss a more concentrated cooperative development project for the Southern Columbia Heights neighborhood. The Southern Columbia Heights Cooperative Housing Development Project was initiated, and a short while later HUD [Department of Housing and Urban Development] awarded a grant to help support this effort—the development of a federa-

Paul Brubaker

*Scenes from the Southern Columbia Heights Tenants Union's recent neighborhood congress.*

Paul Brubaker

Paul Brubaker

tion of low-income housing cooperatives in the neighborhood that were tenant-controlled, tenant-owned, and had a commitment to a limited equity situation where the buildings were not controlled by the market.

*

For the Thirteenth Street property, a "financial packager" was hired to consider the financial options and put together a plan for financing the purchase. The owner owed approximately $210,000 on the property and agreed to continue with the existing mortgage arrangement, so that he would continue to make payments and would, in turn, receive monthly payments from the tenants association. Short-term financing for the balance of the purchase price was provided through the First-Right-to-Purchase Program, which had been created under the District of Columbia Department of Housing and Community Development (DHCD) to help tenant groups like this one complete the acquisition process and to give them time to work out long-term financing. A short-term loan of $185,000 from this source included some money to cover the cost of emergency rehabilitation and to make up for an operating deficit during the first year, when the building was not fully occupied and not yet ready for full occupancy. Since rents were still low, the city at this time asked the tenants to show their good faith by raising their own rents by $10 per month. The tenants complied.

Long-term financing was sought through HUD in the form of Section 8 rental subsidies, a loan for major rehabilitation, and permanent financing for the whole project. The application for this financing was favorably received, but new policies under the Reagan administration forced the tenants to reapply through reorganized city and federal channels. At the time of this writing, these arrangements are still up in the air, but it seems likely that the Section 8 subsidies will be approved and that the complete long-term financing package will be worked out by one means or another.

*

*JIM TAMALIS:* The tenants are, I think, justifiably proud of themselves having come all the way from being pretty insecure in even gathering to have a meeting with the landlord, to going through this entire purchase, and sometimes even needing to go and stand up to these different agencies that are established to assist them. When the Housing Finance Agency [HFA] was going to make their decisions on which buildings to finance, they came up with a ruling that said something about being unable to finance cooperatives, so they could only finance tenants-association-owned buildings. Tenants were really in an uproar, and the tenants from our area and others throughout the city, pretty much on a 24-hour notice, mobilized and went up to the HFA boardroom and demanded a meeting with the director of the HFA and the director of the Department of Housing and Community Development for some clarification on that. One other incident involved the Department of Housing and Community Development, which was administering the First-Right-to-Purchase Program and also the Seed Money Loan Program, which was established to help pay some of the up-front costs of acquisition. The city was just dragging its feet on both of those situations, and finally the tenants wrote a straightforward letter demanding that the DHCD get its act together and get their application processed. The department's response to that letter was a good one; the logjam was broken and things began to move again. So they really have developed a lot of confidence in themselves, and as a group they've learned that working together and working hard will bring results. That kind of experience is really helpful in bolstering the broader tenants union in the neighborhood.

## PROSPECTS FOR A NEW CLT

*PERK PERKINS:* We're immediately hopeful about five buildings, which would be about 150 units, somewhere in that range. And all of that, I think, has grown out of that initial interest that some of us had in the housing issue. So the land trust, even though at that point it didn't serve the need, did get people involved in housing.

Now we need to provide a way to make sure that the housing that we have continues to be available to low-income people. There are plenty of ways you can do that, but we think the best way is the land trust—it makes your intention very clear, and the structure—if you do it right—is rather simple. I can see—and I don't want to put this on anybody—but I can see that tenants who own and operate their buildings may decide to do the same thing. They already are moving in that direction to the extent that a limited equity co-op can only be used to provide low-income housing. Of course, there's a drawback—you could vote that corporation out of existence and create a new one, one that did not limit equity. So the normal bylaws of a limited equity co-op do not protect the building against speculation in quite the same way a land trust does. But it's important that the issue be decided by the people who are in the housing.

A land trust would own the land and the individual tenants associations would own the buildings, paying taxes and the costs of running the property. So the land trust, in that sense, would be a somewhat passive organization. Land trusts in many areas should be activist community organizations, but we don't need to create a land trust for that purpose if the purpose is already served by the neighborhood tenants union.

*

CHAPTER 7

# Community Land Cooperative of Cincinnati Cincinnati, Ohio

As a new urban land trust that has taken the initiative in dealing with housing problems in its community, the Community Land Cooperative of Cincinnati (CLCC) bears some resemblance to the Columbia Heights Community Ownership Project. Its rather sudden founding in 1981—in response to one large family's pressing need for housing—has involved a degree of risk; but unlike CHCOP, the CLCC has well-established roots in the community and appears to have grown from those roots at a favorable time. It has had the benefit of the experience of other urban CLTs. Another advantage that it enjoys, at least for the time being, is that although the West End community is subject to many of the kinds of pressures affecting Columbia Heights, speculation hasn't raised real estate prices so high. Furthermore, the CLCC has alternative sources of capital that were not available to CHCOP.

The West End, several miles from downtown Cincinnati, is a large community of low-income people, almost entirely black. Like Columbia Heights and other such neighborhoods in other cities, it began as a wealthy suburb, later became a middle-income neighborhood, and was finally abandoned to the poor. In recent decades it has been invaded by powerful forces from outside the community. People have been displaced to make room for parking lots and expressways. In the southeast section of the community, houses stand virtually abandoned as a result of urban renewal that was planned but never completed.

Now the threat of gentrification looms as well. In both the southeastern and northern sections of the community, there are many architecturally interesting, restorable old buildings. A part of the northern section has been designated an historic area, and some buildings have been purchased for rehabilitation. The old railroad terminal has recently been renovated as an upper-income shopping mall, suggesting the expectation that upper-income people will be moving into the area. Between the terminal and the Music Hall is a major public housing development, and there is now fear that this housing, so close to these upper-income attractions, may eventually be denied to low-income people.

Though still very young, the Community Land Cooperative of Cincinnati is a vigorous, well-informed, and very hopeful CLT. (*Note:* The group has had to adopt the term *cooperative* because Ohio law prevents such an organization from incorporating as a trust.)

Following, several of the people involved with the Community Land Cooperative comment on the community's history and circumstances today. Rev. Bruce Hinkley and Rev. Maurice MacCrackin are members of the CLCC board of trustees. Willy Watts is director of the CLCC.

*

*BRUCE HINKLEY:* This is Cincinnati's first suburb. It came about as a result of speculative business ventures—Cincinnati was a great shipping area. The people who built the grand houses in this neighborhood were extremely wealthy. Then around those houses grew up a much larger neighborhood of moderate-income persons who came in and built simpler housing. But all of it is such substantial housing that, even though it's a hundred-plus years old, it remains good housing stock. Therefore it has tremendous interest for upper-income people who now wish to live in the city again. However, our problem is that these persons—mostly upper-income, mostly white persons—seem to have feelings that prevent them from wanting to live with the people who are here now. They want us all to leave.

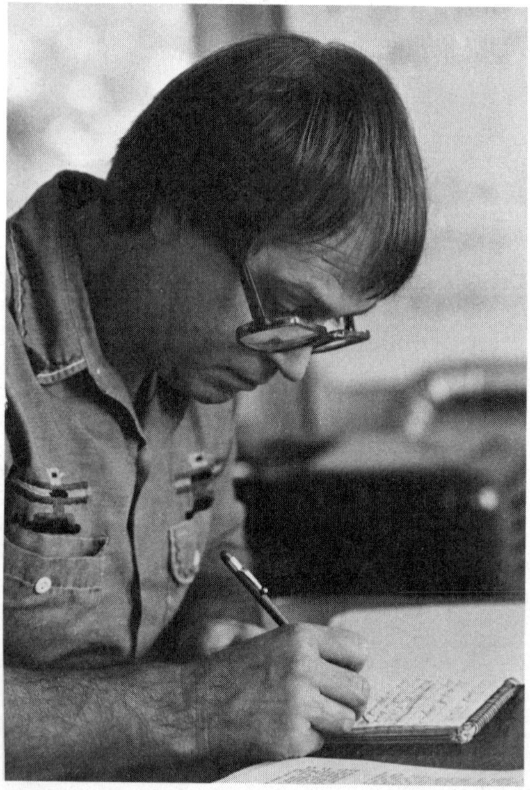

Robert O'Keefe

*Bruce Hinkley.*

*WILLY WATTS:* Back before World War II, this was a German neighborhood. But the peculiar characteristic is that this side of the street was Protestant and that side was Catholic, and it was unsafe for Catholics to cross Liberty Street, right here. This was the dividing line. Then they had a truce about it, and from then on, they began to somewhat explore other neighborhoods, one by one, moving away. This was before the war. Many of them owned property and they left the property, sold it or rented it, and they began to dribble away. They kept on this little dribbling away until, after the war, blacks began to buy, and the people remaining saw that they could make some money and go out and join their friends who had already moved. But some of them had little stores and they kept them. This type of thing kept going until this was nothing but a colony, colonized by people who formerly lived here. People came in and they made the money and took it out. And consequently, the community got a very bad name—crime rate was one of the highest—and everything began to feed upon itself in the West End.

*QUESTION:* You've lived in this neighborhood more than 20 years. What kind of changes have you seen happen since you've been here?

*WILLY WATTS:* When I moved here there was no expressway. This is one of the many areas that was razed. Weeds took it over, wildflowers and everything. Before that there was houses here. And these people, most of them were renting, and they were scattered to the four winds.

Robert O'Keefe

*Willy Watts.*

When the expressway came, the community had a few meetings. The state even sent buses into the neighborhoods and picked up people and brought them down to a big meeting, served them doughnuts and coffee and listened to their bitching for two or three hours, while the expressway kept working. I mean, the meeting didn't have nothing to do with the expressway.

*MAURICE MACCRACKIN:* Ever since I came to Cincinnati 35 years ago, I've seen displacement of people. It was put up to a vote as to whether the urban renewal would be done, and the people in the area were promised that if it went through and they had to be dispossessed, they'd be helped in finding a new location. So all they were doing was voting themselves out of a place to live. I'd have families that were moved—not only once, but then the expressway'd come along and they'd have to move again. And they would buy places which were big and expensive to heat, and the only way they could make payments on them and heat them was to sublet them.

Robert O'Keefe

Robert O'Keefe

Paul Wertheimer

Robert O'Keefe

The government had a relocation office and they would give them moving costs, of course—pin money as far as the need was concerned. If you had a house they would say it's not worth more than, say, $12,000. Well, it's worth far more to the person that owns the house, because it's his own, he built his life in the home, in the neighborhood, and it's a cinch that with that kind of money, even back then, they couldn't get a place anywhere else. Most of those people that were displaced I'm sure never had a home of their own again, and there were quite a number of homeowners in this area. This bulldozer approach to people—it's cruel.

*QUESTION:* And now gentrification is a threat as well?

*MAURICE MACCRACKIN:* Recently, the Miami Purchase group was formed [a private group that buys architecturally significant buildings in the area and rehabilitates them]. They were securing houses and we knew that this was going to result in speculation. Over-the-Rhine [a nearby neighborhood] had been bought and people displaced, and it became very bad.

A real estate friend of mine calls this "resegregation." Whites moved out, mostly because of black people coming in, and now they're moving back. That's one way to displace people—to come in all of a sudden and say, "It's a historical area, you got to fix up this facade, you got to do this, you got to do that." And then the residents check their resources and they can't do it, so the property is condemned and someone who has the money comes in and buys it and fixes it up.

Over at Lincoln Courts, which is right back of the Music Hall, they have public housing. They've put on these fancy roofs and entrance ways so the view will be nice for these people that are parking and coming to the Music Hall. 'Course they didn't put out the money to make it nicer for the people that have been living there and paying all those rents all these years.

I had a preacher friend in my youth, and I heard him say once at service that "Cincinnati should not be called the Queen City; it should be called the Peacock City. It loves its plumage—the arts, the sciences, music! But it hasn't any concern about these ugly feet that are planted in the West End of the city."

*

## CREATION OF THE COMMUNITY LAND COOPERATIVE

The Community Land Cooperative of Cincinnati was created with dramatic speed in the spring of 1980, when one family's extraordinary need for housing coincided with a visit to the community by someone with knowledge on the subject of CLTs. A recently formed coalition of community religious groups provided an organizational base for the effort.

*

*MAURICE MACCRACKIN:* I suppose, if I thought that providence worked in details of this kind, I would say that providence was at work. *Circumstances* were—I can safely say that, all right. It just happened that when this family, a woman with nine children, was desperate for a place to stay, Chuck happened along [Chuck Matthei, director of the Institute for Community Economics]. When I told him about the need of this Mrs. Maxwell and her children for a place, we got off immediately on the land trust idea.

I'd had a call from Mrs. Maxwell. She lived right over about two blocks from the church here, and somebody suggested she call me because I've been around a while and might know of a place. That was on a Tuesday and she was to be evicted Saturday of that week—she and her nine children. Well, even if you have one or two children, 75 percent or so of the places won't take you. And she was absolutely hopeless about finding a place. She had *looked*—she's a very enterprising, wonderful woman; she can cope if there's anything to cope with.

*VIVIAN MAXWELL:* I was living on York Street and my landlord found out how many kids I have, and he wanted me to move. I was paying like $250 a month, and we went to court and he wouldn't accept his rent—he just wanted his house. But I had nine kids living with me, actually ten.

When I had moved in I didn't tell the truth on the lease, because people don't like to rent to nobody with no 10 kids. And I *got* 10 kids, and 15 grandkids. And anytime one of my kids want to come home or my grandkids want to come spend a week here with me, whatever—it's just the house—but people find out, and, "Oh, my goodness, she got too many kids. She got to get out of my house. They'll tear it down, break it up." So anyway we went to court, and I got in touch with Rev. MacCrackin, and I told him how I didn't have nowhere to go. So Rev. MacCrackin helped and we finally found a place in Mt. Auburn. Six rooms, $350 a month, and we had one doorknob in the place—if you'd go in the john and forget to take the doorknob you'd have to stay in there until somebody let you out. This doorknob was the only one in the house and we had to carry it around with us, or if somebody got locked on the other side you'd have to find the doorknob or something to let them out.

And this lady, she gave me a real rough way to go. I had to pay too much rent to get in there, and she wouldn't fix anything. Rev. MacCrackin had to have my bathroom fixed so we could use it. She didn't even give me a door key to the house. And she would come to my house while I was gone—if I was gone to the store or something—and she would curse my kids.

So I looked in the paper—and I was actually looking for a crib for my kids—and I seen this house for $11,000. And I asked Rev. MacCrackin, would he take me out there, because I didn't have transportation. I said I was gonna try to talk the lady into letting me have the house on land contract. And we met with the lady, Mrs. Hamilton—we met with her and she said she didn't think her husband would go for the land contract.

I just fell in love with the house. I'd seen the yard—space for the kids to play in—and I said, this is the home I really need for my children. And I just prayed real hard.

*MAURICE MACCRACKIN:* About a year before this problem came up, we formed the West End Alliance of Churches and Ministries. So when Chuck was here and Mrs. Maxwell's problem came up we called a meeting and got, I think, about four or five of the churches represented. We met right here in the yard—about 40 people, I guess—and talked about it.

Chuck talked. Mrs. Maxwell was there. Her need was so great that people—some of them, I think—felt a little pushed, without maybe understanding the land trust idea that much. So we made it clear that while Mrs. Maxwell's need was very great, we didn't want to hinge it on that. If they became involved in the land trust they certainly ought to understand what it is. So we sort of withdrew that emphasis, but then we had two or three other meetings explaining what the land trust was and Sister Barbara and I put down option money. Chuck made it clear that if that $10,000 was available [through the Revolving Loan Fund of the Institute for Community Economics], which he thought would be coming in, he would loan it.

*VIVIAN MAXWELL:* Rev. MacCrackin called and told me they were going to try to get something started so I could get that house for myself. And they got $500 together, good faith money. And when Chuck came back through, they discussed it again and he promised me—he said, you gonna have that house. And I believed all the time that I was going to get it. I didn't know *why,* I didn't know *how* I was going to get it, but I just *believed,* you know. I just used to lay up and sleep at night and dream about it. Get up in the daytime and daydream about it.

And then Rev. MacCrackin came out one day and told me, "Well, we finally got the money—Chuck sent us the money." And he said, "We'll close this evening. When do you want to move in?"

I said, "This evening!" Because I was staying with my daughter, you know—I had kids spread out all over town. A girlfriend had a couple of them, and my mother-in-law had a couple. And I was pregnant. And my daughter didn't have but four rooms and she got three kids, and I think I had about six or seven of my kids with me, and we slept in this one room. That was, you know, the first time I'd ever had to stay with anyone—it was nerve-wracking. I think I was happier on that day than I'd ever been in my whole entire life.

It's got a big backyard to it, and to me it seems like a lot, like 35 acres. I can hang my clothes out. It's got a basement. It's nine rooms, all together, with three floors, two baths. It's a whole lot of work got to be done, but I feel like I'm on Sugar Hill now. 'Cause I can take my time and get a little at a time. And I don't have to worry about nobody knocking on my door and saying, "Mrs. Maxwell, you got to go 'cause you got too many kids." And I don't have to worry about my landlord telling me, your kids can't play in my yard, or what have you. These things I don't have to worry about.

*

## ONGOING EFFORTS

Not long after buying the house for Mrs. Maxwell, the newly formed CLCC was able to acquire a second property.

*

*WILLY WATTS:* The second house was a multiple place—it has several families living in it. These people had been notified that the building would be going up for sale. One lady who lived in the building came to one of our meetings and said she believed that if the co-op would back her, she could find somebody that would lend us the money.

Now we have obtained the money and have bought the place. The building had to have some work done on the roof. Of course, people are living there and the rain that was coming in has not driven them off, and we intend to get it fixed before this happens. It has a little storefront to it which they call the Contact Center, a very busy place. It is a center for people who are in need of housing, food, clothing. Chances are it would have been moved had a speculator bought the

Robert O'Keefe

*Vivian Maxwell with her youngest child and Maurice MacCrackin, on the porch of her new home.*

place. This is a very good example of what we're trying to do. Now the Contact Center will be there because we own the building. The people will be there; they won't have to move. [The property is leased to one individual on terms that allow her to sublease to the existing tenants, who are not interested in a long-term CLT lease or in having a share in owning the building. This case is mentioned in Chapter 15, where CLT lease arrangements are discussed.]

*QUESTION:* Now that the land trust is organized, what are you, as director, working on?

*WILLY WATTS:* My responsibility is to find houses that we can buy in the target areas we've set up, and find families that can fit into each building, whether it's a big building or a family-size house.

One of the problems I run into is that the people that own the property don't live in town. It's hard to get in touch with them. Another problem is it's hard to talk with some of the people who live in or are renting the place. They've been living there for a number of years, maybe they're elderly people, and they naturally suspect you. We've gotten so we don't write anything down in front of them. We just walk up and start talking about their garden or how're you feeling today. But we don't want to arouse any suspicions. They've been thrown out, maybe two or three times—if they haven't themselves, their friends, their neighbors, their relatives have—and when they see somebody in the neighborhood looking at buildings or asking questions or writing something down, they suspect them right away.

*QUESTION:* What kinds of prices are being asked now for property in this neighborhood?

*WILLY WATTS:* This land is on the speculator's market. There are buildings that are literally nothing but shells. Three or two years ago these buildings were going for $5,000, $3,000, almost anything that you wanted to give. Today, they are asking $30,000 for them. We hope they don't get it and will come on back down to where they're supposed to be, and then we can buy. We have a pretty good chance; I don't know any old shell houses that have actually been sold for $30,000.

*

In acquiring property and arranging financing and lease agreements, the CLCC has been advised by Legal Aid attorney Pat Hornschmeier. Here he discusses some of the problems involved in acquiring property and in matching potential acquisitions with potential leaseholders.

*

*PAT HORNSCHMEIER:* I think one thing that's important—and this isn't really even a legal point—is that the group has to carefully scrutinize the finances of the individual transaction. I think the Community Land Co-op has had transactions very favorable to the co-op and will undoubtedly work out very well. But there's always the danger with an enthusiastic, public-minded group that they will say, "Ah, this is a good deal. These people were going to sell this building for $20,000, and they're going to give it to us for $10,000—so let's sign on the dotted line." Then they find out, for instance, that it will cost $30,000 to rehabilitate instead of $15,000. And the whole thing will just be a total bomb.

Now the co-op here in Cincinnati has enough sophistication so that, for instance, they've already turned down one deal where the guy was just going to give them the house—I guess for one dollar. The guy just wanted to get rid of it. A couple of board members looked at it and said, "This thing is so bad, even if we got it for nothing, to get it so a family could live in it would be more money than the family could possibly ever pay off." I think especially in a city like Cincinnati, where there are a lot of vacant and boarded up buildings, this is going to be a real danger.

I think groups have to not only evaluate the building but also evaluate this particular financing package and this potential occupant. If you can match up the three and make it work, that's what you do. The danger is, in many cases you'll have the three, but the person who needs a place

Robert O'Keefe

this week will not match up with the financing you've got or the building you've got. Then the group has to make the hard choice: Maybe they're not going to be able to give this person this building this week. I think the crucial thing is to have the expertise to make that decision—to weigh out whether this person can handle this building. I think it comes down to taking a look at the 20- or 30-year picture, and putting a figure on how much they need for maintenance of the building, how much for stuff like utilities. Hopefully taxes and insurance would be pretty clear-cut, but maintenance is going to depend on how much people can do themselves, how much they are going to be able to get from low-cost sources, how much they are going to have to go out and pay the full price for. Also, maintenance depends on the current condition of this building. If the building's already got a 10-year-old roof on it, for instance, then you've got to figure that in 10 or 12 years that roof's going to have to be replaced. I've devised a little form for checking out the situation. A co-op needs to have somebody who can fill out the blanks on this form and make their answers stick over 20 or 30 years.

*

Calculating what a family can afford over a 20- or 30-year period is, of course, not easy. Sister Barbara Wheeler, chairwoman of the board of trustees, comments on this difficulty.

*

*BARBARA WHEELER:* One family has been looking at property for almost a month and a half. Initially, he was out of a job and couldn't get unemployment because he was from Kentucky. But he's a pipefitter, and now he's working as a pipefitter again, so he really has a good income. I mean, people can vacillate all the way from having nothing to having a good job. What are you going to do with that? Well, if we don't take risks with those kinds of people, and realize we're not always going to win, then I don't think we're even going to begin to change what's always been the plight of the poor—that they could never get any equity. I think the choice of leaseholders is going to have to do with faith in people and also with the realization that it's not always going to work.

*

## REFLECTIONS AFTER THE FIRST YEAR

Bruce Hinkley, Sister Barbara Wheeler, and Sister Monica McGloin comment on the accomplishments of the CLCC in its first year and on the risks and opportunities they see in its future. Monica McGloin, like Barbara Wheeler, is a member of the Dominican Sisters of the Sick Poor, who has donated part of her time to the CLCC so that she can work on writing grant applications and other fund-raising activities.

*

*BRUCE HINKLEY:* We had never tried to do something like this before. We had been a rather loosely connected ecumenical group of religious folks in the community, and this gave us an opportunity to see if we really wanted to work together in a way that would effect some changes.

One of the things about community organizing that we've found here, and that I have also found in other places, is the greatest risk is not so much trying to bring ourselves together to deal with a particular problem, but trying to stay together when we get together. There is a kind of

*Sister Barbara Wheeler.*

Robert O'Keefe

dissatisfaction and infighting that tends to destroy many good efforts. It's like the old Pogo strip: "We have met the enemy and he is us." When it comes to taking action, it doesn't require some malevolent force from out there to do us in—we do ourselves in. It's really exciting that this hasn't happened with the land trust, because it means that at the very outset of the organization we're succeeding in trusting one another; we're succeeding in saying we want to do such and such and then going ahead and getting it done. This sounds very simple, but it is a very significant step for us, and for most folks trying to organize around some specific issue.

*QUESTION:* Earlier you spoke of upper-income people moving into the community and wanting you all to leave, and of course you are resisting that, but do you see any hope of a mixed neighborhood finally evolving?

*BRUCE HINKLEY:* The exciting possibility is that a mixed-income neighborhood assures that the best services are delivered to the neighborhood. Therefore we are happy to see not just low-income people live in our neighborhood. We feel that a mixed neighborhood is really the way that people ought to live in order that they grow and learn the most about each other and are able to enjoy differences rather than constantly fear or deplore these differences. I think the rub comes when we realize that if we are low-income people and if it's left only to the market to change how real estate is done in this community, then we will all be driven out. And it won't be any great evil tide of ill-wishing people that drives us from the community; it will simply be the so-called housing process. Money will just force us out. Only if we have some control in the market, like the land trust provides, are we going to have the means to cooperate with people of greater power and more income.

*MONICA MCGLOIN:* If we can get some property, it will prevent some people from moving in. At least we will know that *all* the property won't eventually go because we'll have some of it. And it would give some sense of hope to people in the community—a sense of wanting to build and stay, because they would see that there are some ways to maintain some control. You don't have to just sit there and be pushed around.

*QUESTION:* What problems do you see the co-op facing in the future?

*MONICA MCGLOIN:* Because we were faced with an immediate situation we moved very quickly. Maybe that was good because it could have taken us five years to get started otherwise. But I think we need to plan more about the people who become part of the co-op, particularly user-members; we need to have a clear understanding of how we're going to work with these people before they get a home, and how to train people for maintenance of a home. I think one of the things that's really important is the leaseholder's personal involvement in the co-op. Coming to board meetings if you're on the board or coming to membership meetings has got to be as important a requirement as making your monthly payment.

For poor people, there have for so long been people doing things to them and for them and at them, but rarely with them. What's really important is that people have a sense of their own power as members of the co-op. Otherwise, even if somebody has a house, I don't think they've really learned anything—I don't think they're really in a position to do something for somebody else. Leaseholder participation is also important because I suspect that ultimately we're going to run into a situation where someone is not going to make their payment, and we may have to do something that we don't want to do—like say to the person, "Well, this arrangement is going to have to end." I think that if the person is involved in the co-op there's less likelihood that that will happen, because there's a sense of responsibility *for* and *with* the other members rather than just a sense of living in this place. You know, people have always rented—they're not used to owning homes and they need support from each other.

Robert O'Keefe

*Signs of gentrification.*

Robert O'Keefe

Robert O'Keefe

*BARBARA WHEELER:* It's a strange thing—as many times as we complained and picketed, as many times as we tried brainstorming, we never really thought of the possibility that people could own their own homes. It just was never on the horizon. It's strange that it's that new to us who are very much aware of the plight of the poor, and the fact that they would always remain poor until we had some way to build something where they had a regular kind of income. But as for building this kind of system, that could provide equity, that just never really came.

But I think that even more important than homeownership is community. We've been trying to build community for years. That's one of the reasons we [the Dominican Sisters of the Sick

Poor] moved into the neighborhood; one of the reasons why we got out of the whole third-party payment situation with Medicare and Medicaid, because somehow it means more to establish relationships with people on an ongoing basis. Help doesn't mean a thing in any other kinds of terms. I think the whole community aspect of the land cooperative is very, very important. I think, also, one of the drawbacks could be if we got so involved in getting people in homes and getting them equity that we isolate them from each other. Somehow we need to draw together to get this kind of political strength that will help people to be something. It's that sense of community that will hold the whole concept together. I think unless people see it in some relationship to somebody else, it will fall apart and be like any other kind of housing.

*

## UPDATE

Since March of 1981, when the accounts and comments that make up this case study were recorded, the CLCC has continued to make steady progress. As of December, 1981, two more buildings have been acquired: a six-unit apartment house and a two-family house. In addition, two other buildings are in the process of being acquired, and a third, on which an option has been acquired, is under consideration.

The co-op has established its own revolving loan fund to finance new acquisitions. As monthly payments are made by leaseholders and other tenants, the money is returned to the fund and is available for further acquisitions. At present there is approximately $150,000 in this pool of capital, which includes both money donated outright to the fund and money made available through interest-free or low-interest loans.

Because the CLCC has been acquiring occupied buildings, and not all of the occupants have been interested in long-term leases or homeownership, it now has some tenants who rent from it on a conventional basis. An effort is made to familiarize all occupants with the purpose of the CLT and the benefits of the long-term lease arrangement and the opportunity it offers for building equity. However, those who prefer to continue as conventional renters are allowed to do so. The CLCC has displaced no one. (Further discussion of the acquisition of occupied buildings is presented in Chapter 15.)

Several programs have been established to help leaseholders, particularly those in the unfamiliar role of purchasing and maintaining their own homes. The CLCC now has a "family worker" whose sole job is to provide help and counseling for the occupants of the buildings—while business arrangements between the CLCC and the occupants remain the concern of the director. The Better Housing League (from which the CLCC received the Better Housing League Award for 1981) has worked with the co-op in providing home-maintenance training for leaseholders. At the present time, a group of students from an area high school is working on the Green and Vine Street building on Saturdays, doing painting and simple repairs. Teenage occupants of the building are working with them.

The CLCC's greatest immediate concern is with finding money to pay staff to supervise and expand these programs and ensure that they can be maintained. At this point, only the part-time director's job is a paid staff position; all other staff time is donated. A grant that will provide a salary for one additional paid position has just been received, and there is hope of receiving more grant money for this purpose.

# CHAPTER 8

# Cedar Riverside Community Minneapolis, Minnesota

A few years ago, the community of Cedar Riverside seemed doomed. Its people were to be displaced and its housing demolished so that the land could be used for high-rise apartment buildings. The story of how the community successfully resisted this fate is not primarily the story of a community land trust. For the most part, it is the story of other community organizations working to gain control of the local urban renewal process and turn it to the advantage of members of the existing community.

The Cedar Riverside Community Land Trust has only recently been established; it has not played a role in community organizing or planning or development, and it will not be discussed until the last section of this chapter. It is the conclusion of the story, but as the conclusion it is extremely important. In the first part of this book we described, in abstract terms, the way in which a CLT can be the means for a community to capture and retain both the value of its own efforts and the value of public subsidies channeled into the community. The Cedar Riverside CLT is now in position to do these things, and to do them on a very significant scale.

The role that the CLT is now in a position to play in Cedar Riverside is basically the role that has been envisioned for a possible second-generation CLT in Columbia Heights. Simply by performing its essential function of *holding land permanently* for the community, it will make community gains permanent and will keep housing affordable far into the future. The CLT in this case can be compared to the keystone in an arch: It cannot be put in place until other community accomplishments are in place, but the other accomplishments cannot be stabilized for the future until the CLT is in place. The arch of community accomplishment in Cedar Riverside is a large and complicated one. This case study is therefore larger and more technically complicated than those that have preceded it. Perhaps one of the lessons to be learned from it is that if a community is to accomplish what Cedar Riverside has accomplished, it must be willing to deal with complexity.

Cedar Riverside is a community of about 6,500 people in central Minneapolis, between the downtown business district on the west and the University of Minnesota campus on the east. Its boundaries are sharply defined by the Mississippi River and a complex of expressways and interchanges. The area includes the campus of Augsburg College, two hospitals, a junior college, and a part of the campus of the University of Minnesota. In the Cedar West area, there is a high-rise housing complex (the origin of which will be explained) and nearby there is a public housing complex for the elderly. Along Cedar Avenue, in the Central and Seven Corners areas, are commercial buildings housing small, locally owned shops, with some apartments on the upper floors. The rest of the area is occupied primarily by relatively old, single-family houses. Until the 1960s, most of these were owner-occupied homes.

In the 1960s a developer, incorporated as Cedar Riverside Associates (CRA), began buying property in the neighborhood. In 1968, CRA succeeded in getting federal and city approval for an urban renewal plan in which CRA itself was strategically situated as both current landowner and project developer. In 1971, the project was designated the first New Town in Town project, under the New Communities program of HUD. The plan called for replacement of all existing privately owned housing with high-rise apartment buildings. The first stage of the project, the Cedar Square West apartment complex, was completed in the early 70s. Since then, however, much has changed in Cedar Riverside—and not in the way that Cedar Riverside Associates anticipated.

One of the primary instruments for this change has been the Cedar Riverside Project Area Committee (the PAC, pronounced "the pack"). Mandated by federal regulations affecting the original renewal projects, the PAC has evolved into a representative and very influential community organization.

Dorothy Jacobs, a member of the PAC staff, describes Cedar Riverside as it was when the original renewal program first took shape, and as it is today.

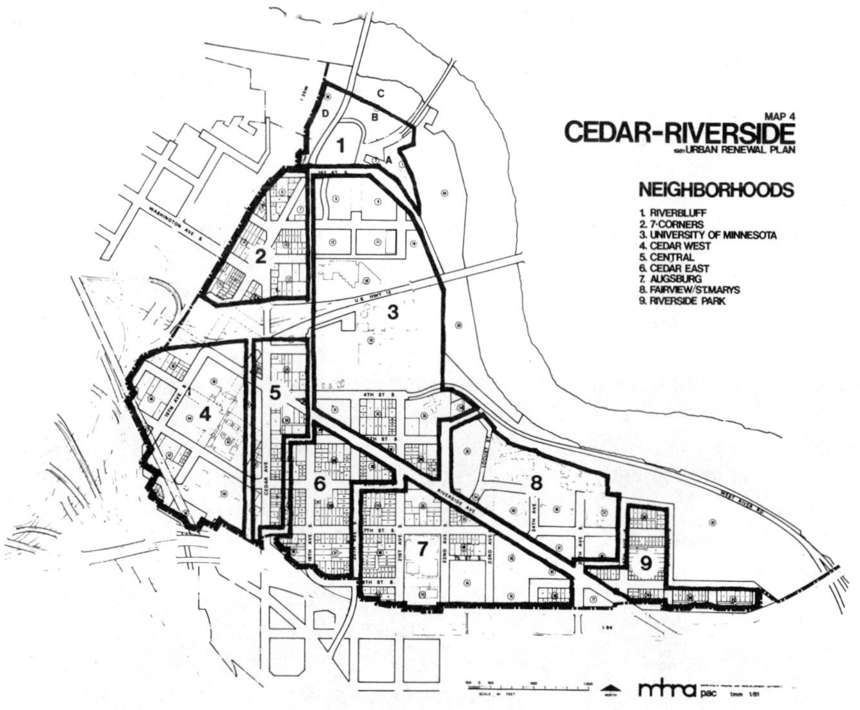

*

*DOROTHY JACOBS:* Thirty or 40 years ago this was a Scandinavian neighborhood, a working-class neighborhood made up of owner-occupant, single-family homes. In the late 1940s and 50s the neighborhood really began to deteriorate. By about 1955 the city planning department was looking at it as something that needed to be dealt with, as far as the city was concerned. The first report on Cedar Riverside came out in the late 50s—that the neighborhood would have to be renewed in some way.

What happened was that a man named Keith Heller, who was president of Cedar Riverside Associates, got wind of this in the late 50s and early 60s, and he and a woman named Gloria Segal formed a partnership. They started to buy up property in Cedar Riverside in the early 60s, and by about 1965 they owned major chunks of property in the neighborhood. Their plan at that time was to build three-story walk-ups for students. It was close to the university and it would be a real lucrative neighborhood for student housing.

*QUESTION:* How deteriorated, really, was the neighborhood at that point?

*DOROTHY JACOBS:* It was *beginning* to deteriorate. A lot of the people were senior citizens who had lived here all of their lives, raised their families here, and they didn't have the money anymore to keep up their houses—and it was beginning to go.

Two major freeways were built, which displaced huge amounts of people. The freeways and the university expansion put a lot of pressure on this neighborhood. It was sort of becoming not a place to live. People were beginning to sell—and Keith Heller did a form of blockbusting with hippies. He would buy a house and immediately rent it to a commune of hippies. This caused incredible problems in the neighborhood, because these older Scandinavian people were fairly conservative and did not want to live next door to hippies.

Towards the end of the 60s, Henry T. McKnight, who was a state senator, started to get involved with Gloria and Keith. At that time, Washington created the New Town in Town Program, and with the help of Henry T. McKnight—the money he had and the political connections he had—Cedar Riverside Associates was successful in getting a contract with HUD to have Cedar Riverside become a New Town in Town. And in 1968, when the city council passed the urban renewal plan, they gave development rights to CRA.

The city council and everybody in the city were real excited about this proposal, and they gave Keith Heller everything he needed. And the federal government came in with loan guarantees, the whole pot, to help this company build this New Town in Town. They were going to build a housing complex that would have involved 12,500 apartments, all rental units, changing the community from a low-density, single-family-unit neighborhood into all high-density, the highest density possible—125 units per acre. The whole neighborhood would have been demolished, all the houses wiped out. They planned ten stages that would have taken place over 20 years. The first stage was Cedar Square West.

There was neighborhood opposition to the plan, but not much official neighborhood involvement. Public hearings were really loaded in the developer's favor. One public hearing went on until five o'clock in the morning, but in spite of the neighborhood opposition the whole thing went through. At that point we had no voice, we were totally powerless. So they went ahead and were successful in completing stage one of their project [Cedar Square West].

*QUESTION:* How much has the community changed since 1968? Does it have the same kind of residents now that it had then?

*DOROTHY JACOBS:* Ironically, it hasn't changed a lot. All of the property is rental property. We all rent our homes from Cedar Riverside Associates, but it's a very stable community. We

John Walkip

*The Cedar East neighborhood as seen from Cedar Square West high-rise apartments.*

did an ownership survey in 1977, and the average length of residency was 6.5 years, which is almost higher than any other neighborhood in Minneapolis, including the owner-occupied neighborhoods. This stability is one of the reasons that we've been able to have the kind of political power this community has.

It's a low-to-moderate-income neighborhood. In 1977, the median income was under $5,000. I don't think unemployment is real high now. I would say that most of the single-parent families living in the neighborhood are welfare families, but if I were going to describe the neighborhood in general I would say it's a working-poor neighborhood.

*QUESTION:* How is it that low-income people can still afford to live here—with CRA still owning all this property and obviously wanting to get all they can out of it?

*DOROTHY JACOBS:* We are now in the midst of our sixth rent strike. The first strike took place in 1974. Four hundred families went out on strike. We settled within six months and we were able to get the landlord to agree to a more-responsible rent increase, and since that time we have gone out on strike five more times. So through the strength of the tenants union we have kept rents extremely low here.

*QUESTION:* You've lived here for 11 years. What brought you to Cedar Riverside in the first place, and what has kept you here?

*DOROTHY JACOBS:* I've lived in the neighborhood since 1970, and started to work for the PAC in 1976. It's kind of funny—I moved here for the cheap housing and the good living situation, and I did not think that I would stay for 11 years—as most people in the neighborhood didn't think they'd stay very long. I'm here because I believe in the power of the neighborhood. I really believe that neighborhoods should determine their own destiny. I think that Cedar Riverside is just an incredible example of what a neighborhood can accomplish, what you can do if people are willing to get involved. The amount of work and the amount of volunteer hours amassed in this neighborhood is incredible. We've got the tenants union, now called the Community Union, which has been the tenant-organizing force. We've got the PAC, and we also have got our own Community Development Corporation (CDC).

*

The West Bank Tenants Union (now the Cedar Riverside Community Union) is the oldest of the three organizations mentioned by Dorothy Jacobs. Jack Cann has worked with the tenants union since its beginning, and more recently he has worked with both the PAC and the CDC in developing alternative plans for affordable housing in the community. He describes the early years of struggle against CRA and the New Town in Town project.

*

*JACK CANN:* I got involved with Cedar Riverside in 1969 because I was working with the citywide tenants organization at the time. The tenants union had started in early '69, and it became clear almost immediately that one of the problems that tenants faced was the enormous demolition of low-class housing that had occurred during the 60s through highway and urban renewal projects. So people who were working with the tenants union decided to try to work with community organizations around the city to reorient city development policies. The first vehicle for doing that was a challenge to the city's "workable program," which at the time was a requirement which the city had to meet every two years in order to get any federal urban renewal contracts signed. We set up a coalition of about 15 neighborhood organizations that wound up holding up about $50 million in federal funding for Minneapolis for over a year, until the city made some real substantial changes. The Cedar Riverside area was one thing we focused on.

Because I was working on this redevelopment stuff anyhow, I got involved with people who were just starting to talk about one last attempt to build a community organization to try to fight the development that was proposed. They looked at it as a last-ditch effort that probably wouldn't succeed. So what we did in Cedar Riverside was planning and organizing for the first meeting of what was to be called the Cedar Riverside Community Union. When that group met [1970], about 150 people turned out, and everybody was so encouraged by the turnout that they decided to go on. They adopted several projects almost immediately. One was getting the People's Center building away from the university and getting a number of community service programs set up there. [The People's Center is an old church building which now houses a number of community organizations, including the PAC and the CDC.] The second was getting involved in this "workable program" challenge—with the specific demand for Cedar Riverside being actually threefold. One was that there be a project area committee set up; the second was that low-income family housing be stressed more in the development plans; and the third was that adequate plans for relocation be made—because at that point all the actual land acquisition had been done privately

*Demonstration on Riverside Avenue, with the People's Center in the background.*

Ken Sower

and there were no plans to pay anybody relocation assistance. The final project was challenging university condemnation that was taking place on a pretty wide scale at that time. The community union started moving on all of those projects at once, and met with varying degrees of success. We won the workable program challenge, and one of the results of that was that project area committees had to be set up for the Cedar Riverside and Nicollet Island projects. What followed was another six or eight months of political hassle about what the composition of the project area committee here would be.

*QUESTION:* What were HUD's guidelines concerning that composition?

*JACK CANN:* It was generally something about being representative of the community affected, including minorities. The implication was that all elements of the community were to be adequately represented. The other kind of guidelines language was that it was to have direct access to the decision-making process.

The big fight was about whether all of the big developers in the neighborhood would automatically be guaranteed seats on the PAC. That is finally what happened: CRA, the Batzli Development Company, all of the hospitals, the University of Minnesota, and Augsburg College all got guaranteed seats on the PAC, and that was automatically about one-third of the seats right there in favor of the project as it had been proposed. We took a delegation of neighborhood people to Chicago one weekend and thought that we had all of that squelched. In fact, we had a letter from HUD saying they weren't going to tolerate that. The next weekend a delegation including the city coordinator and the former mayor of Minneapolis, who was working for Cedar Riverside at the time, flew to Chicago, and there was a new letter the next week saying that it was okay.

*QUESTION:* How did the community eventually manage to change the character of the PAC?

*JACK CANN:* Two things happened. One was that the opponents of the development didn't dry up and go away. They settled in for the long term and started to build alternative institutions in the neighborhood, and those institutions—like the People's Center, the collectively organized Riverside Cafe, and the grocery co-ops—became stable elements in the community. At the same time, the

New Community project started to fall apart of its own weight. It was a project that was ridiculous in its conception—not just in what they wanted to build, but more importantly, it was built on a financial house of cards, with a ridiculous financing mechanism that has failed in virtually every other New Community project. And so by 1974 there were big newspaper stories about serious financial problems and about gross mismanagement of the project. The developer simply was not capable of managing a project on anything like that scale. Money that was supposed to be drawn down over a ten-year period they spent entirely in two years. They didn't do the financial reporting to HUD that they were supposed to. So those two things—the fact that the developers were busy discrediting themselves in the press, and that the opponents of the project were busy building positive institutions in the neighborhood—resulted in a lot of people who had been early supporters of the project becoming disillusioned and realizing that what the opponents of the project were saying made a lot of sense.

The other thing that happened was that initially the representatives for Cedar Square West tended to be toadies for the owners. The owners set up and hired organizers for a tenants organization, and not surprisingly the PAC representatives for the tenants organization tended to be very vocal supporters of the developer. That lasted until the first big rent increase—which was again about 1975—and then a *real* tenants organization formed and took over the organization that the owners had set up, and elected representatives to the PAC who were strong tenants rights advocates. For all those reasons, by 1975 the political climate in the neighborhood had changed completely.

*

In 1973, the community, acting through the Cedar Riverside Environmental Defense Fund, had brought suit against CRA, the New Communities administration, and the City of Minneapolis, charging that the environmental impact statement that had been filed for the New Town in Town project was inadequate. In 1975, the case was decided in the community's favor. As Jack Cann explains, this court decision made it impossible for the already ailing CRA to proceed with the original New Town in Town project.

Ken Sower

*

*JACK CANN:* The decision meant that not only was the development completely bankrupt, but there was no way that whatever alternative was proposed could very closely resemble what was initially proposed—because the judge just said wholesale that what was proposed was completely ridiculous from any kind of sound planning viewpoint. Ever since then it's essentially been the PAC and the Community Union and the West Bank Community Development Corporation, working pretty closely with city government, to get through a completely different set of plans and come up with some way to implement them.

*

Charlotte Fisketti

*Ann Waterhouse.*

## THE CDC

The West Bank Community Development Corporation was founded in that pivotal year of 1975. Ann Waterhouse, first staff person and chairwoman of its board of directors, tells how it was created. In 1980, Ann left the West Bank CDC to become regional director of the National Consumer Cooperative Bank. Based in Minneapolis, she is still in touch with the Cedar Riverside community.

*

*ANN WATERHOUSE:* I moved into the Cedar Riverside community originally in 1969, when I was attending the University of Minnesota, and lived there for about a year and a half—at which point I felt I had become a part of at least a small portion of the community. But I found out—we all found out—that the building that we lived in was going to be torn down by the university in order to build an athletic field. We tried to negotiate with the university as a small group of residents but we failed miserably. The university simply laughed us out of their offices. We were a small group of people with no political or economic clout, and they didn't have to deal with us. So everyone was dispersed. I left town before the building was torn down and was gone for about three and a half years, but that experience of community really stuck with me—of helping to organize the first food co-op, of helping to organize the Cedar Riverside People's Center Clinic, of working with the residents to try to save our building, and I realized that Minneapolis was a place that I wanted to come back to.

I came back in 1974 and began working with the West Bank Tenants Union, which was at that time trying to save the entire neighborhood. I worked as an organizer part-time while I was typing downtown full-time, helping to coordinate two or three of the rent strikes that occurred. But in the process of doing that I realized that rent strikes were only one reaction to a bad situation, and that even the most successful rent strike was not going to solve the neighborhood's problems, that we were still faced with an absentee landlord who owned the land and the buildings. We were still faced with having to react to his decisions, and it was a frustration. I decided personally, along with a lot of other people, that we had to begin working on some action-oriented plan of our own.

There was a conference held in January of '75, which we had been organizing toward for about four months, and it turned out to be the founding conference for the West Bank CDC. About 50 residents showed up that day, amid blizzard conditions—40-below-zero weather and 30-mile-an-hour winds—but there were enough people there so that we did spend the day huddled inside, talking about community-based economic development and exactly what kind of impact the residents could have, what kinds of projects we wanted to undertake. I was chosen along with six other people to form a steering committee, to incorporate the CDC and to establish a grocery store committee. [Residents wanted to do something about the fact that there was no full-scale grocery in the community.]

The first year the CDC operated with literally no funds. Eventually the board of directors was approached by the North Country Co-op—the "mother of us all" co-op, as we refer to it—which was the first whole foods or "new wave" co-op in the Minneapolis area. They said they had salary money available for an extra position, but had decided that rather than using it to help run the store they would donate that salary to the West Bank CDC to hire a staff person. What happened was that I was chosen as the first staff person to work full-time with the CDC, living on this $50 a week donated by the food co-op. The first few months I wrote two grant proposals—one to the city of Minneapolis for community development block grant money, and one to the State of Minnesota, which has a program that funds CDCs.

Both of those grants were funded, and we were suddenly moved into the position of operating on a $92,150 budget the next year. It was quite amazing—about twice as much as I had hoped for. We ended up hiring four staff people. I mean, I can laugh at it now, but at the time it was definitely what needed to happen. We worked on various planning activities, pulling together an overall economic plan—putting the co-op grocery together, getting our feet on the ground, securing development rights to various parts of the neighborhood, doing a lot of organizing, getting the residents involved. There was a constant member outreach and education program, telling people about the efforts of the CDC.

*QUESTION:* What has the relationship been between the CDC and the PAC?

*ANN WATERHOUSE:* The PAC has always maintained that formal contractual relationship with the city, to involve residents of the neighborhood in policy formation for the redevelopment of that area. The CDC has been the implementer, the developer—community-based, with an elected board and all those things, but much more the arm of the neighborhood for specific development projects. So, for instance, if the PAC decided that what the neighborhood needs is 80 units of Section 8 housing co-op, they would look toward the CDC to put together the financing packages, the management structure, funding sources—all of those pieces that you have to have in place to meet that need.

## THE CEDAR RIVERSIDE TAX INCREMENT DISTRICT

*DOROTHY JACOBS:* In 1971, Cedar Riverside became a tax increment district. Tax increment was something created by the state legislature to provide a way for cities to have a development fund for neighborhoods. What it means is that the taxes from the 1971 assessment on this neighborhood are all that go into the general fund for city services. Anything extra that is generated because of higher taxes resulting from development goes to the Minneapolis Community Development Agency for development in this community. If it's not abused it's really a good tool for the city to use to get neighborhoods developed. Unfortunately, in Minneapolis this is the only project that is not a prime example of abuse of tax increment funds. What it has turned out to be in other neighborhoods is just a free pot for big developers. And I think without the strong neighborhood involvement in this project, that's exactly what it would be here, too. We're almost a perfect tax increment district because Cedar Square West was built with federal money and it generates about $800,000 to $1,000,000 a year for this tax increment pot. So now in order to develop the neighborhood we can use this resource to sell bonds. We've got a pot of money that will pay off the bonds, so we're very safe here in terms of financing, and we're extremely lucky—considering what's happening with the federal money drying up for housing. It's a wonderful position to be in.

*

Charlotte Fisketti

*Cedar Square West.*

## THE PROJECT AREA COMMITTEE

Jack Cann has described the early history of the Cedar Riverside PAC. Dorothy Jacobs now describes the committee's present situation.

*

*DOROTHY JACOBS:* The Project Area Committee is under contract with the Community Development Agency. We negotiate a new contract every January and they fund us for one year—and our funds come out of the tax increment money. We're funded at about $100,000 a year.

How the PAC works is that each spring we have elections. We're divided into 5 districts and each district elects 5 delegates. Two years ago we turned out more people for our elections than the city primary did. If there's controversy in the air, our elections are incredible. And then we have 11 delegates that represent special interests. We have delegates from the business community, the religious community, the social service community, the culture community. And the major institutions in our area—the University of Minnesota, Fairview Hospital, St. Mary's Hospital, and Augsburg College—each have a delegate.

*

In its effort to develop an acceptable alternative to the original renewal plan for the community, the PAC has worked closely with neighborhood residents on a block-by-block basis. Tim Mungavan came to work for the PAC in 1976 after graduating from the University of Minnesota School of Architecture, where he had written his thesis on an "infill" housing project similar to the sort of projects then being considered in Cedar Riverside. Infill housing is designed to make use of unused space in a community while preserving existing housing that is sound or can be rehabilitated. It has thus been one of the basic elements of Cedar Riverside's alternative approach to urban renewal.

Since the PAC staff functions as a collective, with all members participating in both administrative and community-organizing activities, Tim Mungavan's work has been varied. His primary focus, however, has been in helping the community to develop workable and acceptable designs for new construction. He comments on this special role.

*

*TIM MUNGAVAN:* I think that it's a real exciting spot to be, but you have to be fairly comfortable with the skills that you have as a designer—that issue has to be fairly unobtrusive. The problem that I see with designers being involved in these decisions is that they become attached to a particular solution too early in the process—at a time when physical solutions should be just experimentation. They have to be able to understand the importance of providing information to people who are making decisions about what should happen in their lives. It's very important that it remain just a technical contribution to the decision-making process and that it not be seen too much as an effort to make your mark in the architectural world.

I didn't have as much confidence in that process actually working when I started as I have after really giving it a chance to work. Now I find that if I can assist people in getting the tools to make the decision, there's a tremendous creative energy in any group that's facing the situation. The key that I have found is that you've got to present the design or physical limitations in a way that's understandable and that they can manipulate, and then I find that solutions arise that I would not have thought of myself and that really do represent a collective vision.

*

## RECENT PLANNING AND DEVELOPMENT

By late 1977, a number of things had happened to make it possible for the community to proceed with its own alternative development projects. Some of these things have now been discussed. The tenants union had succeeded in holding rents down and thus stabilizing the population of the community and encouraging it to act. A strong PAC and a strong CDC had been developed, and both, by this time, were well staffed and had acquired valuable experience and expertise. The tax increment district provided an important financial base for development. The original New Town in Town project was dead and neither the City of Minneapolis nor HUD had much interest in trying to resurrect it. CRA had defaulted on loans guaranteed by HUD, and HUD had paid them up and thus was in a position to foreclose on CRA, but in 1977 these foreclosure proceedings had been delayed by the change in federal administrations. CRA therefore still held title to most of the private land in Cedar Riverside, though as a developer it was paralyzed. A final settlement of this complicated state of affairs was not made until 1980.

In the meantime, however, HUD had approached the City of Minneapolis with a revised renewal plan prepared by an independent consultant. This plan, proposed as the basis for continuing federal assistance, called for a total of 5,000 units of new housing and 200 rehabilitated units, rather than the originally planned 12,500 new units. HUD asked the city to determine, by June 15, 1977, whether the plan was acceptable to the city and other "interested local parties." The city council then created a nine-member task force, on which the PAC was represented, to consider the plan. The task force eventually rejected HUD's proposal and recommended instead a plan including only 1,900 units of new housing and 450 rehabilitated units, in addition to 2,113 existing units. Accepted by the city council, the task force recommendation cleared the way for the PAC and the CDC to proceed with specific planning and put together their own development projects, though a new comprehensive urban renewal plan was not approved by the city until 1981.

The first of these projects, and the beginning of the PAC's neighborhood-by-neighborhood planning program was in the Seven Corners area (see map at beginning of chapter). The project is noteworthy for the ingenuity with which it solves a complicated set of land-use and financial problems.

*

*DOROTHY JACOBS:* [In 1977], the City of Minneapolis Housing Authority got a development proposal from a motel developer that wanted to build a suburban motel on Seven Corners—you know, landscaped like you would out in the prairie. We really got upset about that, because there's only a little over five acres up there to develop on, and he wanted to use the whole thing for a surface parking lot and nice sprawled-out motel. So we said that's not going to happen. That's just a misuse of that land. We asked what would be the best way to utilize that land up there, and how can we come up with a plan. At that time the PAC said, *do* planning in that neighborhood, and then do planning in all the other neighborhoods. So the first subneighborhood planning document that we started and completed was in Seven Corners. We met weekly with all the residents in Seven Corners who would come to the meetings. As a result of that we did get the motel—which is very good for this neighborhood because of the generation of tax increment—but what we got in addition to that is 250 units of affordable housing, and structured parking. So this process allows us to utilize the land so that all needs are met.

*

An important part of the financing was a federal Urban Development Action Grant (UDAG) to the city to be used as a direct subsidy and/or as a loan to developers. The UDAG resulted from a proposal written by Jack Cann as a member of the PAC staff. The financial package in which the UDAG money was utilized is indeed complicated—even more complicated than the following account will indicate—but it is an extraordinary example of the kind of sophisticated financial planning that can make maximum use of federal subsidy and hold down the cost of housing.

*

*JACK CANN:* The mechanism that the CDC is working on for most of at least the initial development projects is a limited partnership with, initially, the CDC as co-general partner, so that the CDC has direct responsibility for all of the planning and lining up of the financing and so on. Then, as rent-up begins, it will turn over its general partner role to a resident co-op. That's been done for several reasons. For one thing, the CDC doesn't have a track record, and the chances of being able to pull off a project of this size on its own, with no ties into the financial network and no experience, are nil.

The subsidy for this project is all Urban Development Action Grant funds. There are two kinds of limits on the extent to which you can use those funds. One is that if you are building housing they will only let you use $15,000 per unit of UDAG money to provide direct subsidy. Since the housing is going to cost a little over $40,000 per unit to produce, we would still be talking about rents in the $400 to $500 range with just the $15,000 per unit subsidy. The second limit is that at the time the grant was awarded there had to be a minimum of three private dollars for every UDAG dollar, so if the housing was only going to be done by itself, that put a severe limit on how much UDAG money we could put into the housing.

We're doing three things to make the money go a lot further than if we just took $15,000 per unit and put it into the construction.

First, we linked the housing with the hotel

development that was being independently proposed for the area, and said, why don't we use an additional hunk of UDAG for the hotel? We'll provide it as a low-interest loan for the hotel and then use the repayment of that money as an additional subsidy for the housing, so that every year for the life of the hotel mortgage, which will be 40 years, there will be a payment of about $450,000 to write down the cost of debt service on the housing.

Second, to make the $15,000 per unit that we can put directly into the housing go further, we decided against putting it in as a front-end subsidy (which is essentially the same as investing it at 12 percent if it's a 12 percent mortgage). Instead, we're going to take the money and invest it ourselves in treasury bills or AA-rated corporate bonds and try to get 15 or 16 percent return and use that money to provide a subsidy.

Third, we'll assume that residents will be able to accommodate an annual rent increase of 7 or 7½ percent, which is lower than the average rent increase in the community, but more than what is necessary to cover the increase in operating costs. What that means is that we can initially accommodate a much lower income level than if we just used the interest on the invested UDAG money or just put it in as a finance subsidy. [In other words, the rent payments will at first be subsidized by the UDAG money (and its accrued interest), but this subsidy will gradually be replaced by the annual rent increase as the pool of UDAG funds is depleted.]

*

The second project undertaken by the CDC in partnership with a private developer involves the construction of 30 units of new housing in the River Bluff subneighborhood (see map at beginning of chapter). This project utilizes Section 8 subsidies that were committed to the community by HUD as part of the comprehensive "settlement" (described later). As in the case of the Seven Corners project, the CDC's role in the partnership will be turned over to a resident co-op. These "management co-ops" will not allow tenants to accumulate equity (beyond the value of a small down payment), but they will allow them to control their buildings. Section 8 was intended to subsidize rental housing and could not be used to subsidize a co-op in which tenants would accrue equity themselves.

In both the Seven Corners and River Bluff areas, development can proceed with minimum effect on existing residents since neither neighborhood was primarily residential to begin with. However, in the other three areas where the community will control development—Riverside Park, Cedar East, and Central—the problems of relating new housing to existing housing are much more intricate. In helping the residents of individual blocks to deal with these problems, the PAC staff has developed a workshop technique using three-dimensional models of the blocks being considered. Tim Mungavan explains.

*

*TIM MUNGAVAN:* We have models of each block that have the basic footprint of the block on them, and then some wooden models of the existing houses that fit on those spaces on the block model, then some models representing new units. In the workshops we just said, "Well, here's your block and here's what we have to put into it—how are we going to do that?" That was the only definition of the problem we began with. People began to look at the building condition and began to make choices, and they were quite aware of what was going on in a building. They knew if it was vacant. They knew if the person that lived there was happy or unhappy with what they had. So we went through the alternatives of how these new things were going to fit on here with much more sensitivity than I could have done in a separate situation. They knew a lot about the block, and all they needed to know besides that was how to move these blocks of wood around on a model. So these plans are very much a product

Charlotte Fisketti

*Joan Sully, Tim Mungavan, and Dorothy Jacobs (left to right), with a block model used in neighborhood planning workshops.*

of a group effort, and people felt that way about them, too, when they were done.

*

In these neighborhoods as well, many houses will be rehabilitated. To determine the need and probable cost of rehabilitation for each house, the PAC hired an experienced contractor to design a worksheet to be used by neighborhood volunteers in their survey. (This worksheet is presented in Chapter 12.) The contractor checked some ratings done by volunteers and found that they had been done quite objectively. The ratings for each building were then used to determine the practicality of rehabilitating the building. Where possible, arrangements will be made for residents to do at least some of the rehabilitation work themselves and thus accumulate "sweat equity" in the building.

## THE CRA "SETTLEMENT" AND THE PROSPECTS FOR A LAND TRUST

The last barriers to community-based development of Cedar Riverside's residential areas were removed in 1980. When HUD had finally foreclosed on Cedar Riverside Associates in 1978, CRA immediately brought suit against HUD and the city. Dorothy Jacobs describes the situation and its eventual resolution.

*

*DOROTHY JACOBS:* CRA sued the federal government for not keeping their part of the contract; they sued the City of Minneapolis for conspiring with the neighborhood group to do in the project. After two years, in June of 1980, the lawsuit was settled out of court. The federal government sold to the First National Bank of St. Paul liens that were worth about $38 million for $2.9 million. They wanted out, and that's how they got out. Now the First National Bank of St. Paul had made to CRA unsecured loans of over $5 million, and they were standing there holding the bag. So they were very aggressive about buying these liens from the federal government, because that was the only hope they had of recovering the debt.

The first deal that HUD was willing to work out with First National was for even less money, with the city getting nothing out of the deal. But this neighborhood sent 500 postcards to the secretary of HUD. We just raised hell, and we were successful through our congressional delegation in getting HUD to back off. The final settlement is the result of a very long series of negotiations with the city, HUD, CRA, the First National Bank, and indirectly, the Cedar Riverside PAC. We were a party to those negotiations even though we were not a party to the lawsuit.

*

The settlement was extremely complicated but at its center was an arrangement between the First National Bank of St. Paul and the City of Minneapolis, whereby the Minneapolis Community Development Agency (MCDA) was given options to buy the Cedar Riverside property on which the bank had acquired liens. (CRA still held title to the property but only the bank could arrange for its sale.) For crucial sections of this property there was the additional provision that the bank would rebate the city 80 percent of the purchase price. Thus the bank's investment was protected, but it was denied extreme profits. The nominal purchase price was maintained at market value, protecting CRA's tax status, but the MCDA would be able to acquire the property at a price that would make redevelopment feasible. Acquisition was to take place over a period of eight years, and only as the MCDA could show that it had a funded developer ready to develop the land. Since no development plans could proceed without approval from the PAC, its control of the situation was now firm.

Other provisions of the settlement included a commitment from HUD to provide 100 units of Section 8 subsidy for housing in the community, and permission for CRA to continue developing in Cedar West around the existing high rises.

It was in this situation, as defined by the 1980 settlement, that the idea of a community land trust made a great deal of sense.

*

*DOROTHY JACOBS:* The reason that we began thinking of the land trust is that we were looking for ways to keep housing affordable in the future. In an urban renewal area you can always have the first sale affordable. However, the second sale is speculative always. So we looked at all the ways that we could deal with that—restrictive covenants in deeds, limited equity co-ops, and all kinds of things. A lot of people in the neighborhood who will be receiving subsidy do not like the idea of co-ops, but they are not opposed to returning that subsidy. And the City of Minneapolis has changed a great deal. In the 60s they used to outlay massive amounts of money for subsidy and never recover any of it—it was just gone. In fact, it was used as a tool to gentrify neighborhoods.

So we thought the land trust would be a way of preserving the subsidy—the equity investment—that the city will make in the neighborhood, far into the future. We asked the city to put that subsidy into the land: sell us the house, put the write-down into the land, and sell the land to the trust. Then the land trust will own the land; the person will own the structure; part of his lease with the land trust would be a limited equity clause, so that when the next family buys in, the subsidy is intact—it's still there—and the first owner doesn't have to sell that house for $20,000 more in order to pay that subsidy back to the city; and the house remains affordable.

*JACK CANN:* As a practical matter, the importance of the land trust is that this neighborhood is probably *the* neighborhood in the Twin Cities with the most potential for gentrification—a huge real estate boom that would last about three years and completely transform the neighborhood. It would happen partly because there's a lot of relatively nice housing that's experiencing deferred maintenance but is basically decent, and because in terms of location it's absolutely the best in the Twin Cities for the gentry to move into. So it seemed real important to take conscious and thoroughgoing measures to head off that sort of speculative land boom, and the land trust idea seemed a good way to do that.

Our concern was sparked partly by the experience of the neighborhood right across the freeway from us, which has almost as good a location. The Seward neighborhood in the late 60s and early 70s had also been designated as a clearance area by the housing authority. A fairly militant neighborhood group fought the housing authority to a standstill and then took control of the planning basically in the same way we have—set up a neighborhood-based development corporation, built a substantial amount of subsidized housing. Still, somehow by the end of the 70s a lot of their efforts at staving-off clearance and keeping the neighborhood like it was went to benefit upper-income professionals, who had bought a lot of the property and made a lot of money selling the property after a couple of years, and who had begun to dominate neighborhood politics and neighborhood culture. So, what was first a working-class neighborhood and then a sort of combination working-class and counterculture neighborhood is now a bastion of the trendies. They have driven a lot of the working-class people out because the property values and property taxes have soared as they have bought and sold houses among themselves.

All of those things happened and they happened almost overnight. We have to take some kind of steps to assure that that kind of thing doesn't happen here.

*QUESTION:* What are the chances of the land trust acquiring enough property to serve that purpose?

*JACK CANN:* I think they're excellent. I think once you've taken the first step, using the anti-displacement argument and the need for low-income housing to convince the MCDA to sell the property to a co-op or the CDC, that the land trust is just sort of part of the process, and justified on

Charlotte Fisketti

*The Riverside Park neighborhood, viewed from the park.*

the basis of already existing MCDA policies about not pissing away subsidies and so on. Then, once it's in there, it's in there. Young professionals can move in, but if they can't speculate on their house they aren't going to make a fortune when they move, and that's going to substantially reduce the attractiveness of the neighborhood for the gentry.

*

In 1981, a new comprehensive renewal plan for Cedar Riverside—finally and officially replacing the New Town in Town plan—was brought before the city council. As it was first drafted and proposed by the PAC, this plan stipulated that, "In any sale which (a) is accompanied by any public subsidy or cost write-down and (b) is primarily related to residential development activity, title to the land will be conveyed by the MCDA to a land trust while title to the buildings to be rehabilitated or constructed will go to the party selected by the MCDA." The nature of this land trust was then defined in terms conforming to the basic CLT model.

At this time the Cedar Riverside Community Land Trust was organized and incorporated, with bylaws emphasizing the goal of keeping housing affordable in the Cedar Riverside community. Meetings were held and written explanations were prepared to familiarize residents with the concept and make them aware of the practical advantages the CLT would offer in the Cedar Riverside situation. The idea was generally well received in the community, and a number of city council members supported it. In fact, at one point the PAC calculated that the proposed CLT clause in the new renewal plan had the support of 9 of the 13 council members. However, the idea was loudly opposed by a few property owners in the community and by a vocal minority in the city generally. Opposition seems to have been a matter of emotion—suspicion of anything that suggests communal ownership—rather than a concern with practical consequences. The issue did become politically sensitive for some council members, and since it was an issue that could be avoided in the renewal plan itself, the plan was finally adopted without the land trust clause. However, a clause was included which explicitly permits development on land leased, rather than owned, by the developer, though specific approval by the city council is required in such instances.

The PAC had, of course, been concerned with all of the features of the renewal plan and with its overall impact on the community. Though there was disappointment at not having the land trust built into the plan, the PAC was generally satisfied with the plan as a whole, and remains optimistic about the CLT's eventual role.

*

*QUESTION:* At the present time the city council has to approve any project in which the developer leases rather than owns the land. Is this likely to be a long-term obstacle for the land trust?

*JACK CANN:* It's more like a long-term problem that's going to have to be dealt with every single time. But we've got a lot of things going for us. One is that there aren't a lot of other neighborhoods pushing for low-cost housing, and the city is under a lot of pressure to produce more low-cost housing. And there's going to be a lot of pressure on the city to do something about speculation—something responsible rather than something negative like rent control—and what's more responsible than what we're proposing? Of course, another basic argument that the mayor's office and the city council have picked up on a lot is that it's a way of holding on to those public subsidies that are initially put into a project to make it affordable to a certain group of people. There's been so much hell raised around the city about wheeler-dealers ripping off city subsidy money that finally the city government, under the mayor's lead, is looking around real seriously for devices to assure that either the public money stays in the project for the public benefit or the city gets all of its money back with interest. And the land trust is almost an ideal vehicle for accomplishing that.

*

For some time the Cedar Riverside PAC and CDC have worked closely with the Minneapolis Housing and Redevelopment Authority and its successor, the Minneapolis Community Development Agency. As has been explained, the MCDA is now *the* entity through which the Cedar Riverside CLT can acquire land owned by Cedar Riverside Associates. Ed Goldsmith, a member of the MCDA staff, comments on the land trust idea as it is viewed by the MCDA and the city council.

*

*ED GOLDSMITH:* My understanding of our renewal process is that a normal renewal project does not preclude the sale of land to a land trust. In fact, there generally is not any restriction on what entities can acquire property. In terms of the Cedar Riverside plan, the original proposal for the land trust hit political opposition, so that the city council couldn't buy specifically placing in the plan a provision that land definitely would be sold to a land trust. In one sense, it could have been left out of the renewal plan entirely and still be accomplished in the future, but the Cedar Riverside PAC, which was promoting the land trust concept, still wanted some comfort language in the plan that would show that the plan would not specifically exclude the concept of a land trust.

We didn't refer to the plan as a land trust, because the *term* became the basis, really, for the opposition. People really didn't understand exactly what a land trust is. They heard the term and they thought it sounded, at the least, socialistic. So we placed in the plan a stipulation that the MCDA could, in fact, sell land with the intention that the land would be leased for development. In other words, it allowed for the land trust concept—that structures built on the land would be owned by the developers of those structures and could be sold, but that the land itself would be leased from some entity and there would be restrictions placed in the lease. The council went further and modified that to indicate that any land disposition of that nature would have to be approved by the city council. There was sentiment, from the opposition in the community and among the council members themselves, that they didn't want any one entity ending up owning a large portion of the land in Cedar Riverside. If that entity was a land trust, then they wanted to basically see how one would operate before approval was given to sell the land to such an entity.

*QUESTION:* What do you see as the land trust's possible importance in Cedar Riverside in the future?

*ED GOLDSMITH:* It has the potential for meeting the objective of long-term continuation of low- and moderate-income housing, under the leasing arrangements and through the involvement of the community in the trust itself. Another option, to do that very same thing, would be for the MCDA to operate in place of the land trust. We could lease the land to the developers with exactly the same restrictions that the land trust would impose on the property. But the initiative for the land trust came from the Cedar Riverside PAC. Their feeling is that this perpetuates community involvement in the neighborhood, and in essence we've gone along with that. We've said, all right, if we do go into this we're going into it with the understanding that this is a mechanism that perpetuates community involvement in the determination of the goals of the land trust. And one of the criteria that the PAC itself has set up is that membership on the governing body of the land trust would include public officials from the city and the MCDA.

*QUESTION:* Do you see any advantages, hypothetically, in having the MCDA rather than the land trust hold the land?

*ED GOLDSMITH:* One definite advantage is that the politics are easier. I would see the agency doing it as a cleaner method of achieving the same ends. The problem obviously that the community sees is that although currently they have a good relationship with the agency, what if sometime in the future there's a disagreement between the community and the agency over the use of the land, if the control is all within the agency? And, of course, it also works vice versa. The agency may become upset with something the land trust wants to do. The other advantage to the agency holding the land is that you eliminate the problem of financing acquisition by the land trust.

But historically, in Minneapolis the agency has not entered into many land lease arrangements. Generally the agency sees its role as getting in, acquiring, assembling, preparing the property for redevelopment, and selling it to a developer. Any restrictions that occur are in the redevelopment contract and in the deed. I think that's why our agency was willing to consider the land trust concept—because historically we haven't gotten into the role of leasing land. Elsewhere in the country it's different. Other cities do enter into long-term land leases with developers.

*

Ann Waterhouse looks at the future of the land trust in the perspective created by both her role as an organizer in the community and her role as regional director of the National Consumer Cooperative Bank.

*

*QUESTION:* Do you see the idea of the MCDA retaining ownership of Cedar Riverside land as a realistic alternative to ownership by a land trust? What disadvantages do you see in MCDA ownership?

*ANN WATERHOUSE:* It is a realistic alternative and was, in fact, the second choice of residents that were organizing in the Riverside Park area [where the land trust idea was first proposed in the course of subneighborhood planning]. I believe there are serious disadvantages whenever a government agency is involved that extensively in a neighborhood-based redevelopment project. I feel, personally, and from my experience as an organizer, that you don't want to put yourself in the position of being dependent upon a government agency for something as important as the ownership and control of the land that you live on. At any point the government may change, different policies may be instituted; there may be a new staff person who is not as favorably inclined toward the community. There are many ways to manipulate the situation when it is taken out of the control of the neighborhood residents. There are too many variables, too much up in the air.

*QUESTION:* It's not yet clear what the land trust would have to pay for land acquired through the MCDA. Tax increment money can be applied to the cost of acquisition, and the cost can be written down to a greater or lesser extent. But the land trust will probably still have to pay something for the land. How do you see the purchase being financed by the land trust?

*ANN WATERHOUSE:* Each particular phase of acquisition would have to be looked at in terms of whether the bottom line could be met—whether the groundleases or groundrents that were going to be generated by the redevelopment would be enough to pay back the acquisition cost of the land. That would be the basis on which the National Consumer Co-op Bank, for instance, would look at financing the land trust. We would look at the land trust as a business, and if the cash flows were enough to meet the repayment terms that we set up, then we'd finance it.

The Cedar Riverside neighborhood is large enough so that it's the scale of model that we could begin to look at for other communities. If it would work in Cedar Riverside, there's the potential that this kind of model could work in other areas.

*

# CHAPTER 9

# The Preservation of Productive Land

The three short case studies contained in this chapter all describe efforts to protect agricultural and forest land from the kind of development that would destroy its productive potential. Each of these efforts is, in one way or another, a community effort. The immediate concern is not with the preservation of productivity on a national or worldwide scale, but with keeping local land in productive use for the continued good of local people. The Ottauquechee Regional Land Trust (RLT), though it has recently become a statewide organization, still works with Vermont communities to help them protect their agricultural and forest land and generally preserve the open space that is an established part of the character of these communities. The Marin Agricultural Land Trust is an effort by and for a community of ranchers in western Marin County, who are trying to preserve their land base against the intense development pressures of the San Francisco Bay area. The Monadnock Forest Land Trust demonstration project represents an effort by a CLT and several other organizations not only to preserve forest land in south-central New Hampshire, but to make the forest more productive in the interest of local communities.

With the exception of Monadnock Community Land Trust, which is a co-sponsor of the Forest Land Trust project, none of the groups examined here is a CLT in the full sense, and none is concerned primarily with providing for people who have been denied access to land. The emphasis, instead, is on helping people to keep and use in appropriate ways land that they would otherwise be forced to sell because of high taxes and other economic pressures. In many cases the people thus helped are not poor; they may, in fact, be well-to-do, particularly by the standards of Clairfield, Tennessee, or Cincinnati's West End. However, when the interests of such people coincide with the interests of the community—when both want to see the land used appropriately and productively and want to see the community itself control its own destiny—the CLT model, or some variation of it, can be an important tool. Today it is not only the "poor" community that is threatened by inappropriate land use and that finds itself at the mercy of economic forces beyond its immediate control. And it is not only the "poor" individual who can be displaced by the forces of real estate speculation.

All of the groups presented here are concerned with controlling speculation and development. None, however, is primarily concerned with acquiring full title to land. Instead, they are concerned with acquiring limited rights to land—specifically, development rights (although the "forest land trust" will be less centrally concerned with development rights). In Chapter 1, we noted that real property has come to be viewed as a "bundle of rights," and that the rights in this bundle can be separated and held by different individuals or organizations. Thus a land trust can acquire the development rights to a piece of land, and thereby prevent the construction of buildings and other improvements (usually with the exception of improvements required for agricultural use), while all other rights to the land remain with the original owner.

In the interviews that follow, various terms are used to describe this process of separating and holding in trust the development rights to a piece of land. In the Ottauquechee case study there is talk of "restrictions." These are restrictions on development that result from the owner giving up development rights. In the Marin and Monadnock case studies, there is talk of "conservation easements." An easement is any right or set of rights that is granted by the owner of a piece of land to another party; thus, to convey development rights to a land trust (or public agency or conservation organization) is to grant a conservation easement. Regardless of the terms used, the process is the same in each of these cases.

The acquisition of development rights has become an increasingly popular conservation technique in recent years. It has the advantage of allowing an organization to protect relatively large areas of land at relatively small expense while permitting the original owners to continue to live on the land and use it in appropriate ways. However, the technique also has some limitations and complications that should be noted. First, the kind of easement that the technique involves may be difficult to enforce legally in the long run. Unlike the kind of easement by which, for instance, a right of way is granted to a neighboring landowner, a conservation easement is designed in effect to retire or withhold certain rights; and there is reluctance, particularly in some states, to recognize a permanent arrangement in which specific rights evaporate, never to be available again.

Second, some organizations—such as Ottauquechee RLT—have relied heavily on the tax-deductability of charitable contributions to encourage donations of development rights. The 1981 tax law, however, has reduced the advantage to be gained by the wealthy donor; and legislation passed in 1980 has raised some still-unresolved questions about the situations in which such donations may and may not be considered deductible. These legislative changes may not present significant long-range problems to organizations such as Ottauquechee RLT, but they do point up the dependence of the technique on changeable tax policies.

Third, although the acquisition of development rights is a proven way of protecting open space, there is real question about its value as a means of keeping productive land productive and controlling the market value of such land. In some cases, land from which development rights have been removed is highly desirable to wealthy individuals who do not want to develop the land but want to own their own open space. The land's desirability for such people can increase its market value beyond what the farmer or rancher can afford. Therefore the removal of development rights from agricultural land is no guarantee that the land will be used for agriculture.

Nonetheless, this approach has proven useful to some communities; and, depending on local circumstances and state and local laws, it may turn out to be still more important in the future. In any case, it reflects the kind of sophisticated approach to landownership that land trusts in the future will almost certainly need to command.

## OTTAUQUECHEE REGIONAL LAND TRUST, VERMONT

The Ottauquechee Regional Land Trust (ORLT) has sometimes been described as a "hybrid" trust, halfway between a CLT and a conservancy trust. But regardless of how it is described, it is an active and distinctive institution that has been shaped by local Vermont conditions and the needs of Vermont residents and communities. The following interview with ORLT director Rick Carbin offers an opportunity to look at the interplay between what might be called the CLT "ideal" and the realities of a particular region.

Though it has become active throughout the state of Vermont, ORLT began in the Ottauquechee Valley in east-central Vermont and is still based in the town of Woodstock in that region. Before becoming director of the land trust, Rick Carbin was director of the Ottauquechee Regional Planning and Development Commission. He describes the region, which in many ways is typical of much of the state.

*

*RICK CARBIN:* It's essentially hilly country, foothills of the Green Mountains running into the Connecticut River Valley. In the past it was primarily an agricultural region—sheep and dairy—but that's changed a lot in this century. Now it's mostly forested land, but with most of the good farmland still open and still used, although a great deal of that land has changed hands from actual farming people to immigrants who are not farmers but enjoy the countryside, who maintain the open fields more for aesthetic reasons than for agricultural reasons.

We have a mix of people—from native Vermonters, who have been basically in farming, timbering, laboring, to extremely wealthy people who have come to Vermont to retire, who can afford to live here on a full-time basis with the money that they have available to them. The tourist industry has had a large impact, particularly since the end of the Second World War. A lot of new people have moved into the area since that time who cater to the tourists, so that now the chief economic enterprise is tourism or tourist-related businesses. Yet those farms that remain are still strong. There's been a stabilization of farming in the last five years or so; we're not losing as much farmland as in the 40s and 50s and the early 60s. But there are pressures still for more vacation-home development, condominium development, suburban-type development. We're close to the Hanover-Lebanon area of New Hampshire where a lot of jobs are being developed. People are now moving into the region who commute, so that a number of the rural communities are becoming bedroom communities.

But even with all these differences over the past 30 or 40 years, there's still a certain feeling about the communities that this amount of development hasn't taken away—the sense that towns have an identity, that each town has its own personality. The type of development that has occurred has generally not been destructive of the environment. There are still town centers that people can relate to. There is still a feeling that we're living in a small New England community.

*

The Ottauquechee Regional Land Trust was incorporated in 1977. Here Rick describes the events leading to its formation.

Robert O'Keefe

*Rick Carbin on the South Woodstock property.*

*

*RICK CARBIN:* In 1975, the Ottauquechee Regional Planning and Development Commission was working with the town of Hartland, in what was called the Hartland Open Space Project, to develop a property tax program for the town at the town's request. The initial impetus for that was concern over a loss of farmland and the potential impact on farmers of property taxes, in the sense that it possibly was unfair to tax farmers at a fair market value determined by development pressure as opposed to taxing land on its use value as agricultural land. The project was looking to alternative ways of protecting open space other than the traditional approach of town plans, zoning regulations, subdivision regulations, and other regulatory methods, because in Hartland, these methods hadn't worked. The town had worked with the Regional Commission from the late 60s onward on a comprehensive town land-use plan. It *was* adopted in the early 70s, but the town had never gotten serious in terms of implementation of the town plan. An attempt was made to adopt comprehensive zoning regulations, but it was not accepted by the voters.

So the Hartland Open Space Project completed its recommendations to the town on various tax stabilization programs, but all of the recommendations were defeated through a town vote. However, there was a lot of feeling on the part of those who had been involved with the project that there was some sense in pursuing nonregulatory alternative techniques in dealing with land-use matters. And that led to looking into other kinds of possibilities.

Then Harvey Jacobs and I started looking at other organizations. [Harvey Jacobs was a planner with the Regional Planning and Development Commission who had worked on the Hartland Open Space Project.] The two different approaches we really looked at were the Nature Conservancy approach, which is basically land conservation, nondevelopment—protecting the countryside both aesthetically and from a natural resources point of view—and the Earthbridge Trust approach [Earthbridge Community Land Trust in Putney, Vermont], which was seeking to gain control of land for social purposes—to take land off the market, and to bring people together in more or less a communal situation to encourage social interaction, and to use the land as a resource to provide food, job opportunities, and so on for the community they hoped they could establish. In our discussions we fell in between. We didn't think, in this area, that a very active social program would be well received. Even though we may have been sympathetic with the goals of the Earthbridge Trust, it just didn't seem to be a concept that would gain much favor here. Yet we were concerned about the resource base, using the resource, so that we weren't looking at the traditional conservancy approach.

As a result of those conversations we decided that we ought to bring a group of people together to explore the land trust idea. We ended up with four or five people who were interested in working on it, and we worked with them for a year. I'm not sure that we ourselves had gotten to the point of feeling what all the possibilities might be with the land trust activity, even though we had some ideas in the back of our heads. I think we held off on talking about them with the group that we had brought together because we saw them as more conservatively oriented in terms of social issues, and that was reflective of the community at large. We wouldn't have been able to get the land trust off the ground if we had started off from the point of view that we're going to have direct impact on social and economic factors.

We recommended to the study committee a set of articles of association and incorporation around the idea of protecting farmland and forest land. The idea was accepted. Three of the committee members incorporated the Regional Land Trust. They also selected the original board of the trust.

*QUESTION:* Now, as you go into your second year as a full-time director, do you have a formal program of the kind of work the organization expects to be undertaking?

*RICK CARBIN:* What we hope to do and haven't been able to do yet is sit back for a little while and say, okay, in this region and around the state what are the important lands to be protected? The reason we haven't done it is that there hasn't been time. People have been coming to us with situations that have all been, from our point of view, important. We're a new organization, so it's going to take time to be really specific about priorities. We're really dealing with specific situations as they come up, and we try to analyze those situations in terms of what's best in each case.

Most of these situations are outside the Ottauquechee region. The board decided early on to become involved in projects if there was no other organization in existence to help out, and if that project met our basic priorities of protecting farm and forest land. [Since this interview took place, the ORLC has officially declared itself a statewide organization.]

*QUESTION:* What kinds of people have been calling you? What kind of projects have they been?

*RICK CARBIN:* There is a general category that they all fit into: Every one of them has a problem that might lead to the loss of the land as a farm and as a unit. There are so many problems—I think that we've found that we're stepping into a vacuum as an organization. That's why we haven't had the time to set priorities. We've been reacting to all these problems that have been out there for a long time.

The most general problem is that people who own land, and have been able to afford to keep that land open, may not be able to in the future, either because they will die and estate taxes or some other force might break up the property, or because they're facing economic problems now in terms of holding on to the land. They're looking for help, looking for alternatives. Most of them want to retain ownership of their property, or want their family to retain ownership of their property. They're coming to us to see if we can work with them in developing a conservation plan, where they would donate restrictions [i.e., development rights or conservation easements] to us, enjoy the income tax benefits, and still keep the land itself.

*QUESTION:* Would you explain these income tax benefits?

*RICK CARBIN:* Gifts of land, money, securities, for conservation purposes or to a charitable organization (which we are), are tax-deductible contributions. And this includes rights in land. The value of rights in land can be deducted from an individual's income tax as a charitable contribution. In many cases that can be a powerful incentive for people to become involved in a land trust program, especially if they are in an upper tax bracket and if what they paid for the property is low. In a lot of cases in Vermont the price was very low. I can think of one case where someone bought land for $14 an acre and it's now worth $600 or $700 an acre. These people can actually make money by giving away the land or by giving the rights of the land away. [This statement was made before the new tax legislation of 1981. Though the financial advantages are not as spectacular under the new tax law, the incentive to make donations, for people who do not want to see their land developed, is still high.]

*QUESTION:* You know that there's been quite a debate nationally about whether we should be trying to protect farmland or farming. ORLC is working to protect the land. Is it doing anything to protect farming in Vermont as well?

*RICK CARBIN:* Obviously there is a whole series of concerns about farming that we can't control, as a land trust organization, even though we're interested in those other aspects. What we can do is keep the land there as a resource. Hopefully in the process we will be able to make sure that it's used as a resource, that we can make land accessible to young people who want to get into farming. We're working on several projects that would, if we're successful, end up in making land accessible to young Vermonters who lack the capital to own their own farm. We would, through our program, be able to reduce the cost of getting into farming at least through the land costs. And that's where our second priority comes in. Our first priority would be to protect the land, and the second priority would be to get people on that land. The type of people that we would be looking for are young Vermonters who want to stay or get into farming, and are capable of doing it.

I would say that our organization is very pragmatic. We have a general ideal, things that we want to see happen, but we also have a realistic responsibility in terms of financing that has to be met in any particular project, so we're going to look at what works best in that particular situation. In the case of South Woodstock, for instance, there may have been a number of ways to have worked out the end result of protecting that property. We chose one because we had a specific offer that was consistent with our general objectives and let us meet our financial obligations.

*

The Regional Trust's involvement in the hamlet of South Woodstock is a good example of how the organization, with its pragmatic and sophisticated approach to financial matters, can serve the interests of a specific community. The land in question was a 330-acre piece that belonged to the South Woodstock Country School. With the closing of this school the land was to be sold, and a large-scale vacation-home development was projected for it—a development that would have drastically changed the character of the community.

*

*RICK CARBIN:* We were involved with South Woodstock at the community's request—the community being just about everyone in South Woodstock. Their goal was to simply not have development take place on the hillside outside the hamlet. It wasn't to protect farmland; it wasn't to protect forest land in terms of productivity. That was not part of their thinking, at least not until we got involved. Everybody in South Woodstock from the gentleman farmer on the hill to the superintendent of the country school property was involved—the snowmobile club, the community club, all types of people, a cross section of the community. They all participated actively in the project.

We needed to borrow, in order to purchase the land, $565,000 in the traditional way, by going to the bank. In order to do that, we broke down the amount of money that we needed into $6,000 units, and we went around to people in South Woodstock and asked them, could they support through their financial statements a loan of at least $6,000? And we got enough people together. Some people said they could do $6,000 worth, others said $30,000. We got their financial statements to the bank as backup for the bank's consideration—and we borrowed the money. The land trust borrowed the money but the land trust has no assets, so all of the people in South Woodstock who provided their credit to the trust were co-signing a note.

Because of that, the trust board, all of us, felt that the community had to have direct input into whatever final decision was made on the use of the property. They elected representatives to the planning committee. In the planning process we did raise the question of the productive nature of the farmland, ways that land could be used and ways that the forest land could be managed, as well as ways to meet the financial obligations of the community. There were some very real financial problems that had to be dealt with. We had paid the developer's price for a piece of property that may have really been worth half of what we paid for it. Because we had to borrow the money at a high interest rate, debt was piling up. At 19 percent interest, borrowing $565,000 can mount up to an awful lot of money pretty quickly, which makes it harder and harder to work out a solution financially.

We did a thorough planning analysis, and we did concentrate on the farmland and made recommendations on what kinds of farming should go on there. But there were some basic problems. The farm had been broken up by the country school, and the facilities were no longer there. It was a financially impossible situation for anyone trying to get into farming. So we had to find another way to get the land into farming, and that meant finding someone with the resources to provide that capital investment. When we were made an offer by someone with those financial resources, we accepted that offer.

Our intent is to restrict what we think is important farmland or good forest land on a piece of property. We want to take the development potential off that land. By doing that, we're reducing the value of that land, but we can put some of

Kerry Mackin

*The South Woodstock Country School property, saved from condominium development.*

that value back into other portions of the land by permitting development to take place. In South Woodstock, we allowed additional development to take place on the land. We identified where that development could occur and located it in a way that wouldn't interfere with the good farmland or the good forest land. We're not taking the position that we're protecting land against any kind of development. We are taking the position that if development occurs, it should not occur in a way that would ruin the farming potential or the forestry potential of the property.

The land trust has been responsive to the feeling that there's a basic structure in our communities that should be protected. The hamlet of South Woodstock has a sense of community. The people that live there saw a threat of losing that sense through rapid growth, through fast change as a result of development pressures. There was a consensus that that was a bad thing, and that there were better ways to see things happen than to see a vacation settlement in the middle of what is now a fairly stable community.

I'm coming from a background of the regional planning efforts that have gone on in the area. And over 10 or 15 years now, an awful lot of effort has been put into planning for the region. An awful lot of thought went into what the region ought to be like, and a number of conclusions were made as a result of that process: the idea of town centers, small-scale communities rather than large; trying to maintain a mixture of open land to developed land. And basically what the land trust is trying to do is to see the goals that people have talked about and agreed to actually happen on a practical level.

*

## MARIN AGRICULTURAL LAND TRUST, MARIN COUNTY, CALIFORNIA

The Marin Agricultural Land Trust is more specialized than Ottauquechee RLT both in the area that it serves and in the types of land and land use with which it is concerned. Geographically it is limited to Marin County. Its goal is to preserve land for agricultural use, particularly land now used by local dairy and cattle ranchers.

Marin County lies just across the Golden Gate Bridge from San Francisco. Development pressures are of course intense, yet in the western part of the county there are a number of dairy and cattle ranches, using approximately 130,000 acres of land and supplying about 25 percent of the fresh milk consumed in San Francisco. Most of the ranches are owned by families—the majority of them Swiss-Italian families—who have been there for three or four generations and have a strong desire to see their children continue to use the land as it has been used. In recent years, as younger members of these families have applied modern agricultural techniques, many of these ranches have become highly sophisticated operations. Yet they face some very serious problems. The market value of the land has risen to the point that estate taxes will, in many cases, make it financially impossible for the next generation to continue ranching. As productive land is then sold to developers, the total land base of the dairy industry may shrink to less than what is necessary to maintain supply and market systems that are critical to the industry's success.

The idea of creating a land trust to deal with these problems was first proposed by Ellen Strauss. She and her husband own a dairy ranch, now managed by their oldest son, in the town of Marshall. For a number of years she has been active in local affairs, particularly on conservation issues. She describes the history of land-use planning in Marin County as it affected the ranchers.

*

*ELLEN STRAUSS:* We had gone as far as we could go with zoning. Originally, agricultural land had been zoned one house per 7,500 square feet or something like that, but it slowly evolved to one house per 60 acres, which was revolutionary at the time. It wasn't very well accepted by the ranchers. They thought that it was confiscatory and that they were providing open space for the urban areas at no cost to the urban areas. They thought it would make it very hard to convert the land to nonagricultural uses in case they wanted to retire or in case they needed additional capital. But eventually they came to accept it. They saw that land values weren't really going down at all, because we were so close to an urban area. The pressure came from very wealthy people moving out into the country and wanting ranchettes. Sixty-acre parcels were very attractive to them, and they

John Marriott

*The Strauss family.*

Trust for Public Lands

*Ellen Strauss.*

didn't care how much they cost. They were putting down $400,000 and $500,000 for houses there. Land prices were being driven up tremendously by that kind of demand.

It also meant that those 60-acre parcels were really out of agricultural use, and with those houses there you can never get the land back into agriculture, even if you could put all the parcels together. I don't think the county ever considered it a very efficient use of land. It's not the way you want to do your housing. So conversion into those parcels is getting to be a big problem. We couldn't have exclusive agricultural zoning—that is considered confiscatory. So we just needed some other kind of vehicle. I knew that we had to acquire the development rights in order to preserve the land, and that's why I thought of a land trust that would be in the position of buying conservation easements. The idea has been in my head for a long time. It's not such an original idea; I've just applied it to agriculture.

Phyllis Faber and I started three years ago seriously pursuing the matter, and it took a long time because we wanted to have more public support. We wanted to have it initiated from the ranchers themselves. We knew that we could at any time incorporate and have a land trust. It's very easy—you just get a board of directors, file the papers, and that's that—but it wouldn't have worked without support from ranchers.

Very early on we had a meeting with county officials and people from conservation organizations—the Nature Conservancy, Coastal Conservancy, Conservation League, Environmental Action Committee of West Marin. The Trust for Public Lands was our advisor, and they were there. The land-use committee of the Farm Bureau was there, and the Farm Bureau president. The ranchers were very skeptical and they asked us to show them how they could benefit from a land trust.

*

As is suggested by the groups represented at this meeting, there was potential support for the idea in an emerging coalition of ranchers and conservationists—with help also from sympathetic county government. The deeply rooted ranch families were concerned not only with their own economic well-being but with the preservation of their agrarian way of life and its necessary land base. Conservationists recognized the appropriateness and practicality of agriculture as a way of preserving open space against increasing development pressure, and were also interested in preserving the food-producing capability of the area. Ranchers were effectively represented in the county government and had already received strong support on several matters. When the Environmental Protection Agency required on-site treatment of dairy wastewater to prevent pollution of Tomales Bay with high concentrations of manure, the county paid for a substantial part of the necessary engineering as well as 25 percent of the facilities that were required. Later, during a drought, the county arranged for water to be hauled to the ranches. They also backed the dairy industry's efforts to gain higher milk price supports.

The Trust for Public Lands (TPL), from which Ellen Strauss and Phyllis Faber had sought advice, was able to supply crucial expertise as the effort to form a land trust was getting under way. Jennie Gerard, land trusts director for TPL, describes that organization's role.

*

*JENNIE GERARD:* They said what we need to do is show the dollars and cents—what participation in a land trust would mean to dairy, beef, and sheep people—so we said we will do the numbers crunching if you put together the profile of a couple of operations. They could be hypothetical, but we want ones that everybody you want to persuade can identify with. And on top of that, you arrange for a presentation to the Farm Bureau which they request us to make. It took a long time to do the work, because although we had a lot of tax analysis capabilities for income tax benefits, we did not know very much about estate tax benefits associated with farming operations. We looked for a long time for a CPA who could advise us and finally found somebody who was willing to work with us on it.

In the meantime, the county Farm Bureau had just elected a young man named Ralph Grossi as their president, who is very progressive in his thinking. The Farm Bureau usually wears two hats—farming, and farmland owner's rights. A farmer could farm, but nothing should get in the way of his last crack at a subdivision. But Ralph's point of view has been that there's no future to farming if we lose the land base. Phyllis Faber and Ellen Strauss then got him interested in the land trust idea, and he basically brought the Farm Bureau along.

We made a presentation to the land-use committee of the Farm Bureau. They were skeptical, but basically it hit home to everybody that each of them either had the hope that their children could stay and continue the operation, or they had the hope that they would see more young people get into farming.

*

Eventually, on the recommendation of its land-use committee, the Farm Bureau passed a resolution calling for the formation of a land trust.

John Marriott

*Jennie Gerard.*

John Marriott

Marin Agricultural Land Trust (MALT) was incorporated in 1980 and received a grant for $60,000 from the San Francisco Foundation to hire staff. A full-time executive director and a half-time secretary were hired. Ralph Grossi, who is now chairman of MALT's board of trustees, discusses current and projected activities.

*

*RALPH GROSSI:* At this point we have staff and we're in business and we're trying to develop our policies and our priorities. We're doing an inventory of all the aglands in Marin County—their current status, what the likelihood is of their selling or turning over in the near future, and so forth—so that we can start pinpointing the areas that need to be worked on the most. At the same time, we're working on brushfires that keep popping up—quick developments, proposed developments, that sort of thing.

We want to take the conservation easement as the centerpiece of our various techniques and use that as a method of encouraging people to keep the land in agriculture rather then developing it to acquire their full value. We can accept donations of easements, which of course gives a tremendous tax write-off if the owner is in a position to *take* tax write-offs. Most ranchers are not, but a few landowners are. So that's one possibility. We also want to develop a fund-raising program so that we'll have money to actually buy easements, purchasing the development rights off the property on critical parcels. One method of raising money is, of course, membership, but you don't raise a lot of money with membership. One is to try to appeal to various foundations for monies. Another is to go to private corporations.

One thing we're looking into—we have to be careful because we do have tax status to protect—would be to incorporate a separate for-profit entity which would turn monies over to the nonprofit. That, apparently, is legally possible. The question still rises: Where do you develop that money? It's possible to do limited development projects, where the for-profit entity is actually developing land where land *should* be developed—say, near the

101 corridor—and then using the profits from that to come out in west Marin and buy off the development rights.

The transfer of development rights is also very much a possibility. The county has adopted it in concept. That would allow a landowner to actually sell his development rights to another landowner, so that within a given valley, if one end of the valley is semideveloped or is basically out of agriculture already, then the other part of the valley that is still agricultural could sell their development credits. If a rancher has the right to build ten homes on his ranch, he can sell those ten units to a landowner in the other end of the valley, who then could increase the number of units he could build by that number. That's kind of an interesting concept because it raises all the money from within the private sector. It's very much a free enterprise kind of thing, although it needs *some* regulation or it can obviously get out of hand. That is a possibility, even though it is very controversial for lots of reasons. MALT doesn't really get involved in taking sides on that issue. It's pretty much left up to the advocacy groups—the Farm Bureau and environmental groups—who have been nudging it along.

In addition, MALT wants to do more than just preserve land for agriculture. We want to develop a support mechanism to encourage agriculture. We want to develop methods of helping people with estate tax planning—a serious problem in Marin County. We want to develop a program where we can actually assist young ranchers getting into business, financially. The capital costs of starting a new dairy are horrendous. But there are examples in other parts of the country where groups have been put together with four or five—or whatever it takes—investors. Outside investors are brought in as limited partners who can take advantage of all the tax benefits of starting up a new operation; then gradually they would be phased back out of the operation, with the farmer winding up with the business. They put up the capital and capture the tax benefits; he puts up the expertise and working knowledge for the operation. That kind of thing is a possibility and I think we'll see them in the fairly near future.

So it's really a twofold thing: one to protect the land and the other to try to develop a support mechanism. The problem is that eventually every ranch sells. It either sells to another member of the family or it sells to an outside buyer. MALT's job is to be there, to assist, at the time of the sale. Those selling want to achieve maximum dollars for the equity they've built up over the years. Those that are buying, if they want to stay in agriculture, can only afford a certain value. We hope that MALT can offer an opportunity to get those parties together, without the sale having to go to a separate developer to capture the full value. I think that's the appeal of the land trust idea—that we might be able to develop a system where the seller can capture *nearly* all his value and still be able to sell it to an agricultural individual in the next generation.

*QUESTION:* The purposes stated in MALT's bylaws are broader than what you've been describing. Is there a problem in limiting your purposes officially to protecting agriculture?

*RALPH GROSSI:* The current tax law allows tax deductions for donation of an easement for a number of things, including the preservation of agricultural land. But the value of the donation is on much firmer ground if it has other values to the general public than just protecting agland—if the land has scenic or historic value for preservation. The IRS has not yet accepted fully the idea that it's in the public interest to be protecting land just for its agricultural value—even though I think that's very obvious. It hasn't been challenged. In Marin, of course, there is a great deal of scenic and historic value in protecting the ranches, so that is a part of the goals and purposes of the trust. It's not really the problem for us that it might be in some areas.

*QUESTION:* What would you like to see the land trust being in 10 or 20 years?

*RALPH GROSSI:* In ten years, the land trust ought to be an organization that every landowner respects as a working partner in developing land-use plans, programs for protecting agriculture. Twenty years from now I would hope that the land trust will be holding easements over very large segments of west Marin—easements in perpetuity. To me, that is the ultimate goal—to assist the ranchers and end up with an easement that permanently locks the land into agricultural use. That's the kind of stability we need. Without that stability agriculture won't survive in this county.

The greatest problem in agriculture just about anywhere you go is instability. If developers and planners are constantly telling farmers that their land is going to be developed in 5 years or 10 years, or that there's going to be a highway through in 12 years, then there's going to be a tendency for the efficiency of the operations to drop drastically, and of course that has a domino effect. Up in Sonoma County, there's a large apple-growing area in the Sebastopol area, but the cities of Santa Rosa and Sebastopol have allowed development to start creeping out into that area, and the landowners are kind of caught—they expect development to take over their property. But particularly with orchards, you need constantly to be making new investments and planting young trees. They don't *do* that sort of thing because they don't see any need to put long-term capital investment into a property that is going to be developed. So the orchards are getting old, they're not being properly cared for, and of course their productivity is dropping off drastically. And as the productivity drops off, the landowner cries more about not being economically viable any more so he needs to develop his property—and the whole thing just goes. That's the problem.

*

As land trusts director of TPL, Jennie Gerard has worked with a number of groups that have created, or are interested in creating, agricultural trusts.

*

*JENNIE GERARD:* I don't see the land trust as being *the* answer to the loss of agricultural land. I see it as a logical complement to other kinds of activities. An agricultural land trust is appropriate where there is strong community sentiment—ideally, in a county with enlightened regulations and action—but if there isn't the leadership in the county, there's no way we can get involved in trying to set up a land trust.

Back in 1979 we had a small conference of agriculturalists in Colorado where we described our work with land trusts and asked if anybody thought we could be helpful in their community. An orchard grower from Mesa County was there, and he said he'd like very much for us to come to Mesa County. Now it's an enormous and very agricultural county on the western slope, and there are 2,000 acres of extraordinary orchard land. What we found there was practically a guerrilla force—a bunch of growers who had been showing up at the planning and zoning commission meetings, and for three or four years had been holding off the county commissioners from permitting subdivisions, and had defeated a bond issue to extend the sewers into the area, which of course would have increased the value of the land for housing developments. But they were beginning to see the same parcels of land come up for reconsideration, and it seemed that was not enough. They needed something more permanent.

It's unique growing land, but they're very much at critical mass. There are packing plants there now, but they only have to lose so many acres before the packers move out and then they become a you-pick operation. Their concern is that the pressure for energy development—synfuel, oil shale—will lead people to buy that land for house sites. It's either energy development or recreation development—folks who just come in and buy second homes for skiing. The growers don't have much truck with them.

Their concern is just keeping out the developers right now. Easements are not the only possibility, but some of them have been very excited and have endorsed the idea heavily. There are a couple of them who are eager to convey easements right now, because they just don't want anything else done with that land.

That group and the Marin County group I think are the best and purest examples of agricultural land trusts. There are others that have an agricultural component and also a land conservation or recreation component. For instance, Eagle County in Colorado, where Vail ski resort is located, is an agricultural community that has been completely busted apart; and the people who are getting involved in that land trust are ranchers, but also people who have moved in more recently, so it has that kind of dual nature. Their interest is in seeing that the hay meadows along the streams stay in production. But some people aren't so interested in that for the production of hay as they are because it's beautiful there. You need to build coalitions in a lot of different ways, and I'm interested in how people do that.

*QUESTION:* What is the actual role of a land trust in overseeing the conservation easements that it holds, in seeing that the land is used according to the terms of the easement?

*JENNIE GERARD:* The easement is a very practical document with a lot of description of what are allowable uses and what are not allowable uses, and that becomes a contract between the holder of the easement and the holder of the underlying fee. Say, I am the land trust holding the easement and you are the landowner: Every year I go back and we basically renew the vows, and I say, "Okay, no, it says you don't sell off the water rights," and so on. Each one of those elements in the easement involves a monitoring obligation on the part of the land trust.

*QUESTION:* Can it be a problem maybe two generations from now when the owners of the land don't understand the easement?

*JENNIE GERARD:* Well, that sure has happened with the U.S. Forest Service on easements along the Appalachian Trail. They didn't show up for years, and ownership passed from one generation to the next, and then people began challenging them and saying, "Pappy never understood what was happening when he signed that; you all just snookered away his rights." The really successful monitoring is done annually. The Society for the Protection of New Hampshire Forests I think is just superb at that. [An account of these monitoring practices appears in the following case study.]

*

# MONADNOCK FOREST LAND TRUST DEMONSTRATION PROJECT, NEW HAMPSHIRE

The primary subject of this case study is a demonstration project being carried out in the Monadnock region of southern New Hampshire, under the joint sponsorship of the Monadnock Community Land Trust, the Society for the Protection of New Hampshire Forests, and the Institute for Community Economics. The model being demonstrated and evaluated through this project has been labeled the "forest land trust" (FLT); however, the term is somewhat misleading. The forest land trust model has been designed as a cooperative forest management program that would bring together a number of small forest-land holdings into one management unit in order to make possible sound forestry practices, efficient selective harvesting of forest products, and long-range protection of forest resources.

Kerry Mackin

Ownership of the land would remain with individual participants, so the program would not literally be a land trust, though it is certainly consistent with the aims of many land trusts and may, in fact, be initiated by a CLT, as has been the case in the Monadnock region.

The basic features of the model are these. A limited partnership would be formed, with, perhaps, a CLT and a regional nonprofit organization serving as general managing partners, and individual landowners participating as limited partners. The value of each landowner's share would be based on the long-range value of his or her forest relative to the value of other holdings in the management unit. A forest management plan for all holdings would be implemented through a professional forester. Profit gained from the harvesting and sale of forest products would be divided among the partners each year according to their respective shares in the partnership (and not according to whose timber was harvested in that particular year).

Advantages for landowners would include the benefits of professional management on tracts of land too small to make such management otherwise practical, an increased yield from the land, more effective marketing, an income distributed from year to year rather than concentrated in a single harvest year, and protection of the land through environmentally sound use. Advantages for the community would include protection of the local environment, an increased supply of fuelwood and other products, and the creation of jobs in the harvesting and distribution of these products.

The New Hampshire demonstration project was initiated in the spring of 1981. Ward Stoops, a member of the Monadnock Community Land Trust and of the steering committee for the demonstration project, describes the local events—including the founding of the Monadnock CLT—which led to the current project.

*

*WARD STOOPS:* I think it was in the fall of 1978 that a group of us were brought together through the Institute for Community Economics and Bob Swann—a group of diverse people who had contacted the Institute about the land trust movement. The next year we met again and pooled our ideas, and decided that we were a group that could work together in this region, making a community land trust where everybody in the community could be represented. We incorporated in 1979 as the Monadnock Community Land Trust.

At about the same time, a group of people who also involved one of our founding members, Ross Jennings, decided that they would try to save a piece of land in Wilton from improper development—a farm which had been run as an organic farm for several years. The owner wanted to see it used in some ecologically sound way, and was willing to sell it to someone who would use it that way at below the commercial value of the land. This group began to think of it in terms of a community of their own. A part of this farm has become the Rural Education Center that Samuel Kaymen started. The other 90 acres, approximately, is now the Hearthstone Community. The members of the community wanted to see their land stay in a more permanent situation so that if they ever broke up it would still be preserved in the best possible way for homesteader and forest usage. For that reason they had a meeting of the minds, and Ross brought us together—their Hearthstone group and our Monadnock Community Land Trust—with the idea of using Monadnock Community Land Trust as the holding organization for the land. This gave us, I think, viability and a goal. Until then, this had been a group talking theoretical ideas.

Then sometime in 1980, at one of our meetings, we were approached by Bob Swann on the possibility of our being involved in a forestry land trust, and the preliminary model of a limited partnership with shares given out to small landholders was proposed. We had reservations about spreading ourselves too thin, getting involved in other things besides holding the land, and for that reason didn't get involved heavily right away. But then we began to see that there *were* opportunities. We contacted people at the Forest Society [Society for the Protection of New Hampshire Forests], and they were interested in the concept. We also talked with people at the Harris Center, which is a conservation center in Hancock, and they were interested in sponsoring a meeting. So we brought together the whole group under the co-sponsorship of these organizations, and had a meeting of landowners last September [1980], at the Harris Center.

*

The meeting at the Harris Center was attended by more than 30 landowners who were interested in the forest land trust idea and asked for more information about the effects that such a program would have for individual landowners and for the region. The demonstration project was designed to provide this information. By spring of 1981 the steering committee had been formed, and letters were sent to all people owning a hundred acres or more within 15 miles of the village of Peterborough, inviting them to attend a public informational meeting. This meeting was attended by more than 80 people.

Twenty owners have now committed a total of 4,977 acres of forest land to the project. Individual holdings range in size from 49 acres upward; the majority are between 100 and 200 acres; the largest is a 2,000-acre tract owned by an institution.

Once these landowners had agreed to participate, the Forest Society solicited bids from professional foresters for the job of conducting forest inventories and preparing management plans for all land included in the project. Forester Robert B. Todd, of New Boston, New Hampshire, was selected to do the work. Landowners—to whom the information will be useful regardless of whether they finally participate in a forest land trust program—have agreed to pay individually for the inventories and management plans. As of October, 1981, the forest inventories had nearly been completed.

The next phase of the project will involve making projections, based on the individual management plans, to determine the practical limits and advantages that would derive from the pooling of these forest resources for a 15-year management period. Individual analyses will then be made to indicate the economic advantages for each landowner, including potential tax advantages. At that point, if the analysis indicates a favorable situation, a detailed proposal for the forest land trust itself will be prepared.

For the present, since projections have not yet been made, a number of practical questions remain unanswered. However, the project is far enough along to suggest some of the ways in which the model might work in the Monadnock region. Forester Robert Todd and steering committee member Rocky Beek discuss the matter. Rocky Beek is also a member of the Monadnock CLT and is on the staff of the Rural Education Center.

*

*QUESTION:* What is it about this particular area that makes the forest land trust appropriate?

*ROCKY BEEK:* When I learned about this project I was working as a salesman for industrial wood-burning equipment, and we began to see a need in our industry for a more organized local fuelwood procurement mechanism of some kind, whether it was small woodcutters or large companies coming in with big equipment. The point was that we needed to be able to assure supplies of wood chips to the customers of our wood-burning equipment. There were very few sources of that supply, and the biggest reason was that most of the land in the southern part of the state is owned in small woodlots, and the owners of those woodlots don't do a harvest themselves and the woodlots aren't big enough to make it worthwhile for them to hire someone else to come in. About the time that we were concerned about the wood supply, we learned about the forest land trust model, and it sounded to me like a good mechanism for making larger sources of wood available.

*

Eighty or 90 percent of the Monadnock region is forested. So far there has been little development pressure in the area, although some nearby areas are experiencing a great deal. Thus, although the size of most landholdings is not extremely large, it is still large enough to make the FLT practical, as Bob Todd explains.

*

*BOB TODD:* As far as what makes this particular area appropriate for the application of the model, I think it is because the area has a lot of fairly large ownerships; it's rural; we still have the opportunity to keep it rural; and there seems to be a predominance of people that have the right attitude to accept the idea, perhaps more so than in some other parts of the state where you've got a more mobile society, perhaps a less affluent society.

*QUESTION:* You'll have a better idea when the study is completed, but what do you estimate is the minimum practical size for landholdings?

*BOB TODD:* We don't have any cutoff point, but I have a gut feeling that 50 acres will be the

Kirby White

*Bob Todd, Rocky Beek, and Ward Stoops on Stoops's land.*

minimum that can be economically managed. Other people have different ideas—some say 25 acres. I think it also depends on the state of the technology in harvesting and utilization. Perhaps the more sophisticated we become, the larger the tract is going to have to be.

*ROCKY BEEK:* But there are situations in which smaller plots—for instance, neighbors' lands which are contiguous—could be included.

*QUESTION:* What do you see as the most important forest products from this land, and what would be the most important factors involved in harvesting them economically?

*BOB TODD:* I think that the most important economic return will be from the sale of hardwood saw logs. Second highest, and perhaps very close, would be the harvest of softwood sawlogs. Next would come fuelwood in the form of roundwood—or chips, if the technology is applied to this area. Finally would be pulp. There's not a good pulp market right now in this area for woodlot-harvested material. Pulp would be harvested in conjunction with a sawlog harvest. I see that there is going to be an increasing amount of firewood harvested in the future, and it's going to be much more important than pulpwood.

I see the land trust as developing its own production mechanism. We talk about low-value products harvesting—fuel and pulpwood—which is needed to thin and make room for the sawlog trees to grow faster. If we had a 5,000-acre management block, I think that there would develop a crew, or more than one crew, with specialized equipment and training, that could go in and harvest low-value material and at the same time improve the quality of the woods.

I'm not even going to rule out horses as an alternative—horse logging, getting back to bunching small trees with single horses, for instance. I think a man and a horse can operate and make a living if he's got the land base to work on, and some management guidelines.

*QUESTION:* What kinds of marketing advantages would the forest land trust offer?

*BOB TODD:* Maybe a concentration yard from which all products would be marketed would be feasible, somewhere in the center of the forest land trust's lands. For instance, suppose Ward Stoops's property had three trees that were of veneer quality. The potential of those trees wouldn't be realized by a harvest of just the trees on his land, because the buyer would see expenses involved in getting those trees somewhere to get veneer-quality prices, so he wouldn't put them into that use; he would put them into the local sawlog market. But if you had a yard where you could bring those trees and let them sit until you had enough quantity to make a load, then you would take that load to where you could get the highest price and get the full potential from those logs.

*QUESTION:* What are the advantages of the model as far as conservation is concerned?

*ROCKY BEEK:* I think the region also has a strong need for a mechanism to defend the woods from being overharvested. That's a real threat with the growth of the market for fuelwood. We've seen a lot of roadside cutting and indiscriminate cutting that is detrimental to the long-term yield of the forest in this region. And it's out of the character of the state, and certainly not my preference, to have regulations passed to try to control cutting. I like the feature of the land trust that it's sort of a self-imposed discipline on woodcutting.

*QUESTION:* There's been talk of people maybe donating conservation easements in connection with the program. What part might conservation easements play in the forest land trust?

*ROCKY BEEK:* At this point, the transfer of easements would not be a requirement for joining the trust. We'd like to leave the landowners as much leeway to do what suits their needs as possible. Their commitment is that they would contribute their forest resources but retain title to their land and also access to their own woods for cutting firewood for their own use. Joining the partnership is like investing capital in a business. They're investing timber resources in the partnership.

We're interested, obviously, in having people donate conservation easements because that represents a long-term commitment, but we don't want to give the impression that they're going to be locked into this. We thought that if it were easier to get out, people would be more willing to get in. We also hope to structure it so that if people leave the program, there would be a penalty representing a portion of the value of their timber.

*

The Society for the Protection of New Hampshire Forests is an old, widely respected, and very active conservation organization. Jan McClure is a Forest Society staff person and serves on the forest land trust steering committee. In her work with the Forest Society she has had a good deal of experience with conservation easements.

*

*QUESTION:* How successful do you think a forest land trust in the Monadnock region might be in attracting donations of conservation easements?

*JAN MCCLURE:* Some of it will depend on

Internal Revenue Service tax policy and how that relates to the donation of conservation easements. Not that altruism doesn't come in at all, but if the landowners don't have any intention of developing the land, and if it's shown that the tax deduction that they might be able to take advantage of would improve their economic picture, I think it will be more likely that we can look at easements on many of the parcels. I don't think we can presume to get easements on all of them, or on that much acreage at once—at least not initially. It may be something that develops with time, but putting an easement on land, more or less forever, is a pretty strong commitment for a lot of people, and they're not always willing to do that.

*QUESTION:* The forest land trust itself would not hold those easements because it would not be a nonprofit organization. Are there assumptions at this point about what organization would hold those easements?

*JAN MCCLURE:* I think there are no assumptions. The Forest Society's general policy on easements is that we would prefer to see a local organization be the grantee—be the organization that accepts them—because we feel that they have a greater local responsibility and that they make better monitors because they are there on the scene, while the Forest Society, being a statewide organization, is not as available to really keep an eye on things. We often retain a sort of backup role so that, if for some reason the local organization ceases to exist, we could step in. If the Monadnock Community Land Trust held the easements, in this case, we might have an executory interest.

When New Hampshire passed the enabling legislation for conservation easements [in 1973], we accepted grantee responsibility on several, and it's only been in the last two or three years that we have stepped back and taken a look at what our long-term responsibilities might be, and what our job is here— and that is to encourage local stewardship more than acquiring easements on our own. We're trying to help local groups get started that could accept easements.

*QUESTION:* Jennie Gerard of the Trust for Public Lands has mentioned that the Society for the Protection of New Hampshire Forests does a particularly good job of monitoring the easements that it holds. You've been responsible for monitoring those easements. What have your methods been?

*JAN MCCLURE:* Initially we took easements and didn't really think about how we were going to monitor them in the long run. What I developed was a regular yearly process. Most of our easements now we monitor from the air. We fly over all of the properties on which we hold easements, in the spring before leaf-out but after the snow's off the ground, so that you can see down to the ground quite easily. In the plane with us we have aerial photographs of the property that we had taken the first year we held the easement, which we can compare to what we're seeing. Afterwards we send each of the grantors or current landowners a card indicating that we've flown the property and we didn't see any problems. We also ask them if there's been any change in ownership. There's a notification in the easement, but we ask just to make sure that we catch any changes.

With easements in which we hold an executory interest we send out certified letters to the grantees, with a copy of the abstract and a return postcard. We ask them to indicate that they have monitored the property during that year, and whether there have been any ownership changes, and we ask them to verify that they are the individual or organization that we should continue to be in touch with. I think it's been kind of an incentive for them to go out and do it. So far it's worked very well.

The other thing that we've done is establish a conservation easement monitoring fund that helps defray the cost of the annual monitoring and also provides a reserve for any potential legal enforcement costs in the future. We don't require that easement donors contribute to that fund, but we make them aware that it is there and hope that they will do that. It does demonstrate our recognition that it's not going to get cheaper in the future; it's going to get more expensive to maintain the obligations that we've established on these properties.

*

As Ward Stoops has mentioned, Ross Jennings has been active in both the Monadnock CLT and the Hearthstone Community, where he is currently building his own house. He is also a member of the steering committee for the forest land project. Here he comments on the relationship he feels among these several projects.

*

*ROSS JENNINGS:* In the same way that a forest influences the weather of a whole area and doesn't just affect the creatures that live within it, I think trying to do things like this is important because the spin-off from it is greater than what goes on within these 90 acres. We have people coming here frequently now to see what we're doing, and I think it's inspirational for people to see something carried this far. It's also inspirational for us to have someone come and say, "Hey, look what all you got done!"—when all that we can see is what remains to be done.

*QUESTION:* Do you see the forest land trust project as part of this spin-off?

*ROSS JENNINGS:* Yes, most other organizations really are looking at things in very conventional terms and are not long-range enough in the way they're looking. This idea of pooling resources, for example, means you don't just think about when you're going to make your killing, but you really are tied up with the productive cycle of other pieces of land, and it begins to encourage a longer vision than what we're used to having in this country.

I'd like to see the forests of New Hampshire like the forests in England—well cared for, productive, and a place that walking through just, you know, *lifts* you. And that isn't impossible. We're going to do that here on this 90 acres. We're going to be doing more than just forest management here. What we're going to be doing is what I hope the forest land trust will grow into eventually—to really advise people in how to develop the right relationship to the earth.

*

# Section III

## A Practical Guide

# CHAPTER 10

# Organizing, Research, and Outreach

The CLT is a community-based institution, intimately involved with the people and problems of its immediate environment. It is a vehicle for controlling the use of land, and land is central to its founding purpose. Its ultimate base, however, is not the land, but the community for whom the land is held and to whom the trust is accountable. This is why we begin our technical section, the "how to" part of the book, with a chapter on organizing, research, and outreach. The social base on which the CLT is built must be organized; research informs and guides the local effort to bring the CLT into existence; outreach weaves the CLT into an organizational web of community affiliation and mutual support. These are tasks which are done together. They are done before, during, and after the founding of a community land trust.

## ORGANIZING

> As an organizer I start from where the world is, as it is, not as I would like it to be. That we accept the world as it is does not in any sense weaken our desire to change it into what we believe it should be—it is necessary to begin where the world is if we are going to change it to what we think it should be.
>
> *Saul Alinsky (1971)*

There are many paths to a CLT. New Communities, Inc., grew out of the civil rights struggle in the South. A CLT was established in Clairfield, Tennessee, after years of local organizing around issues of health care, day care, and economic development. A CLT was established in Cincinnati in just five weeks when people were spurred to sudden action by the eviction of one of their neighbors. The Central Roxbury CLT emerged out of a successful community gardens program organized in one of Boston's inner-city neighborhoods. Other CLT's have had their origin in local efforts to preserve farmland, protect the environment, or create jobs and housing for persons urgently in need of both. In short, nearly any issue that brings people together to improve their community may prove fertile ground for a CLT.

Community land trusts have also arisen as a result of efforts by other organizations. Created by existing community-based groups to complement their own activities, these CLT's serve as trustees for properties that are acquired or developed by more-activist organizations. Thus, in Minneapolis a CLT has been established to hold land on which redevelopment projects planned by the PAC and implemented by the West Bank CDC will be located. In Columbia Heights, tenants organizations and the Cooperative Housing Development Corporation may initiate a CLT to hold the land on which tenant-owned buildings are situated. In Detroit, a local church is planning to organize a CLT to hold in trust the land beneath an unusual assortment of residential units. Detroit's Church of the Messiah, in pursuing shelter for its own staff and for victims of a fire that left homeless dozens of local residents, has come to own six cooperative houses, five duplexes, and a 24-unit apartment building. Wishing neither to serve as a landlord for these units nor to return them to the speculative market, the church prefers to turn this housing over to the residents as individuals or cooperatives and entrust the land to a CLT.

These examples are not cited to prove that an *indirect* approach to organizing a CLT is the only course to take. A group of people who wish to start a CLT does not necessarily need to spend several years rallying people around *other* issues before raising the question of a CLT. On the other hand, the experience of those who have been successful in organizing CLTs does suggest that one must "start where the world is"—beginning where people happen to be in their own attitudes, commitments, needs, and concerns.

This may mean that a community is not yet ready for a CLT. Either its residents have not reached a point where they consider land and shelter a serious problem, or they are already involved with other issues which, for now, are considered more important. Starting with the world "as it is" also means that the ideal model of a CLT which an organizer may have in mind may be subjected to many changes before it becomes a reality. One of the main virtues of the CLT is its flexibility—its capacity for being shaped and fitted to meet the needs of the surrounding community. The community is not badgered to accept an ideal model that is delivered ready-made into its midst.

There is no single strategy for organizing a CLT, nor any one best way to begin. Since each community is different, an organizer's own knowledge of local conditions will be the best guide to where, when, and how to proceed. Use your own good judgment but consider the following as you begin the process of establishing a CLT.

**Don't move too fast.** Remember that a CLT, first and foremost, is a group of committed people concerned about their community. Before incorporation, take the time to build understanding of the CLT among people and organizations in various sectors of the community. If incorporation is begun too fast, by too few, it may be harder to recruit members, resources, and support later on. Organizing a CLT is not a one-person show. Make sure that people who are interested in the trust feel that it is their own, something they are building with their own hearts and hands. If there is not yet a sufficient base of interest and support in the community, you may want to continue working with existing organizations and issues until understanding of the CLT grows and the time is ripe.

**Know your community.** Learn as much as possible about the community in which the CLT will be located (and from which most of its members will be drawn). A vital community has both a *physical* existence (business, banking, production, and construction activity, as well as goods and services provided by units of government, and a *social* existence (including all of the groups and organizations that carry on the religious, political, recreational, educational, and cultural life of the local area). More will be said shortly about researching these elements of the local community. For now, let us merely point out that before the organizers of a CLT begin reaching out to the broader community, going beyond their original "core group" to interest other people in the prospect of a CLT, they must have a clear idea of who those people are and what their circumstances might be.

**Personalize your message.** Identify key members of the local community—leaders, activists, and other persons with a reputation for neighborly cooperation and community pride—and pay each of them a personal visit. There is no substitute for face-to-face contact, particularly in the early stages of organizing a CLT. Not only does the organizer need to explain this new idea, this new institution, to persons who may never have heard of a CLT, but she or he must also listen to what they have to say about adapting the trust to local conditions. Personalizing the CLT therefore has to do with how the story of the trust is told to members of the community, and how the community is allowed to shape the CLT to meet its own conditions and needs.

**Cite examples.** Use newspaper clippings, bylaws, leases, and real-life stories from established CLTs in presenting the CLT model to local residents. These examples reassure your audience that CLTs have already been organized by people like themselves, in communities like their own. Other CLTs are also valuable sources of information concerning incorporation, board selection, property acquisition, and a host of related CLT concerns. Organizers of a new CLT would be well advised to visit other CLTs, or to invite representatives of other CLTs to address their group. An alternative source of firsthand information is found in extended case studies of existing CLTs (which build on the case studies included in the previous section), available from the Institute for Community Economics (ICE). Local groups may also consider inviting a member of ICE to explain the CLT model and to give examples of its application around the country.

**Don't wait too long.** Move deliberately to put together a strong, diverse group, but don't expect everyone with similar concerns and involvement in the community to jump right onto the CLT bandwagon. Some people will be happy to leave the CLT's formation to others, while they continue with their own community efforts. Keep in touch with them and look for ways to work together in the future. Some may wait for results, for visible evidence that the CLT model can work in their community. Remember that it's still a rather new idea, even if it has very old roots; some will wait to join the CLT effort until its potential for dealing with local problems has been clearly shown. Some will never join at all. Too much time spent in preparation, and too much talk, can lead people to question the capability of your group and the practicality of the whole idea. When you've become a solid core group and begun to interest others in the CLT model, when you know your community and see real opportunities for acquiring land and housing, then move ahead.

# RESEARCH

> What is research? Research is digging facts. Digging facts is as hard a job as mining coal. It means blowing them out from underground, cutting them, picking them, shoveling them, loading them, pushing them to the surface, weighing them, and then turning them loose on the public for fuel—for light and heat. Facts make a fire which cannot be put out. To get coal requires miners. To get facts requires miners, too.
>
> *John Brophy (1921)*

Research and organizing, as a veteran organizer once put it, "go together like gum and shoe." Community research is a necessary ingredient of any organizing effort. Research is, as well, an ongoing part of the land acquisition and community outreach activities of an established CLT. A good organizer knows that research starts early and goes on forever.

Most of the facts that a group may need to start and sustain a CLT can be unearthed by anyone with the desire and perseverance to dig them out. Specialists like lawyers, planners, or social scientists may be helpful in obtaining particular kinds of information, but their assistance is, for the most part, hardly needed. Local residents can learn to research their own communities, and should be given the training and encouragement to do so. By involving as many people as possible in the collection and discussion of needed information, the research process can become in itself a means of educating, motivating, and mobilizing an entire community.

As we suggested earlier, there are three main areas of fact-finding that the organizers of a CLT should cultivate: research regarding the land and buildings that give a community its physical character; research pertaining to a community's real estate market and other aspects of the local economy; and research directed at discovering certain characteristics of the population, groups, and organizations that make up a community's social environment.

**Research on the ownership and control of real property.** Most of us know surprisingly little about who owns and controls the real estate in the communities in which we live. We are likely to know more about who "owns America"—i.e., the largest corporations and the richest families—than about who owns the land and buildings that are right around us. Our relative ignorance regarding local property questions stems, in large measure, from the right to privacy which has historically accompanied private property in the United States. Personal privacy is a legitimate interest that individuals have in certain property, and should be respected and protected. Privacy, however, tends to become confused with secrecy, despite the fact that public disclosure of information about the ownership of land, the use of real property, and the payment of local taxes is guaranteed by law. Researchers will often encounter screens of privacy, reflected in hard-to-use public documents and tight-lipped public officials, even when seeking ownership information that is a matter of public record.

The basic information sought in landownership research includes the *identity* of those who own the land; certain *background* charac-

Robert O'Keefe

*Willy Watts inventorying vacant buildings in Cincinnati.*

teristics of property owners; the present *use* of the property; and the *assessed value* and *taxes* paid on the land and buildings of a specific parcel, neighborhood, community, or region. The identity and background of the owners of local property reveal the owner's legal status (individual, partnership, for-profit or nonprofit corporation), place of residence (inside the community or outside the community, state, or country), primary occupation or business, relevant organizational affiliations (membership on the boards of banks, businesses, or nonprofit institutions, public positions or offices held, etc.), and any other information that might assist a local group in inferring what plans an owner might have for the property in question. Preprinted index cards, like the one pictured on the next page, will be a great help in recording, storing, and retrieving such background information. Each parcel of land in the "target" area should have its own index card, filed under the address of the parcel or the name of the owner. The identity and background of the parcel's owner is recorded on Side 1 of the index card. Adapt this card system to your own circumstances and needs.

Information pertaining to the *use* of each parcel can be included on Side 2 of the index card, along with the property's assessed value and tax bill. A description of the land's use should be supplemented by description of the physical condition of any structures that are located on the land. It is also important to note any constraints on the property's use (zoning, historic preservation, protected wetlands, etc.) and any specific rights in the bundle of property rights that are no longer part of the deed (such as mineral rights and development rights). Assessments on the land are periodically made by a public official known as the tax assessor. They are a rough estimate of what the market value of a parcel's acreage and improvements is believed to be. (Since assessments are not performed every year, the actual market value is usually higher than the assessed value.) The assessment is the basis on which the taxes on a parcel of property are figured.

Another device that is helpful in recording ownership information is a map of the community or area under investigation. Maps may be used in conjunction with the card system just described. Beginning with a single base map of the area, researchers may superimpose sheets

## INDEX CARD (Side 1)

Address of parcel: ____________________

Name of owner(s): ____________________

Address of owner: ____________________

Phone: ____________________

Name & address of manager or leasee: ____________________

____________________

**Owner information:**

a. Legal status: ____________________

b. Occupation/business: ____________________

c. Affiliations: ____________________

d. Describe other property owned: ____________________

____________________

e. Comments: ____________________

____________________

## INDEX CARD (Side 2)

Lot size/acreage: ____________________

Tax Map No.: __________ Assessment (Yr. ___): __________ Taxes: __________

Principal use & acreage: ____________________

Secondary use & acreage: ____________________

Physical description (land & bldgs.): ____________________

____________________

No. of rental units: __________ No. of unoccupied rental units: __________

Principal use of neighboring properties: ____________________

____________________

Zoning: __________ Other land-use constraints: __________

____________________

Rights sold or leased: ____________________

____________________

Comments: ____________________

of a clear plastic, such as Mylar, on which are recorded information about the ownership, use, value, and condition of specific parcels. Overlays might also be prepared which indicate zoning restrictions, absentee ownership, critical areas (historical, environmental, or cultural), and the social composition of the area's population (discussed at a later point in this chapter). A check with local planning officials may reveal that useful maps of your area already exist.

Where else does one look for basic ownership information? The place to begin is usually with local people, those who live and work in the area under study. Long-term residents sometimes know a remarkable amount about the financial interests and earlier ventures of the community's largest landlords and landholders. Recent residents, particularly those who have just purchased property in the area, may know a lot about other properties in the same community. Admittedly, some of this information will be secondhand gossip that must be checked with other sources, but most will later prove useful. Moreover, even if the *content* of such face-to-face, door-to-door research is somewhat inadequate, the *process* of doing it will provide a fine opportunity for the organizers of a CLT to meet local people, discover their needs, and spread the word of the prospective trust. Such research can be easily done by a team of people, armed with the kind of cards we have already described.

Having obtained initial exposure to the community through informal interviews with residents and other selected informants, members of the research team should plan a series of visits to the offices of key public officials, probably in this order: local officials like the tax assessor and the recorder of deeds; regional offices such as planning and development agencies and the Agricultural Stabilization and Conservation Service (ASCS); and, finally, the secretary of state in your own state. The data collected in these offices will mostly go on Side 2 of your index cards.

## Urban Mapping Service

For many years, the Sanborn Company has published an insurance atlas providing useful technical details for most urban neighborhoods. The maps include scale drawings of existing buildings on their urban lots and contain information on street width, utilities servicing the area, building use, height, shape, materials of construction, lot size, building date, and owner of record for each structure. These maps may go back many years. They are available to real estate firms and insurance underwriters on a costly subscription basis. Contact these outlets to arrange a loan or inspection, or check with local libraries and planning offices. As a last resort, contact the Library of Congress in Washington, D.C., where a complete set is available. Be sure that the Sanborn map you see coincides with the period for which you need information.

For tangible returns, a researcher is well advised to begin in the tax or land books of the tax assessor's office. Land parcels are listed there by address as well as by the owner's name. Find and record the tax map number for the parcels you are concerned with. Should you ever need to contact the assessor for further information at a later time, the tax map number will enable you to get the information you need over the phone. Also record the property taxes and the assessment (before comparing them, determine whether the assessed value is entered into the tax books at full value—100 percent—or some lesser percentage of full value). Be prepared to encounter different methods of data storage in different offices—cards, microfilm, computer tapes or printouts. Ask for help when information is not self-evident; it is public information and most public employees will offer cordial assistance.

Now go to the recorder's office and ask to be shown the general index of property deeds. Here are listed the names of all sellers ("grantors") and buyers ("grantees") of real estate, as well as references to other critical documents pertaining to a piece of land. The most important of these documents is the deed itself. The deed usually reports the address and legal description of the property, the date of transmission from seller to buyer (both named), and "alterations" in ownership—these include mortgages, liens, leases, foreclosures, or other financial arrangements complicating simple ownership.

Ownership research at the local level takes persistence and creative thinking. It can be complicated by the practice of recording the property under the name of the owner's spouse or relative. Following are other complications that might arise.

Taxes and holdings by utilities may not be in the county tax books. In some states this information is not public, in others it is recorded and maintained by a state agency. Ask the local assessor or recorder of deeds for guidance.

Property may also be recorded under corporations: partnerships, syndicates, fiduciary trusts, and associations. Sometimes it is recorded under the name of a title company, bank, or escrow company holding title until a sale is completed. Assessors usually file a list of corporate holdings in a county with the state's secretary of state. You may request the list at either level. Since not all tax books show addresses, ask who maintains addresses for mailing tax bills, then request those that you wish. The Securities and Exchange Commission (SEC) is another valuable source of corporate information; you can contact them directly or through your congressional delegation.

Often, a "local" corporation will be a subsidiary of an absentee out-of-state corporation. Local residents may provide clues on this, as may local realtors, attorneys, or title insurance investigators (all of whom frequent the county court house in their work). Once you get a lead, some library work in *Standard and Poor's Who Owns Whom* or *Moody's* will help trace the correct address of the parent company.

Information on nonprofit holdings may not be available in the assessor's office, since such lands usually do not produce revenues. If the institution is public, consult local, state, or federal planning agencies for leads as to where the ownership data resides. Private nonprofit information, even if not recorded by the assessor, will be known to most assessors because of local concern over tax-exempt holdings.

When comparing ownership or tax data from several counties or states, be alert to data quality—differences in the ways that information is categorized and in the ways that tax assessments are made. Be aware, in rural areas, that policies vary considerably in recording mineral rights. Such information will be quite thorough in some localities and spotty in others. Uneven quality is, for that matter, a fact of life for much of the ownership data that is available from these agencies.

Control of local property is less explicit and less manifest than ownership. Yet it can be just as significant as ownership and demands attention. Private individuals, whose names may be tucked away in the property deed, may exert control through easements, restrictive covenants, or deed restrictions. Lending institutions, investors, and insurers, for instance, exert control through mortgages which are publically recorded in bound volumes in the office of the recorder of deeds.

Regarding *public* restrictions on land, zoning administrators are valuable repositories of information about present (and pending) land-use regulations as well as variance practices. They can describe the powers, behavior, and composition of local planning boards and municipal zoning boards. They can tell you of pending land-use legislation, public works, and utility plans and, like the assessor, what tax delinquent lands might be available in the area. Additional land-use regulations can be documented by talking with planners at the local, regional, and state levels, and with federal officials charged with administering floodplain, mine reclamation, costal zone, or public lands programs.

Finally, information available from the ASCS is helpful in researching both ownership and control when the property of interest is rural. Specific names, addresses, or other information about individual parcels will *not* be recorded at the ASCS. Yet it is a good source of data for documenting *absentee* ownership. This is because the owner's place of residence is indicated (i.e., in or outside the county, outside the county but in the state, outside the state and outside the nation). Recorded, too, is the number of owners, the number of owner-operators, the number of renters, and the number of acres for each type of owner. Such data will later prove useful in verifying the pattern of ownership that begins to emerge as researchers learn more about individual parcels of land.

**Research on the real estate market and the local economy.** The second area of community research is less concerned with describing the current pattern of property ownership than with analyzing the market through which that pattern is created, sustained, or replaced by another. Less attention is devoted to who owns individual parcels than to how the buying and selling of real property might affect the price and use of those parcels. By combining a general analysis of the local real estate market with the kind of ownership research discussed above, the organizers of a CLT should have enough information to identify the most influential actors on the local real estate scene, to identify the most pressing land-related problem facing the local community, to discover properties that the CLT may later acquire, and to detect trends in the market for housing and land that may affect the entire community.

This last item is especially important, for people are not always aware of major market changes slowly occurring all around them. Mortgage and home improvement loans may gradually become unavailable to residents of a certain area, or a landlord may make fewer and fewer repairs. Disinvestment through redlining or perpetually deferred repairs can go on for months or years before its impact is noticed. Conversely, realtors and developers may gradually buy up many parcels of land before investment becomes obvious. Disinvestment or reinvestment can quietly gather momentum until the day that either suddenly appears as an agent for devastation or displacement—a land-related problem that local residents must belatedly try to solve.

Market analysis means different things in different communities, but there are several kinds of information which no researcher should overlook. These include data on vacancies, tax delinquencies, foreclosures, liquidation, and abandonment; information on the credit practices of local banks; indicators of local business activity; data on changes occurring in the assessments, prices, and rental fees for local land and housing; and information on current construction and rehabilitation going on in the area under study.

The sources of such information are varied.

but quite accessible. City and regional planning offices collect much of this data as a matter of course, as do the housing agencies of large and medium-size cities. In rural areas, local officials of the Farmers Home Administration and the ASCS may be able to provide some of this information. Real estate boards, post offices, and utilities conduct periodic surveys to determine local vacancy rates. The building, fire, and health inspectors of city government must periodically evaluate the state of repair of rental units. Cities also issue building permits for new construction and major repairs; most cities maintain a monthly record of the number issued for each district.

Information on the credit practices of banks and savings-and-loans has been made easy to obtain by two pieces of federal legislation: the Home Mortgage Disclosure Act (HMDA) and the Community Reinvestment Act (CRA). These acts cover most depository institutions in the United States which are either chartered or insured by the federal government. The HMDA requires banks, savings-and-loans, and credit unions with offices in metropolitan areas to release a publically available disclosure statement. For each census tract in which an institution made at least one loan during the year, it must report the number of loans and total loan dollars for each of five mortgage and loan categories. (*Note:* HMDA disclosure does not apply to institutions in many rural areas, nor to very small institutions.) The CRA requires all federally regulated lenders to make public an annual "CRA statement" which contains a map delineating the area in which the lender makes (or is prepared to make) loans and a list of the *types of credit* the lender is prepared to extend to communities within this area. Under the CRA, federal approval of a lender's request for changes in its ongoing operations is contingent upon the lender's performance in meeting the credit needs of local residents. Written comments received by the lender that relate to its record in meeting this obligation must be kept for two years in a public file. (Guides to using HMDA and CRA data in community research are listed in the bibliography at the end of this book.)

The real estate market is affected not only by the credit practices of local lenders, but by the level of business activity in the local economy. The performance and potential of the local economy will, of course, also affect the lives of the people to whom the CLT will look for membership and support. Researchers should be sensitive to signs of economic growth and decline since both will cause fluctuations in property values, disposable income, and the morale of local residents. Planners, banks, and chambers of commerce are potential sources of data on monthly business trends and local economic activity. Researchers should also acquire the publications of Federal Reserve banks for their region and make contact with the research arms of universities and unions. The latter two, in particular, may have forewarning of plant runaways or planned cutbacks in local production.

Finally, researchers should discover the extent to which property values, taxes, and rents are moving up or down. Such information is necessary not only for understanding the problems that families face in obtaining shelter and making ends meet, but for revealing the hurdles that the CLT will face in meeting the costs of acquiring and holding local property. Tax assessors, local realtors, and the real estate department of local banks will all have some idea of the changing costs of local land and housing, as will municipal housing or planning offices. This is also an area in which local residents are quite knowledgeable. They know more about the bills they pay and the burdens they bear than all the planners, bankers, and realtors in town.

**Research on the population and local organizations.** To understand a community one must ultimately know what kinds of people live there, work there, move there, and leave there. What, for instance, is the age distribution of the population? How many elderly live in the area, and do they own or rent the property they use? What kinds of racial, ethnic, income, and occupational groups make up the community? What percentage of the population is made up of tenants? Facts like these should be at the organizer's fingertips. They are not difficult to get.

Local population figures are available from a number of public agencies. School officials, health departments, welfare agencies, and local planners routinely collect and use statistical information describing the people and groups that populate their region. Researchers may also obtain such information from any library that has a copy of the U.S. Census. The 1980 Census gathered population and housing data at the national, state, county, and "minor civil division" level. This means that some cities (those participating in the Census Bureau's Neighborhood Statistic Program) will have complete census information all the way down to the level of the neighborhood block. Be aware, however, that official population counts are often misleadingly low in neighborhoods with a high proportion of black or Spanish-speaking residents.

One other comment: It is important to obtain population data for more than a single point in time. The social composition of an area, as it now exists, is only half of the picture that an organizer needs. Current population figures should be compared to those of the previous decade (or the previous year) to get a sense of how the population is changing. Is there a trend of growth or decline? Is the income or age of the population rising or falling? Who is migrating into or out of the community? Population research is a moving picture which must be examined again and again, not a snapshot that is taken once and put away.

Finally, in researching the community's social environment, the organizers of a CLT must not ignore other groups and organizations which already exist. The kind and number of organizations which a community happens to have says much about its identity, prospects, and concerns. But a CLT must go beyond regarding other organizations as merely facts of community life, researched like any other fact. The CLT must find ways of reaching out to these other groups.

# OUTREACH

> In 1854, Chief Seattle, the leader of the Suquamish tribe in the Washington territory, marked the transfer of ancestral Indian lands to the federal government with a speech that included the following words: "Man did not weave the web of life; he is merely a strand in it. Whatever he does to the web, he does to himself."

The community land trust becomes a part of the community's life at the most basic physical level, gathering to itself land, shelter, and (in some rural cases) the means of subsistence. Whatever the CLT does with these resources will affect not only itself, but the rest of the community as well. At the same time, whether it chooses to or not, the CLT becomes an important part of the community's social fabric, one strand in a complicated organizational web. Whatever the CLT does to this web, it inevitably does to itself.

Almost every community, urban or rural, contains a varied assortment of institutions, organizations, and associations whose interests and activities are intricately interwoven. There are agencies for real estate, for welfare, and for work; associations for the preservation of this, and for the promotion or prevention of that. There are churches, Boy Scouts, banks, and bars. There are businesses and commissions and enough clubs of Mooses, Lions, and Elks to fill a zoo. There are departments for every duty and disaster. All of these—and all of the criss-crossing relationships among them—make up the CLT's "organizational environment."

As with the natural environment in which the CLT finds itself, the organizational environment serves as a general setting for the CLT's activities, offering a mixture of resources and scarcities, opportunities and constraints within which the CLT must operate—and with which the trust must strike a sort of ecological balance. Within this setting, outreach begins as organizing. The effort to build a base of community support and to personalize the message of the CLT is an exercise in reaching out to individuals and organizations throughout the community, enlisting their support for the CLT. Once the trust is established, however, the importance of outreach does not diminish. Outreach becomes what might be called "community and political relations"—the ways in which a CLT will choose to interact, cooperate, or formally affiliate with other groups in its organizational environment.

There are several reasons why community and political relations should be a central concern of the CLT. The first of these has to do with the CLT model itself, for the community land trust is ideally portrayed as an integral part of its surrounding community. The ongoing interrelationship between a CLT and the community-at-large is part of what *defines* an organization as a CLT. The community land trust is not an enclave, not an island of guarded lands and privileges from which the larger community is routinely excluded. It is, instead, a locally based institution guaranteeing broad participation in the use of its resources and in decisions concerning their use. This necessarily makes community relations one of the CLT's most important concerns.

A second reason for believing that community relations must be a high priority is that the CLT will not be ignored by the rest of the community even if it wishes to be. In most communities, the establishment of a new institution for acquiring and holding land will not go unnoticed—or, perhaps, unchallenged. Dominant economic and political interests may regard the CLT as a threat to their local positions of power, for the CLT promotes popular sovereignty over land-based sources of power and wealth. Homeowners may suspiciously associate the CLT with public housing, urban renewal, or other programs of the public sector; or they may group the CLT with the speculators, developers, and affluent promoters of gentrification. Local organizations involved in tenants rights, welfare rights, housing, and environmental issues may regard the CLT as an intruder or competitor for scarce resources and similar constituencies. Agencies and officers of local government, baffled by the unfamiliarity of this new organizational form of land tenure and control, may innocently harass the CLT with inappropriate regulations, restrictions, or codes. Any of these situations may create serious problems for the community land trust. Consequently, whether the organization of the CLT provokes opposition, suspicion, regulation, or merely curious interest, the CLT must consider community relations a necessary and continuing concern.

The most persuasive argument for placing a high priority on community relations, however, involves neither an ideal definition of the CLT nor a strategy of defense. Simply stated, community relations are necessary because the purposes of the CLT are most readily achieved through cooperation with other community organizations committed to similar goals. Supporting or allying with other community groups may be the CLT's surest and shortest route to successful realization of its own plans. At the same time, the CLT may lend considerable assistance to its organizational allies and do much to promote *their* programs and plans. Examples of such cooperation and mutual aid are plentiful.

On *economic development issues,* CLTs have found common ground with local cooperatives, worker-managed businesses, and community development corporations (CDCs). In Tennessee, the Community Land Association is planning to build several homes with construction assistance provided by the Home Makers, which, like the CLA itself, is a member of the local association known as the Mountain Women's Exchange. In Georgia, New Communities is a supporting member of the Federation of Southern Cooperatives; the federation helps to market some of the commodities produced on the CLT's farm. The CLT being organized in Minneapolis will become an integral part of community development efforts that are already underway, initiated by the Cedar Riverside Project Area Committee and the West Bank CDC.

On *environmental issues,* CLTs have worked cooperatively with local groups who would pre-

Robert O'Keefe

*PAD, People Against Displacement: community coalition around housing issues.*

serve or protect aglands, open space, wetlands, woodlands, wildlife, and natural resources of other kinds for future generations. The Marin Agricultural Land Trust, for example, has been working side-by-side with the local Farm Bureau, local conservation groups, and the county government to preserve farmlands threatened with development. The Monadnock Forest Land Trust project is being carried out under the joint sponsorship of the Monadnock CLT, the Institute for Community Economics, and the oldest conservation group in the state, the Society for the Protection of New Hampshire Forests.

On *residential displacement issues,* CLTs have joined with other community groups to fight redlining, control gentrification, and stop displacement due to both disinvestment and reinvestment. The CLT in Cincinnati, for instance, is participating with other local groups in a suit to challenge insurance redlining in their neighborhood. Board members of the same CLT have helped to organize a homeowners association that will work with the Community Land Cooperative to oppose gentrification in Cincinnati's West End. In Minneapolis, a tenants union that has long been active in the struggle against high rents and gentrification is supporting the development of a CLT to complement the union's own activities, a means of consolidating some of the gains it has made.

On various *public policy issues,* CLTs have had some rather unusual relations with one of the most important actors in their organizational environment: local government. Most interaction between CLTs and municipal officials has been marked by benign indifference, with neither part doing more than is minimally required to meet whatever legal obligations each might have with regard to the other. On several occasions, however, their interaction has been more substantial. The Monadnock CLT was recently invited by the local planning board to assist in drafting a new zoning ordinance that would permit the kind of residential ownership and development that is common to CLTs. The CLT that is being developed in the Cedar Riverside community is expected to have close relations with the Minneapolis Community Development Agency, a public housing authority that may eventually transfer a number of properties to the trust. Perhaps the most interesting case of cooperation between a CLT and local government occurred in Boston, where the city encouraged three competing neighborhood organizations to jointly organize a CLT. The incentive for this unlikely alliance was a large Community Development Block Grant which the city was willing to make available if a CLT were formed to be the recipient of this federal money. Whether or not this strategy proves successful, it is indicative of the interest that local government is beginning to take in working together with CLTs. (Noteworthy as well is the fact that an increasing number of the requests for information about CLTs received by the Institute for Community Economics comes from public officials.)

Examples such as these are merely suggestive of the kinds of formal or informal relations that CLTs might establish with other community-based organizations. Community land trusts around the country have used many additional means to make community outreach an ongoing part of their operations. Some, for instance, publish regular newsletters, distributed free or for a minimal charge to their own members, local residents, local organizations, and (occasionally) to supporters outside the community. The most ambitious of these was the *Maine Land Advocate,* a 16-page bimonthly publication that was distributed nationally for seven years (1973 to 1979) by the Sam Ely CLT. Another bimonthly paper, *This Time,* is published by HOME Co-op, the parent organization of Covenant CLT. Less-formal newsletters, prepared mostly for internal circulation among the trust's members and supporters, have been used by the Community Land Cooperative in Cincinnati and the Valley CLT in Franklin County, Massachusetts.

A final element of community outreach deserves special emphasis. Outreach should be more than a means by which the trust parades its accomplishments before the eyes of its neighbors. Community relations is a two-way street. Outreach, therefore, should also allow the surrounding community to impress its concerns and desires on the CLT.

The issue here is accountability. By its structure, policies, and personal style, how open is the CLT to participation by persons and organizations that reside nearby? Through its open membership, democratic elections to the board of trustees, and perhaps by reserving seats on the board for representatives of certain organizations or interests, the CLT can build an element of accountability into its very structure. (These structural questions will be discussed in the next chapter.)

The *policies* of the CLT determine the content of community relations: what kinds of cooperation or assistance will be extended to other community groups; how much time and effort the CLT will devote to initiating contacts with individuals and institutions not listed already among the trust's supporters. Finally, by its personal style and public attitude toward the rest of the community, the CLT communicates either a readiness or a reluctance to accept "outsiders" into its midst. The greater the disparity in dress, manner, education, or wealth between those who initially organize the trust and those who reside around it, the greater will be the social distance that must be bridged. But even without such personal differences, the CLT can convey an attitude of self-centered distance and exclusiveness that pushes its neighbors away.

Community and political relations keep the CLT directed outwards, toward the rest of the community. At the same time—through an open structure, cooperative policies, and a receptive style—the CLT welcomes the community inside its own domain, opening itself up to wider scrutiny and closer supervision by the community at large. This, in the end, is the purpose of outreach: that the CLT may resist becoming an isolated island of self-interest and privilege—remaining, instead, an active part of the local community which contains and sustains it.

CHAPTER 11

# Internal Organization

To inexperienced people, the process of organizing a CLT as a legal entity is sometimes intimidating. However, incorporation is not a confrontation with The Law. It is a contract, a covenant, among all of the members of the CLT. It is a commitment to work together for the common good, and a statement of the way the members have agreed to work together. This chapter is meant to demystify the process and documents of incorporation, help CLT members think through the key issues, and prepare them for an experience which can be interesting and even exciting. When it is completed, the CLT will be ready to begin property acquisition and development, to meet community needs, and to take charge of its own future.

## BASIC CONSIDERATIONS

**Why incorporate.** A CLT is typically organized as a nonprofit corporation. Organizing as a corporation gives a group a common identity and legal standing and allows it to do business as a single body. Within the corporation, the legal liability of individual members is limited (except in cases of intentional wrong doing or serious mismanagement); they are not personally liable for claims against the corporation. As a corporation, the CLT has an identity and existence longer than the life or involvement of any individual member. The CLT can preserve its rights, carry on its activities, and fulfill its responsibilities as individuals come and go. As a nonprofit corporation, the CLT is eligible for tax-exempt status, which will open additional sources of funding, reduce operating costs, and enable the CLT to make use of low-cost property acquisition techniques.

**Who should incorporate.** In most states, the number of people legally required to form a nonprofit corporation (the "incorporators," whose names are recorded in the "articles of incorporation" and submitted to the state) is very small—usually two to four. But incorporation should be a real group process; all of the initial members of the CLT should understand and ratify their founding documents. Nevertheless, the technical process—reviewing sample legal documents, discussing the many clauses and the issues they raise, trying to imagine and provide for future problems, and finally formulating a set of documents tailored to fit the specific group and community—will be time-consuming, and may be frustrating for some; and a large group may be an unwieldy tool for hammering out the many minor details. Therefore, the founding membership may want to appoint a drafting committee to prepare a set of legal documents. While the committee, with the help of an attorney and other technical assistants, works on the legal drafts, other members can continue their outreach and neighborhood research, and begin to identify likely property acquisitions.

The drafting committee should report to the entire group periodically, reviewing their progress and soliciting the advice and direction of the group on specific issues. When the document drafts have been completed, the committee should present them to the membership, with a copy for each member, and should review the documents, article by article, in a general discussion. This is a very important process since individual members (even those with little or no legal experience) will often bring fresh perspectives and valuable insights into the process. In a diverse membership group, different individuals will recognize the likely impact of the proposed agreements upon themselves and their own interests. With these various interests represented, a CLT can be created that will fairly balance the interests of the various constituencies in the community. The CLT's attorney should be present throughout these discussions, which will give her or him a deeper understanding of the concerns and objectives of the organization.

After the initial presentation and discussion of the proposed documents, members may want to take them home for further study and informal discussion. Another meeting should then be scheduled for a final review and formal ratification.

## PREPARING FOR INCORPORATION

As the members of the drafting committee approach their task, they should obtain copies of the forms and laws regarding nonprofit corporations in their state, and copies of the federal Internal Revenue Service's publication 557 and form 1023 for application for tax-exempt status. The incorporation forms and applicable laws should be available from the office of the secretary of state. They will describe the information and structural features required of a nonprofit corporation in the state (these vary somewhat from state to state, but are generally similar); they will outline the process of management, financial accounting, and periodic reporting required by the state; and they will specify the process and fee required for registration of the corporation.

After reviewing the legal requirements, the drafting committee may want to visit or talk with members of other CLTs, if that is possible, and discuss with them their own process of formation and incorporation, their practical experiences, and how these experiences have compared with their original expectations. The committee might also review this group's documents with them.

Perhaps even more important, the drafting committee may contact a representative of an organization such as the Institute for Community Economics (see end of book) which provides technical assistance to CLTs—someone who is familiar with the legal issues of incorporation and the documents and practical experiences of many CLTs. The committee should ask for a copy of the organization's model articles of incorporation and bylaws to use as a point of reference in drafting its own documents. Before the committee begins to write, it can be very helpful for members to think carefully about the particular purposes, features, and experiences of CLTs, and the potential opportunities and pitfalls which may affect the structure of the organization. A good technical assistant can help the committee to do this. They may want to make arrangements for the technical assistant to work with them throughout the drafting process, assisting and training both themselves and their attorney. If the group does not have an attorney, the technical assistant can help write the document drafts, and these can then be taken to a capable local attorney for review.

Here in the beginning and throughout the life and work of the CLT, committee members should learn to understand the legal issues involved in the formation and development of a CLT, and learn to do some of the legal work for themselves. It is not as difficult as it may first seem, and it will enable members to work more efficiently and effectively, whether on their own or with the help of their attorney (and may save money). And they just may be surprised at how many new and good *legal* ideas *they* might have!

## WORKING WITH AN ATTORNEY

An attorney is one of several professional friends, advisors, or assistants a CLT will need as it develops. He or she may assist with incorporation, property acquisition, leasing, and other matters. After the preparation suggested above, a sympathetic, capable local attorney should be sought who will familiarize herself or himself with the purposes and needs of the organization and will provide continuing advice and assistance. Your own advance preparation will help you to identify the right attorney and to know whether you're getting good advice. A good attorney will appreciate your preparation and respect you for it.

The matters on which a CLT may eventually need legal advice include not only organization and maintenance of a nonprofit corporation, but also income, gift, and estate taxes and deductions; real estate acquisition and development (finance, zoning, building codes); and landlord-tenant laws. An attorney may be found who is already knowledgeable about these issues, or at least willing to learn in order to assist you. Ask about the attorney's previous experience and skills. Corporate bylaws and lease agreements are not unusual legal instruments; however, specific provisions of these documents may be unusual or unique as they relate to the particular purposes and structures of CLTs. Even an experienced attorney may not fully understand the philosophy and goals of a CLT and their legal implications, and may unintentionally give insufficient or mistaken advice. A skilled CLT technical assistant can be helpful in orienting and preparing an attorney for a valuable ongoing relationship with the CLT.

One particular matter of terminology should be immediately clarified when a CLT begins working with an attorney. Although the term "community land trust" is becoming more widely recognized and understood, it is often confusing or misleading for lawyers and others who are accustomed to legal terminology. The CLT is not typically a legal trust, but rather a nonprofit corporation. The word "trust" in "community land trust" is used not for its legal meaning, but for its everyday meaning, to convey the spirit of the relationship between the members of the CLT and between the people of the community and their land. Be sure to explain this clearly to your attorney when you first contact her or him to assist in organizing the CLT, as well as to others who may be confused.

In any event, find an attorney whom you trust and with whom you can work easily. In Cincinnati and some other communities, the Legal Aid Society has provided free legal assistance to neighborhood CLTs. Other CLTs have received help from faculty members of local law schools or from private attorneys. Some large firms do a limited amount of pro bono (without charge) community service work. You may want to consult with other nonprofit groups in your area if you do not already know an attorney. Some groups have received legal assistance without cost; others have paid legal fees. Establish a clear understanding with your attorney regarding fees, and specifically identify your needs.

## OVERVIEW OF THE LEGAL DOCUMENTS

The documents of incorporation consist of the articles of incorporation and the bylaws of the corporation. The articles are a shorter document. Their purpose is to establish the existence and identity of the organization as a legal corporation. They must be submitted to the state for approval and registration. If the articles are later amended, these amendments must also be approved and recorded. The purpose of the bylaws is to define—for its own members and board of trustees, and for the legal authorities—the CLT's organizational structure, division of rights and responsibilities, process of decision-making, and method of operation. In most states, they do not need to to be filed and approved, but the CLT is legally required to have them and to abide by them. If the bylaws are later amended, these amendments need not be recorded with the state.

In addition to these legal documents, the CLT may wish to develop a set of policies or guidelines which describe in more detail its principles, goals, strategies, and procedures. These are not legally required. They may be written in a style that is less formal or technical than the legal documents, and they may be useful as a public description of the aims and activities of the CLT. Because they can be more easily amended to fit changing circumstances and needs, they can be more detailed.

## ARTICLES OF INCORPORATION

The articles establish the existence and identity of the corporation; they may state the principal elements of the organization's structure, but not the details of its operating procedures. Most states provide a short and simple form for this purpose. The drafting committee should ask for it when they request a copy of the state laws regarding nonprofit corporations from the office of the secretary of state. You are not required to use this form; you may write your articles as you wish, provided that all of the required information is included.

The nature and amount of information required in the articles varies somewhat from state to state (with the balance of information on the corporation and its operation left to the bylaws). Provisions not specifically required by law may be included but you will probably want to leave them for the bylaws, where they will be easier to amend if that becomes necessary. In some cases, it is possible to withhold certain requested information from the articles by simply stating "... as provided in the bylaws of the corporation." You may want to consult your attorney or staff persons in the appropriate state office concerning this possibility.

It is likely that the information required or requested for the articles of incorporation will include:

- Name of the corporation.
- Address of the principal office and/or name and address of the registered agent.
- Purposes.
- Names of the incorporators.
- Categories of, and qualifications for, membership.
- Number and/or names of initial trustees (may be different from the incorporators).
- Procedure for amendment of the articles.

Most of this information will be easily stated, with perhaps the exceptions of the information regarding membership and the purposes of the corporation. Membership issues are covered in greater detail in the bylaws and we will discuss them later under that heading. The statement of purpose deserves more attention at this point.

## PURPOSES OF THE CLT CORPORATION

The statement of purpose may be a general statement of the principles and objectives of the CLT. It need not be very detailed, and it should not include every planned activity. The articles of incorporation are not usually a document for general circulation; you will probably produce an informational brochure or other literature which describes the CLT and its purposes more fully to interested people. Nevertheless, this requirement for a statement of purpose is an opportunity to clarify and state publicly the CLT's goals in the community.

Be sure that these "public" purposes of the CLT are clearly stated. Make it clear that the CLT is not a homeowners association or an organization primarily concerned with the personal interests of a limited group of members—that it has a commitment to the well-being of the community as a whole. In general terms, such public purposes might include: providing access to land and decent housing for low-income people, conservation and responsible management of land and natural resources, development of an economic base in and for the local community. It should be made clear that the activities of the CLT will go beyond the business of real estate acquisition and management, and will include education, community service, and support for cooperative development throughout the community.

A clear statement of public purpose is particularly important if a CLT plans to apply for federal tax-exempt status. The IRS will want to be sure that it is a charitable or educational organization, chartered to act in the public interest. If you do plan to make such an application, you should consult the specifications set forth in IRS form 1023 before drafting your statement of purpose. You may need to include additional provisions, either as part of your statement of purpose or in a separate article which is frequently called "powers and limitations," and which further defines the corporation's purposes and the activities in which the corporation is forbidden to engage. The wording of these provisions will play a large part in the determination of the CLT's tax status by the IRS; they should be written in language and format which conform to the specifications for exemptions in form 1023. As a safeguard, many groups preface this statement with language such as, "To initiate and administer programs exclusively for charitable and educational purposes within the meaning of IRS Section 501(c)(3) and, in furtherance of such purposes but not in limitation thereof, to . . ."; or will end the statement with language such as "... and other activities consistent with these purposes and permitted under IRS Section 501(c) (3)."

The Internal Revenue Service must be assured that no part of the income or assets of the corporation will be distributed to the members and that, in the event the corporation is dissolved, its assets will be transferred to another tax-exempt, nonprofit corporation (or corporations) with similar purposes. These restrictions may be included in the statement of purpose or the powers and limitations, or in a separate article governing "disposition of assets in the event of dissolution."

If, at the time of incorporation, you are not sure whether you will apply for tax-exempt status, but do not plan to engage in any activities which are expressly forbidden by IRS regulations, then you should phrase your articles in such a way that you might later qualify, without having to amend your articles before you apply.

## BYLAWS OF THE CORPORATION

The bylaws may address some of the same issues as the articles, but they are usually much longer and more detailed. They set forth the division of responsibility and operating procedures for the CLT corporation. They are its "constitution." Although the states do not provide forms for corporate bylaws, you should read and familiarize yourselves with the state law regarding the organization and operation of nonprofit corporations. This law may have an effect on some of the provisions you will draft, but you are free to include any provision you choose if it is not specifically forbidden by state law.

Remember that the bylaws are not simply a legal document—they are an agreement among all the members of the CLT. Include whatever provisions you feel will be necessary to ensure responsible and democratic management of the CLT. On the other hand, do not make the required procedures so numerous or complex that members cannot fully understand them. Make sure that all members are treated fairly. Give the board of trustees sufficient authority to manage the affairs of the corporation and fulfill their own responsibilities effectively, but guarantee that the voice of the full membership will always be heard. Ultimately, the success of the CLT, as of any organization, depends on the trust of its members in one another and their commitment to a common purpose.

There are many details which may be included in the bylaws, as you will see when you review a set of model bylaws, but there are several critical issues and features which should be considered carefully as the CLT is being shaped.

**Membership.** By definition, a *community* land trust is an organization which seeks to include people and land throughout the community, to link them together, to build bridges between the various legitimate individual and public interests. No matter what specific activities it undertakes, its membership is open. Its form and functions are in many respects similar to those of local government.

CLT members are not necessarily residents of CLT lands, as are members of the typical housing cooperative. The CLT membership will include those whose needs are not yet met, and others in the community who share the CLT's purposes. The bylaws may, however, recognize the different interests and perspectives of these members by identifying more than one category of membership with equal rights and standing ("land-user" and "general" member, for example).

You may decide to require some qualifications for participating membership in the CLT—a minimum age requirement, for instance—but make sure that these qualifications are reasonable and necessary and do not limit the ability of the CLT to serve the community as a whole. You may require periodic membership dues, an orientation program for prospective members, and some measure of continuing participation (comparable, in some respects, to the requirement that voters be registered before voting in an election). Again, be sure that these requirements are reasonable and affordable, that they do not prevent any group of community residents from actively participating in the CLT. The bylaws may contain a nondiscrimination provision, an explicit statement that the CLT will not discriminate against any of its members for reasons of race, creed, sex, age, political belief, or ethnic background.

The CLT may restrict membership to residents of the geographical community it has chosen to serve, but the question of how to define this community has posed some difficulties for a number of groups. It is best to focus on a geographical area whose residents already have a sense of themselves as a community—an urban neighborhood, or a rural valley, town, or county. On the other hand, the population of the area should be large enough to provide a "critical mass" of interested members. (As individual CLTs and the CLT movement grow, there may be a further evolution—CLTs with large initial service areas may decentralize and CLTs representing small areas may affiliate in federations.) If a CLT decides, for any reason, to acquire land in an adjoining community where there is not yet a local CLT, it will want to offer membership to some residents of that neighboring community. To date, some CLTs have adopted a geographical restriction on membership; others have not done so. Those that have not done so have received very few applications for membership from people outside the community, but there is, of course, no guarantee that this might not later become a problem.

One way of dealing with the different levels of interest and commitment among community residents is to establish two different types of membership: "participating" and "supporting." Supporting membership gives community residents, and perhaps people outside the community who are unable to play an active role in the CLT, an opportunity to pledge their moral and financial support; but it does not confer the same voting rights as participating membership.

The bylaws will also describe the rights of members, provide for an annual meeting of the membership and for other meetings, establish procedures for those meetings and for the decision-making process, and identify those critical issues on which the entire participating membership will be called to vote. Responsibility for the daily mangement and development of the CLT is assigned to the board of trustees (or directors). Individual members can take an active role in shaping these policies and activities through service on the board or various committees.

**Board of trustees.** The board will make or approve decisions regarding property acquisition, financing, land-use planning and development, leasing, and management. Obviously, its membership should represent fairly the various interests and perspectives represented in and by the CLT. For this reason, when selecting trustees, the CLT's membership may want to give thought to the balance between men and women and among various age groups, and to the representation of low-income and minority members, various land-use constituencies (residential, agricultural, commercial, etc.) and other legitimate interests in the community. It is possible, of course, to mandate patterns of representation in the bylaws, but there are problems which often accompany such requirements. One person's representation may be, or be perceived as, another's disenfranchisement. A young CLT must be certain that it has a sufficient membership base from which to maintain an active and capable representation for any specific category that it establishes. In many instances, these questions of equality and justice may best be addressed through an educated sensitivity in the membership as well as operating policies or guidelines to assist the board in its work, rather than through specific provisions in the bylaws.

Those who lease and live on or use CLT lands are protected through properly drawn leases; further, to avoid a negative landlord-tenant relationship, CLT bylaws usually guarantee leaseholders direct representation on the board of trustees. In this way, leaseholders are more owners than renters.

But leaseholders certainly are not the only group with a legitimate and personal interest in the CLT. Others in the community still persevere in that traditional rental situation, and they may hope to enjoy someday the security, equity, and legacy for their descendants which the CLT provides; also, a CLT's neighbors are affected by the trust's use of the land, and some land uses or abuses affect the entire community. To provide for the present and future interests of other community residents, CLT bylaws guarantee representation on the board to those members who are not currently leaseholders. The CLT is neither a "landlord," nor a protective enclave of limited self-interest for those whose needs have already been met.

Basic to the CLT concept is the recognition that land (and its natural resources) is a timeless trust, which must be shared justly today and preserved or enhanced for those who will come after. To incorporate this long-range perspective in the CLT's decision-making process, as well as to represent other interests in the community or to add particular skills and human resources to the board, the bylaws usually provide for "public interest" representation on the board. These representatives may be people chosen for their record of community service or for particular skills which will aid the board in its work. They may include one or more members of other CLT's or CLT assistance organizations—people who bring understanding of the CLT's goals, an objective perspective on issues in the local community, and a sense of the local CLT's relationship to a larger community. A local community, of course, relates to surrounding communities and to a region as its own members and neighbors relate to one another. Involvement of representatives from other CLTs on the board looks forward to the eventual formation of regional federations of CLTs (at which time the federation may be asked to appoint these board members).

This public interest category also opens a door for possible links between CLTs and local governments. The activities of a CLT parallel some of the critical functions of local government—planning, zoning, taxation, public assistance—and there are opportunities for the two to work together. With the financial resources of government, its landholdings (particularly in low-income neighborhoods), and the influence of public policy in land use, disposition, planning, and development, such opportunities for cooperation can be very important. Depending on their local situations, CLTs may choose to offer a seat on the board to a person appointed by the local government, or to include some local officials as individuals.

The provision in the bylaws for representation on the board for leaseholders, other community residents, and the public interest is one of the principal means by which the CLT fulfills its goal of fairly balancing the legitimate interests of individuals and their communities in the possession and use of land. Over time, the proportionate representation of these groups may be shifted—as the percentage of community land and population in the CLT shifts and other circumstances change—but the commitment to maintain a just representation of these various legitimate interests must be basic and unchanging.

In addition to establishing the composition of the board, the bylaws describe its duties, powers, and limitations. They assign to the board the responsibility for oversight and management of the corporation, and give its members the authority and specific powers they will need to fulfill the purposes of the CLT. This is typically done through a specific list of the principal powers, followed by a general authority to "exercise all other powers necessary to . . . further the purposes of this corporation in conformance with the articles of incorporation and these bylaws." The bylaws also provide for the board's ultimate accountability to the membership and define its working relationship to members, committees, and staff.

The principal limitation on the powers of the board, aside from its legal obligation to operate within the structures and procedures established by the articles of incorporation and bylaws, is usually a requirement that it seek and receive the direct approval of the entire voting membership before taking action on major decisions—such as the removal of board members, sale of land, incurrence of substantial debt (other than acquisition of land with a mortgage encumbrance), amendment of the articles or bylaws, and dissolution of the corporation. In addition, conflict of interest provisions are likely to require trustees to disclose their real estate and other holdings in the community, and to require them to abstain from voting on any matter in which they, or a family member or business partner, have a personal financial interest. The bylaws provide for regular meetings of the board (typically open to all members) and describe the procedures by which these meetings will be called and conducted, and decisions made.

The sections of the bylaws dealing with both members and trustees also provide for their resignation or removal. If faced with a motion for removal, they must be assured of a fair process of judgment and the opportunity for an open hearing. Removal is, of course, a very serious action which should be undertaken only in extreme situations.

**Land stewardship.** Stewardship of the land, together with allocation of rights to its use, is the principal purpose of a CLT and thus the critical responsibility of the board and other members or representatives of the corporation. Though in many respects the bylaws of a CLT are similar to those of any other nonprofit corporation, a special section of the CLT's bylaws may be devoted to land stewardship.

In this section may be stated the principles which should guide the board, or designated representatives (a leasing committee composed of members, for example), in leasing CLT lands. The statement of principles may be very general (with interpretation and implementation left to those who will make the individual decisions), or it may attempt to establish specific criteria or procedures. General principles may include a commitment to providing access first to those in greatest need, to concern for the environment and preservation of the land itself, and to the land-use or development needs of the community as a whole.

The definition of these principles is difficult. There is, of course, a considerable potential for change in the membership and prevailing attitudes within the CLT over time. The founding members can be justly concerned that someday their successors may neglect or turn away from one of these principles, jeopardizing the land itself or the legitimate interests of a particular sector of the community and membership; or that a particular interest group within the membership will seek to dominate the processes and dictate the decisions of the CLT. On the other hand, the CLT, as empowered by its bylaws, must be flexible enough to respond to a wide range of opportunities, and to meet needs of people and land throughout the community through changing circumstances. It is important not to hamstring the corporation or its trustees in their pursuit of common objectives.

A number of CLT founders have first been inclined to place within the bylaws (where they are difficult to amend) acreage limitations and narrow environmental guidelines on all leaseholds. While these may be consistent with the philosophy and spirit of the CLT, and an understandable reaction to the absentee ownership, monopolization, and environmental abuse which infect so many communities, they may also have quite unintended and counterproductive side effects. For instance, the CLT may be offered land as a donation or partial donation (bargain sale) in exchange for a lifetime lease to the present owner. If that owner's landholding, or current use of the land, does not conform to the provisions of the bylaws, the CLT will be unable to accept the donation—and will lose what might be a valuable, long-term opportunity to redistribute and responsibly manage the land. Generally, there should be care taken that the values and limitations that are built into the CLT can be understood and respected by a significant portion of the local community. If they are not, the organization's ability to build a strong and diverse membership may be seriously compromised. If a group faces widespread misunderstandings and resistance in the community, it may be that the immediate task should be education and outreach, rather than incorporation.

The provisions for land stewardship may also describe the process by which the board will make land-use or leasing decisions. Decisions with a particularly serious or long-term impact, such as the commercial use of vital or nonrenewable natural resources, may require a larger majority, with support for the motion from trustees in each category. Likewise, a decision to mortgage or otherwise encumber land—which may be a reasonable and effective tool to expand land acquisition and meet community needs but does potentially jeopardize the CLT's custody of the land—may require the same stronger approval from the board as well as the assent of the current leaseholders of any land to be mortgaged.

Finally, there is the question of sale of land. Many conservation organizations and conservancy trusts regularly acquire and resell land, often removing the development rights on some or all of it before reselling. Most CLT members, on the other hand, regard land sale as contrary to the philosophy and purposes of a CLT. However, it cannot be legally prohibited. Some states allow a landowner to prohibit the sale of land for a period of time, even several generations, but no state permits an owner to stipulate that land can never be sold. Nevertheless, the bylaws can make the decision to sell CLT land very difficult by requiring a unanimous or high-majority vote of the board and the approval of a substantial portion of the membership.

**Amendment.** The bylaws should provide a procedure for their own amendment (and for amendment of the articles, if that has not already been provided in the articles themselves). As a CLT develops and accumulates experience, improvements in its structure or further clarification of its purposes may be appropriate and useful. For such a significant decision, the approval of the membership is usually required, along with an affirmative vote of the board. It may also be required that the membership receive prior notice of the proposed amendment, or that the motion be presented at two or more consecutive meetings before a vote is taken, to ensure that it has received careful consideration.

It may be that some elements of the CLT's structure or procedures are so essential to its purposes that they should never be amended. The bylaws may designate some provisions as unamendable. Once again, however, such decisions should be made cautiously. They are very long-term decisions, and the CLT will almost certainly encounter many unforeseen circumstances in the years to come. It may be better, in some cases, to require the agreement of a greater majority of the trustees or members before a particular provision can be amended.

**Dissolution.** If the articles of incorporation have not already made provision for disposition of the assets of the corporation (including the land owned by the CLT) in the event that it must be dissolved, then the bylaws must do so. If dissolution should occur and the CLT must give up its stewardship of the land, the principal concerns must remain the same: to ensure that the land itself, the interests of the community, and the legitimate interests of current leaseholders are protected.

By law, the assets of the corporation cannot be distributed to its members or trustees. CLT bylaws usually provide that the assets be transferred to another CLT, a regional CLT assistance organization or federation, or another nonprofit corporation which agrees to administer these assets (care for this land) in accordance with the purposes of the original CLT, and to honor any outstanding lease agreements. The bylaws will describe the process by which the trustees and members of the CLT will choose its successor.

Leaseholders may be further protected by a stipulation in their leases that the lease agreement will remain binding in the event that ownership of the land changes. As a last resort, if a willing corporation with similar purposes and commitments cannot be found, the CLT land could be sold to its current leaseholders, on reasonable terms, and the proceeds given by the CLT to another nonprofit corporation with appropriate purposes.

While the articles of incorporation and the bylaws certainly constitute a binding charter (all of the members, trustees, and agents of the corporation will be held legally accountable to their purposes and provisions), no legal agreement can provide an absolute guarantee that any corporation will remain true to the spirit and goals of its founders. The integrity and success of a CLT will ultimately depend upon its members—their commitment, good faith, perseverance, tolerance, and even sense of humor. The CLT is more than a legal entity, as it is far more than a real estate business. It must be a community, of people and their land; it must be a social, educational, even "political" organization. It must bring people together, offer them vision and values, strengthen and support them. This understanding must be present, and must guide the membership through the process of incorporation and throughout the development of the CLT.

The process of incorporation should be carried out thoughtfully and carefully, but it need not be very long or difficult. When the articles of incorporation and bylaws have been approved by the founding membership, the articles must be filed, by mail or in person, with the office of the secretary of state for your state. A small filing fee (usually $10 to $30) may be required, and there may be a brief waiting period before certification is complete. Once that occurs, the CLT is fully incorporated and ready for business.

## TAX-EXEMPT STATUS

As the first order of business after incorporation, a CLT may wish to apply for federal tax-exempt status. (This action does not have to be taken at this time, however; the CLT will be just as eligible in the future as it is now.) The application procedure consists of completing the IRS form 1023, attaching to it certified copies of the articles and bylaws, and mailing them to the Exempt Organizations Division of your regional IRS office. The bylaws must be signed by a corporate officer or legal representative of the corporation, attesting to their authenticity. No fee is required with this application.

Tax-exempt status under IRS Section 501(c)(3) offers significant advantages to CLTs. This classification makes the CLT eligible to receive grants from foundations, and allows others to receive a charitable tax deduction for their donations to the CLT. Both of these features will substantially enhance the organization's fund-raising abilities. The tax deduction can also be a valuable tool in acquiring property, as will be discussed in the next chapter. Another advantage is that this status eliminates the CLT's legal obligation to pay federal tax on its program-related income, including lease fees and membership dues. (Even a tax-exempt nonprofit corporation is liable for taxes on income from sources unrelated to its purposes.)

There are, however, some limitations imposed by this status, principally limitations on the political activities of the CLT. The tax-exempt CLT may not support any candidates for elective office, or enter into the electoral process in any way. It may lobby on pending legislation, but may not devote any more than 20 percent of its budget or resources to such efforts. However, these restrictions do not apply to individual CLT members when they act alone or through other organizations.

The IRS will respond to the application for tax-exempt status several months after it has been filed. You will receive a letter at the corporate address either confirming tax-exempt status, denying such status, or requesting further information before such a ruling is made. A letter of confirmation will also contain instructions regarding the kind of substitute tax return that the organization will be required to file yearly with the IRS.

When the early CLTs first made application for exempt status, they received mixed responses from the IRS, and several were denied the classification. These difficulties discouraged some trusts from applying; other groups refrained for philosophical reasons (objecting to government standards for eligibility which recognize some organizations but deny others, although they, too, may be engaged in activities vital to the interests of the community). However, in recent years a number of CLTs have received

501(c) (3) classification without difficulty. It should be emphasized, once again, that the IRS must be assured that the CLT has clearly "public" purposes and intends to carry on activities of a "charitable" or "educational" nature. The IRS is quite familiar with organizations whose purpose is to provide various kinds of assistance to low-income people and others in need, and is also familiar with organizations dedicated to conservation and preservation of land, resources, and wildlife. Many groups of both types have received tax-exempt status. A CLT may refer to the list of permissible activities in the IRS informational materials and bear them in mind as it formulates its statement of purpose and its application for tax-exempt status.

Everything said above applies to *federal* tax status. State and local taxes are entirely separate legal obligations, and separate provision must be made in regard to them. In most states, if an organization has received a 501(c) (3) classification from the IRS, it can easily qualify for exemption from state income taxes (and perhaps sales taxes as well), but a separate application to the appropriate state agency is required.

Property taxes are local taxes. Some local governments regularly grant property tax exemption to organizations which have a federal tax exemption and make application for the local exemption; some require additional information and review; others only rarely grant this exemption. Regardless of local policies on this issue, however, CLTs have chosen to pay local property taxes and not to request exemption. A CLT's failure to pay local taxes would place an unfair burden on community residents (some of them CLT members). Over time, as landholdings of the CLT increase, this burden would become heavier and ultimately unsupportable. A request by the CLT for property tax exemption is both unreasonable (with CLT lands in use, the organization and its leaseholders should assume the same obligations as other community residents) and a poor strategy for community organizing and membership development. Exemption may alienate other residents, while voluntary acceptance of the obligation will earn respect and support for the CLT. If CLT members recognize inequities in the local property tax structure, the organization may lend its support to their reform. In public presentations of the CLT model and the activities of a particular CLT, it is important to make this distinction between federal, state, and local tax responsibilities quite clear; many people will quickly assume, upon learning that a CLT is exempt from federal taxes, that it pays no local taxes either.

# CHAPTER 12
# Acquisition

This chapter is rather brief—not because land acquisition is unimportant but because it is so closely related to matters treated in other chapters. Here, however, we do want to review some of the things that should be considered as a CLT approaches acquisition, and some of the techniques that can be employed.

## TIMING

At what point in the development of a community land trust should it begin acquiring land? One logical answer is: not until a great deal of organizing and planning has taken place. But in certain situations, acquisition should be considered at an earlier stage. For instance, the community may be threatened in a way that calls for immediate action, or real estate prices may be expected to jump, or a bargain parcel may have come on the market. Another reason for considering early acquisition is the fact that actual ownership of property can stir interest within the community, give substance and credibility to the idea of the land trust, and thus provide a strong base for further organizing and planning.

The Clairfield Community Land Association is a good example of a CLT that acquired land very early in its existence and used its ownership of this land as an organizing tool. Its land is also a good example of the kind of property that can safely be acquired with a minimum of preparation (although, of course, some kinds of preparation had been under way long before the CLA was founded). It was a low-risk acquisition—first, because it did not cost the CLT any money, and second, because the land was unoccupied and had no improvements on it. The CLA thus took on neither a financial obligation nor a responsibility for maintaining existing buildings or providing for existing tenants. It could acquire the land and then take as much time as necessary to bring people together to consider how it should be used and who should use it. At the other extreme in this respect is the Cedar Riverside CLT, which will not, and cannot, acquire land until planning is complete and a fully financed development project is ready to be implemented.

Clearly the question of timing is one that each CLT will have to answer for itself as it weighs the advantages of immediate acquisition against the advantages of a slower, more methodical and cautious approach. A rash and ill-considered acquisition not only can waste financial resources, but can also compromise the reputation of the organization and discourage potential supporters. However, it is possible to go too far in the other direction: an overcautious group that goes on studying and discussing its situation for too long may miss important opportunities and earn a reputation for inefficacy. As with the question of when to incorporate, the CLT should try to time its actions in accordance with community attitudes—neither pushing too far ahead of what the community is ready for, nor moving too slowly when the community wants action.

## TARGETING

Whether a CLT acquires land quickly or slowly, it will be important for it to have a definite acquisition strategy—an idea of what kind of property it wants to acquire, what specific geographical areas it is interested in, what ought to be acquired first and what later, and so on. Depending on a CLT's particular goals and community situation, the strategy may be a rather simple one or it may be quite complicated, but in any case it should be based on more than the mere availability and immediate attractiveness of the property. The acquisition strategy should take into account all of the things that can significantly affect the CLT's ability to reach its long-range goals.

**The land's inherent potential to serve the long-term goals of the CLT.** The importance of this factor is obvious, yet there may be times when people are tempted to treat it lightly. If the land that best serves an organization's long-term goals is expensive and difficult to acquire, there may be a temptation to compromise too quickly—to acquire more readily available land even though it is not the right land for the long run. This is not to say that a CLT should always hold out for the ideal piece of land—which, if it can be found at all, may simply not be affordable. It would be a mistake to begin the search for land with a rigid idea of exactly what is needed. Often, with study and some imagination, ways of utilizing a piece of land may be found that are not immediately obvious. (The question of how to determine the most appropriate uses for particular pieces of land is discussed further in Chapter 14.)

**Perceived needs in the community.** When consistent with its long-range goals, a CLT may give a high priority to the acquisition of property that meets the needs most clearly perceived by the community. In communities where these needs are extreme and pressing—where residents are concerned with immediate threats to their health and security, as has been true, for instance, in Columbia Heights—it will be difficult for a CLT to build support for acquisition policies that serve long-range goals (such as future control of gentrification) rather than solve current problems. Part of the success of the Community Land Cooperative of Cincinnati may be due to the immediate usefulness of its first two acquisitions—the first meeting the dramatic need of a displaced family, the second preventing possible displacement not only of several families but of an established community service organization (the Contact Center).

**Relevance of a property for potential community leaders.** Neighborhood politics can be an important consideration. If, for instance, a decision must be made concerning which of two residential properties to acquire, and if there are particular tenants in one building who have a strong interest in remaining in the building and would be active and persuasive supporters of the CLT if the CLT made it possible for them to remain, then there would be an obvious advantage in giving a high priority to this building. In Cincinnati, it is worth noting, Vivian Maxwell was not simply a needy case; she was, and is, an active and persuasive person who now believes strongly in the community land trust idea.

**Geographical strategy.** In deciding *where* to acquire property, it may be useful to think of acquisition as a type of chess game in which you may achieve your long-range goals by arranging your land holdings in a strategic pattern. If your aim is to prevent gentrification in an urban community, you may want to scatter your holdings in order to develop support throughout the community and to keep gentrification from gaining momentum in any one part of the area. On the other hand, if your aim is to secure a land base for an agricultural community, you may want to consolidate your holdings as much as possible. In Georgia, New Communities chose to invest not in a number of isolated holdings but in a single large tract of land that will support larger-scale cooperative farming operations. In most communities, too, there will be particular properties that have particular strategic importance—perhaps because of their development potential, perhaps because they can shield or buffer neighboring property. Also, it can be said that a geographical strategy should normally be flexible. As in a chess game, you want both to anticipate your "opponent's" moves and to respond to the moves that are actually made—as the Cedar Riverside community did when an inappropriate motel development was proposed for the Seven Corners area.

**Financing and affordability.** Obviously, the question of whether a CLT can afford a particular piece of land is a primary consideration, but affordability is not simply a matter of price. A small purchase for which a CLT must pay cash and which cannot be counted on to generate income may be less affordable than a large purchase that is financed on reasonable terms and can be leased for enough money to cover the loan payment. In the latter case, the question, of course, becomes not simply what the CLT can afford but what the intended leaseholders can afford. If the CLT's purpose is to provide land for low-income people, it must either find land that can be financed on terms the leaseholders can afford, or else find a way of subsidizing the purchase from another source. If the aim is to provide housing as well as land, then the total cost to the leaseholder/homeowner must be kept affordable.

The CLT should also investigate all possible opportunities for acquiring land at less than full market price. The Community Land Association in Tennessee acquired its first piece of land at no cost from an inactive nonprofit organization, and its second at no cost from a

Robert O'Keefe

*This house was a good buy at $11,000.*

Robert O'Keefe

*This house was refused by CLCC even though it was offered for $1. The cost of rehabilitation made it unaffordable.*

regional land trust. Other CLTs may not have these particular opportunities in their communities, but the chances are good that they will find others if they search for them.

## SCOUTING

As a CLT approaches the point of actually acquiring property, the information that has been collected concerning property in the community (as discussed in Chapter 10) will clearly be useful, and it will be important to continue collecting and updating this kind of information, with a special emphasis now on the questions that have a direct bearing on acquisition decisions. As in earlier research, it will be useful to involve as many community members as possible in the "scouting" process—both because the process can stimulate community interest and involvement, and because it will increase the number of contacts and sources that can be utilized. Different people will know different kinds of things about different properties, and much of it will be information that cannot be gathered through official channels.

In order to make the best use of these scouting activities, it may be a good idea to put together a kind of "scout's handbook," so that community members will know what they should be looking for, what kinds of questions need to be answered. The development of such a handbook also provides a meaningful occasion for CLT members to agree upon a targeting strategy.

The contents of the handbook will vary as these strategies vary, but generally the criteria set forth will be concerned with the *usefulness* of a piece of property in meeting both the short-term and long-term goals of the CLT, and with the *affordability* of acquisition and development (or redevelopment) of the property. The next two chapters, Financing and Land Use Planning and Development, will help in formulating the kinds of specific questions that should be asked about the affordability and usefulness of property.

The first and most obvious question that must be answered is whether the owner of a piece of property is interested in selling (or perhaps donating or arranging a bargain sale to the CLT). In trying to answer this question a CLT should do more than simply look for "for sale" signs, but in communities where absentee ownership is common, the difficulty of contacting absentee owners can be a particular problem—as Willy Watts in Cincinnati has mentioned (see Chapter 7). Once the names and addresses of such owners have been collected, it may be a good idea to prepare a letter that can be sent to all of them, explaining the CLT's interest in acquiring property and inviting them to contact the CLT if they have an interest in selling.

Other sources of information concerning property that might be acquired include local newspapers and real estate agents. Newspapers should be checked regularly not only for real estate advertisements and announcements of public auctions, but for reports of real estate transactions and other events that may influence or reflect the market. Though property can sometimes be acquired more cheaply without going through a real estate agent, the role that agents play and the knowledge that they have cannot be ignored. A good relationship with trustworthy and sympathetic agents can be very useful.

## ACQUISITION TECHNIQUES

As was suggested in the first chapter of this book, the idea of property ownership as it applies today is not as simple as one might assume. We have noted that property can best be understood as a bundle of distinct rights

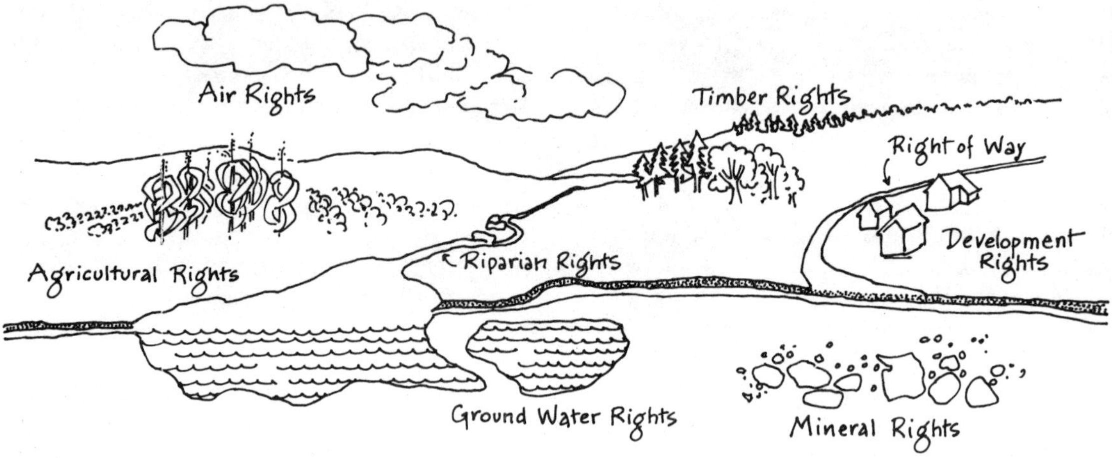


which can be separated from one another so that the person who holds one right does not necessarily hold the others. Therefore, when a CLT acquires property it will need to know which rights are important to its purposes, and which it can, in fact, legally acquire. In Chapter 9 we described some land trusts that are concerned with acquiring only certain limited rights, specifically development rights. Most community land trusts, however, will be primarily concerned with "outright," or "fee simple," acquisition—in other words, the acquisition of the entire bundle of rights, or at least the part of the bundle that is normally conveyed from one owner to another (certain rights normally remain with the public). In the remainder of this chapter we describe some basic techniques as they apply to outright acquisition, though most of them can be applied to limited, or "less-than-fee-simple," acquisition as well. For more-specific information concerning the acquisition of development rights, refer to Chapter 9.

**Straight purchase.** The most common way of acquiring property is through "straight purchase"—by which the title to the property is received in exchange for a specified amount of money. The ways in which a straight purchase can be financed are numerous, and are discussed in the next chapter.

**Donation.** This can be a most desirable way to acquire property—as long as the property itself is useful to the CLT. However, as suggested in the Cincinnati case study, CLTs should beware of accepting donations of property that will require expensive rehabilitation of existing buildings, or involve other burdens. Nevertheless, donations can be very important to a CLT, particularly to a newly founded CLT lacking the resources and track record that would make straight purchase possible. Among the more likely donors are other nonprofit organizations owning land that they are not in a position to manage or make use of, and property owners who can take significant tax deductions for the value of what they donate to a nonprofit institution. As noted in Chapter 9, these tax advantages are especially great for people whose income places them in a high tax bracket and whose land has so significantly increased in value that they would be liable for large capital gains taxes if the land were sold. Particularly for the person who sympathizes with the goals of the CLT, these potential tax savings may tip the balance in favor of a donation. If certain CLT members are knowledgeable on tax matters, they can help the potential donor to calculate the tax advantages, and in that way perhaps arrange a donation.

**Bargain sale.** A bargain sale is a combination of outright sale and donation. The owner sells the property for a price lower than its market value, thus in effect donating that portion of the property's market value that is not paid for. Such a person is eligible for income tax deductions for the value donated.

**Installment purchase.** Sometimes called a "land contract," this arrangement allows the buyer to pay for property through a series of agreed-upon payments over an extended period of time. The advantage for the buyer is that usually no down payment is involved. The disadvantage is that the buyer does not receive title to the property until the last payment has been made. If for any reason payments cannot be made, the contract is voided and the value of previous payments may be lost; therefore the buyer has no equity until the entire amount of the contract has been paid. Installment purchase may make sense as a way for a CLT to acquire property when the owner is willing, when no more favorable form of financing is available, and when it is fairly certain that the payments can be met.

**Life tenancy.** This arrangement may take various forms—involving straight purchase, installment purchase, donation, or bargain sale—but in every case there is an agreement that the original owner will be allowed to continue to use the property for the rest of her or his life. This person may either have exclusive lifetime rights or may share the use of the property with the CLT, or with CLT leaseholders, in some agreed-upon way. Life tenancy arrangements can be an ideal means of acquisition when a CLT wants to prevent speculation and inappropriate development, and to achieve long-term control of the land while preventing displacement of the present owner. Elderly homeowners with limited incomes and rising property tax bills can secure their own interests through such arrangements and still allow the CLT to acquire the property on favorable terms. Elderly farmers can remain in their established homes while allowing a CLT to lease much of the farm to others who will make appropriate use of it.

**Sale-and-leaseback.** In some cases the effect of sale-and-leaseback arrangements will be similar to life tenancy arrangements. The original owner will continue to occupy or use the land, but as a leaseholder—with the rights and responsibilities of other CLT leaseholders—rather than as an owner. With people who are committed to the idea of the CLT and who want to see their land protected from future speculation, it may be possible to arrange the transaction so that little or no money needs to change hands—having purchase payments and lease payments offset each other.

**Joint acquisition.** Normally a CLT will want to acquire property in its own name and avoid the complications of co-ownership. However, there may be some situations in which the organization cannot finance an important acquisition on its own but could do so in partnership with another party. If the other party has objectives consistent with those of the CLT, or if it has compatible short-term interests—perhaps concerning improvements on the land—but is willing to leave long-term control of the land to the CLT, then joint acquisition might be considered. Though it did not involve a CLT (at least initially), the partnership between the West Bank CDC and a private developer in acquiring and developing land in the Seven Corners area in Minneapolis is an example of one sort of joint acquisition arrangement that *might* be made by a sophisticated CLT.

**Lease.** A CLT's concern with leasing will usually be as a lessor rather than as a lessee, but there may occasionally be a situation in which the only way a CLT can gain long-term control of a piece of land is to acquire a long-term lease. Since the aim of a CLT is not ownership of land as such but rather to make possible long-term community control of land, there is no reason necessarily to rule out such a lease arrangement.

**Options and rights-of-first-refusal.** These are not in themselves forms of outright acquisition; they are very specific rights in the property bundle. However, they can often be important first steps toward outright acquisition. An option is a right to purchase a particular piece of property at a specified price within a specified period of time. A right-of-first-refusal alows the party holding it to acquire a particular property by matching whatever price is offered by another potential buyer in the future. Both of these rights can often be acquired at nominal cost from property owners who are sympathetic with the CLT and would prefer to see it, rather than another buyer, acquire their property. The Ottauquechee Regional Land Trust acquired a 90-day right-of-first-refusal on the South Woodstock County School property for the sum of one dollar, and was thereby able to prevent a condominium developer from acquiring the property.

The acquisition techniques just described—and perhaps others as well—may be combined in a variety of ways to create the particular arrangement that is best for a given situation. A community land trust that is imaginative and persistent enough to explore a wide range of possibilities may sometimes succeed in making important acquisitions when at first there seems to be no opportunity at all.

## LEGAL ADVICE

Even when a CLT's members or staff are able to handle other legal matters by themselves, it is generally considered wise to have a lawyer handle the final legal details of acquisition. A lawyer at this point can make sure that the organization knows exactly what property rights it is acquiring and that there is no misunderstanding about any aspect of the transaction on the part of any of the people involved. It can be especially important to have a lawyer's professional presence when the overall arrangement involves the immediate leasing of the land and the sale of housing or other improvements to leaseholders. (Such arrangements are discussed in Chapter 15.)

Even though a lawyer may be retained, CLT members—and particularly board members—will still want to educate themselves as thoroughly as possible about the legal aspects of acquisition. No organization should have to consult a lawyer at every turn. As is true with other professionals whom a CLT may consult, more value will be gained from a lawyer's time if it is understood what the attorney can do and what is needed from him or her in a particular situation.

# CHAPTER 13

# Financing

Finance, like war, suffers from the fact that almost all those who have technical competence also have a bias which is contrary to the interests of the community. When Disarmament Conferences take place, the naval and military experts are the chief obstacle to their success. It is not that these men are dishonest, but that their habitual preconceptions prevent them from seeing questions concerning armaments in their proper perspective. Exactly the same thing applies to finance. Hardly anybody knows about it in detail except those who are engaged in making money out of the present system, who naturally cannot take wholly impartial views. It will be necessary, if this state of affairs is to be remedied, to make the democracies of the world aware of the importance of finance, and to find ways of simplifying the principles of finance so that they can be widely understood.

*Bertrand Russell,* The Modern Midas *(1930)*

Finance, to paraphrase Bertrand Russell, suffers from the fact that those who *know* won't say (except for a price), and those who *need* don't know. Those who have a bias which is consistent with the interests of the community do not often have the financial competence to defend and promote those interests. Unfortunately, we cannot succeed in simplifying the principles of finance in one short chapter. We can, however, stress the importance of finance and offer a few rules-of-thumb that CLTs might follow in planning for the acquisition and development of real property.

Our approach has been to emphasize "appropriate financing" for CLT projects, as opposed to the "miracle financing" that has prevailed in the past among many community-based organizations. Appropriate financing relies upon prior financial planning to match particular types and sources of funds with particular needs and uses for funds. Miracle financing awaits the lucky arrival of adequate funds to meet immediate needs; like manna from heaven, such funds may be urgently needed and patiently awaited, but hardly expected or prepared for. The latter cannot, of course, be lightly dismissed. Considering the remarkable accomplishments of numerous grass-roots groups operating on shoestring budgets with little hope of long-term financial support, the miracle theory of finance must be credited with many good works and substantial social progress. Miracles do happen. We believe, nonetheless, that local groups will have a greater chance of eventual success in establishing, managing, and maintaining a CLT if they devote a greater degree of attention to the planning and preparation that goes into a program of appropriate financing. They will even be better prepared to take advantage of any miracles that do come their way.

## APPROPRIATE FINANCING AND LENDER BIAS

Appropriate financing begins with a proper appreciation of the attitudes and biases of most financial lenders. How a lender views the world—and the prospective borrower—is a factor that must be taken into account as the CLT becomes involved in financial planning. Many CLTs, of course, will set out in search of grants rather than loans, and will seek funds from public or charitable institutions instead of banks or savings-and-loans. Most of what we have to say about lender bias, however, is generally appropriate to the financial officers of foundations, churches, and public agencies, as well as those of commercial lenders. The goals of these institutions are different; the mentality of their officials often is not.

The CLT must recognize, for instance, that most lenders have an extreme aversion to risk. Banks tend to carry this aversion the furthest, but risk avoidance is something of an obsession with almost every institutional lender. Risk is gauged, first and foremost, by the extent to which a loan is *secured* by the borrower. A secured loan is one that is backed by collateral—liens (claims) against the borrower's property, savings, investments, or other assets—which, in the event of default, can be seized by the lender and applied to the unpaid portion of the loan. Unless a CLT can provide security, its chances of receiving a loan from conventional sources will be nearly zero. An unsecured loan is far too risky for most lenders to consider. (Unsecured loans are made by some lenders, but they are always made as short-term loans and are only available to privileged borrowers who have proven themselves especially creditworthy over a period of years.)

For most people, backing a loan with substantial security would be enough to banish the spectre of risk, but this is not so for most financial officers. Their conception of what is "risky" goes beyond the ordinary meaning of the term. They perceive risk in unusual forms of ownership or unfamiliar forms of organization, in new products, innovative projects, or newly established organizations. The fear of being first permeates the lender's role, bringing a bias against all who sail in unfamiliar waters.

There may also be bias against places, groups, politics, and projects that are not a comfortable part of the lender's world. What is *alien* is seen as *risky*. Accordingly, some neighborhoods are not perceived as safe for mortgage or home development loans. Women are seen as a greater risk than men, blacks as a greater risk than whites. Politics and projects that are seen as controversial are among the greatest risks of all.

An institutional innovation like the CLT is obviously going to rub such a fretful sensibility the wrong way. What, then, can the CLT do to get around the barrier of lender bias? There are two general strategies: one confrontational, the other amicable. The confrontational approach has been most frequently employed in the struggle against redlining. Community groups have intentionally confronted, embarrassed, threatened, and forced banks and savings-and-loans to make mortgage and home improvement loans in areas that have been systematically denied such reinvestment. This approach has been extraordinarily successful, particularly when grass-roots action has been combined with the kinds of documentation and legal challenge that are now made possible by the Home Mortgage Disclosure Act and the Community Reinvestment Act (see Chapter 10). Confrontation—or the threat of it—is an option to which community-based groups must sometimes turn. Some lenders cannot be reached any other way. Most, however, can be handled with a somewhat softer touch. The amicable approach might be called "know your banker"—or, more to the point, make sure that he knows *you*. Based on the recognition of lender bias, this approach tries to make what is alien more familiar. Some of its maxims are:

- Establish contact with a lender long before you ask for funds. Use requests for information or financial advice to initiate early interaction and to build basic relations.
- Personalize the relationship. In America, money still passes hands on the basis of gut feelings and personal confidences, as much as on the strength of a computer printout. Like a judge in a courtroom, the bank officer must enforce certain institutional rules but is left with much individual discretion. A face-to-face relationship will help to assure that the lender's judgments are made in your favor. If possible, establish that relationship outside the lender's institutional setting and role, on your own turf. Conduct all significant transactions in person with the same officers. (One organization that we know makes a point of delivering its monthly loan payments on the day before they are due, hand-carried to the bank officer who originally approved the loan.)
- Deal with higher authorities within the institution. The individuals with the most power are also the ones with the most flexibility. The lowly loan officer cannot step outside the bounds set for him or her by those above. Go higher. Persons with power enjoy showing they have it by bending a rule now and then.
- Build a credit record slowly over time. Borrowing small amounts that are promptly repaid (as scheduled) can set the stage for a larger request at a future date.
- Use intermediaries to intercede on your behalf. Reputable third parties who are known by the lender or who are credible as financial advisors can plead your case in contacting the lender or accompany you in visiting the lender.
- Be prepared. Prepackage the project that is being proposed in ways that are understandable and familiar to the lender. A familiar package around a new venture is wonderfully reassuring to a cautious lender. Preparation and packaging are, in fact, what the rest of this chapter is all about.

## THE FINANCIAL PLAN

Before the CLT even begins the search for funds, it should have a written plan stating the costs of the project, the resources that are already available to the CLT, and the extent to which the CLT must look outside itself for funds to subsidize the project's costs. Such a plan is important, first, for evaluating the project's feasibility, and then, for demonstrating the project's soundness to outsiders who may be asked to fund it. A financial plan, therefore, is for both internal and external use.

**Cost.** The financial plan should include a summary of all of the costs of a specific project, including (1) the cost of acquiring the property in question (excluding, for the moment, any financing costs), (2) the cost of putting the property to use, (3) the cost of maintaining the property in good repair, and (4) the administrative cost of carrying out the project. As we move from the first cost category to the last, we must rely more upon *estimates* of future costs; hence, there is a temptation to dispense with these last two or three items, putting them aside for later consideration. For organizations that daily live with an urgent sense that something must be done to solve the land and housing problems that surround them, the tendency to focus upon acquisition as the only relevant cost is understandable and often justifiable. Nevertheless, we recommend that equal attention be given to all four categories of cost.

Acquisition costs include not only the property's negotiated price but any other expenditures that must be immediately made to close the deal. In addition to various closing costs, the CLT may be expected to assume tax, utility, or special assessment liabilities that already encumber the property. Particularly important for the CLT's cash flow situation will be the proportion of the property's selling price that must be paid "up front" as earnest money or as a down payment. Earnest money is partial payment to the seller of a piece of property, made as an indication that the buyer will obtain the full amount. It is required by the *seller.* A down payment is required by the *lender* to reduce the portion of the total acquisition price which the lender will need to provide.

The cost of putting the property to use must take into account everything that must be done to repair or rehabilitate the property in question. The cost of such improvements may be borne by the CLT, the leaseholders, or by both, but they must be considered a part of a project's total cost. Timing is especially important here, for the CLT must set priorities for the work that should be done and must estimate the project's costs at successive stages of development. In doing so, the CLT must be careful to distinguish between essential improvements that must be made before the property can be put to its intended use, and improvements that are not immediately necessary.

The cost of maintaining the property in good repair includes both the cost of physical maintenance and the cost of guarding the property against possible damage or destruction. The latter expense might involve the cost of property insurance and protective devices, such as fences and fire extinguishers. Again, these costs may be borne by the CLT, the leaseholders, or any combination thereof, but they should be counted among the project's total costs. (For common property, the CLT may want to establish an emergency fund that is capitalized through assessments on individual leaseholders. A similar pool might be created to handle the CLT's tax bill—another cost of "maintaining" the property.)

The final category is not often considered a relevant—or legitimate—project cost by community-based organizations. We are referring to the project's overhead costs, the ongoing expense of administering the project from start to finish. The CLT should give serious consideration to adding salaries for staff support to any major project. But even if the CLT does not need—or is not willing—to use project funds to partially subsidize a working staff, it should assign a dollar value to any materials or labor that will be required to launch or sustain the project. Whether directly reimbursed or not, such project support should be counted among the project's costs.

Adding together all four of these cost categories, the CLT can determine the *total cost* for the project under consideration. Dividing the total cost by the number of leaseholds or the number of housing units contained in the project will indicate the project's *unit cost.* Both figures will be useful in completing the financial plan.

**Capability.** Once the costs of a project have been determined, the CLT should begin identifying the resources that it already has to meet those costs. The main question here will be how much the projected users of the property can afford to pay. Any contribution that the CLT can make as an organization is, of course, also relevant and should be counted. But the question of capability revolves around the ability of the users to pay for the property that is being considered for acquisition and development. What can they contribute—in lease fees, mortgage payments, materials, and their own labor—to help meet the project's unit costs?

The simple but not-so-obvious answer is that even the poorest families can probably contribute a great deal, given the right conditions and terms. Without considerable help, a low-income family cannot currently afford to buy a home. Aside from the fact that inflation and speculation have pushed the price of most homes far beyond their real value, the poor cannot purchase homes because they do not have the down payment and cannot obtain loans on reasonable terms from conventional lenders. (The poor are no longer alone in this. A recent study by the Harvard-MIT Joint Center for Urban Studies found that less than one-quarter of U.S. households can now afford to buy a home, compared to two-thirds in the 1930s.) This does not mean, however, that low-income families have *no* resources, for they do pay rent; furthermore, many low-income families will actually pay out, in a lifetime of renting, an amount equivalent to several times the purchase price of a decent home. The CLT must find ways to put these resources to work in meeting the unit costs of a secure and decent place to live.

In computing the potential contribution of a prospective user, the CLT should include not only current income but an estimate of projected income over a period equal to the financial life of the project. Admittedly this may be a difficult task, but if there is a reasonable chance that a family's earnings will increase sometime in the future, then the terms of financing may be written to take this into account. The CLT should also take into account any personal subsidies for which the individual family may be eligible, such as low-interest loans or other forms of housing assistance, and any labor or materials which the users themselves may contribute.

Once the CLT has calculated the total contribution that may be expected from a prospective user (or class of user), it should add whatever contribution the CLT can itself make. Remember: If overhead costs have been included in the calculation of the project's total costs, then it will be necessary to place a dollar value on any labor or materials which the CLT can and will contribute, even if these are contributed free of charge. The inclusion of such costs and contributions is important both to give the CLT a realistic estimate of its own ability to afford the project, and to give outside investors and lenders a complete picture of the CLT's own financial commitment to that which they are being asked to fund. Funding sources, whether public or private, are generally reluctant to subsidize all of a project's costs. The CLT—and those who will use the property—should carefully document their own contribution to a proposed project, *before* turning to outside sources of funds.

**Subsidy.** By comparing costs and capability, the CLT should be able to make a fairly accurate estimate of its need for outside subsidies. This may be done for the project as a whole or on a per-unit basis. If the former, then the CLT itself would probably become the primary seeker and receiver of outside funds; if the latter, then outside subsidies will likely be sought primarily by the individual leaseholder, with the help of the CLT. The financial plan, in other words, must identify both the *gap* to be filled by the outside funds and the *agent* that will bear prime responsibility for acquiring, spending, and (perhaps) repaying whatever subsidy is sought.

Our own bias is that the CLT, as an organizational entity, should play the leading role in most negotiations concerning outside subsidies. Even where personal mortgages are sought for individually owned homes on CLT land, the CLT should be actively involved in the process of seeking the loan and writing the terms of the loan. To the extent that the CLT has established a clear reputation for creditworthiness, it can also act as an intermediary in securing loans for a leaseholder whose own credit record is not as strongly established. We shall continue to speak, therefore, of a single project for which the CLT must plan and for which the CLT must find a source of outside funding.

## THE PROJECT PROSPECTUS

The project prospectus is a formal and systematic way for the CLT to tell its story—and the story of the project that is being proposed—to lenders, foundations, government agencies, and other funding sources. The prospectus serves as an introduction to the financial plan, a justification for the project that the CLT is trying to fund; yet the prospectus must feature not only the proposed project but the CLT itself. As an institutional form, the community land trust will be unfamiliar to most institutions and individuals who might provide funding. Consequently, the CLT's own stability, solvency, and credibility will be as central an issue in any application for funding as the feasibility of the project being proposed. The prospectus places the project, and the project's financial plan, within the context of both the community in which it will occur and the community-based institution that will carry it out. The following information is typically included.

**The local community.** Describe the geographic area in which the CLT operates and in which the project will take place. A map of this area, denoting the boundaries of the community and the specific location of the property to be acquired and/or developed, is a useful addition.

What is the nature of the community of which the CLT is a part? Generally describe the kinds of groups, occupations, enterprises, and activities that characterize this particular community. (The CLT should have much of this information already in hand as a result of the kinds of research described in Chapter 10.) Most important, what are the special problems or needs of this community that have prompted the organization of a CLT and that now spur the CLT to undertake the current project?

**The CLT.** What is a community land trust? When, why, and by whom was this particular CLT established? Describe the legal status, the organizational structure, and the principal constituency of your CLT. Relate the origins and goals of your CLT to the nature and needs of the community described above.

What progress has the CLT made toward achieving its short-term objectives and long-term goals? Review the CLT's track record to date. It is important to describe previous undertakings in enough detail to give the reader a sense of the CLT's competence to undertake the project that is now being proposed.

What is the CLTs current financial situation? A brief summary of the trust's principal assets and liabilities should be supplemented, in an attached appendix, by a balance sheet, a statement of revenues and expenditures, and an operating budget from the previous (or current) year.

What is the CLT's technical capacity? Describe the reservoir of experience and expertise from which the CLT may draw in undertaking the project under review. Professionals and skilled workers with a formal relationship to the CLT—staff members, board members, leaseholders, or persons under contract to provide specified legal, financial, or architectural services—might be given special note.

What kinds of formal relationships have been established with other organizations and institutions in the region? These should be mentioned only if relevant to the ongoing stability of the CLT or the expected success of the proposed project. It is sometimes useful to include, probably as an appendix, letters of support which attest to the CLT's integrity and the community's need for the project under review.

**The project.** Describe in some detail the property that has been selected for acquisition and/or development, including an explanation of any repairs or improvements that must be made. Again, a map or blueprint might be useful here.

How will this property be used? Who will the users be? It is important to show how this project will further the goals of the CLT and meet the needs of the persons who will be the project's beneficiaries. At this point, it is often advisable to personalize the discussion as much as possible. One device is to make use of a large box, inserted into the text, in which a typical family who will benefit from the project is described. Mention the family's current situation, their prospects if the project is not undertaken, and the benefits they will derive from the project if it is completed.

It may also be useful to provide examples of similar projects, carried out by CLTs or other community-based organizations, that have been successful in the local community or elsewhere. As we have previously said, financial officers have an abiding fear of the untested, the unconventional, and the new. A project that is "tried and true" is more likely to be funded than one at the cutting edge of innovation. (*Note:* While this is usually the case where loans are involved, it may not be true for some grants. Some foundations prefer to fund only new, innovative projects. The CLT should try to discover the particular bias of a funding source before applying for support.)

Finally, add to the project prospectus the financial plan that was developed earlier, summarizing the costs of the project, the capability of the CLT, and the financial subsidy that will be necessary if the project is to be completed.

## SOURCES OF FUNDING

The project prospectus, along with the financial plan, documents the *need* for outside funds and specifies the use to which they will be put. This represents one side of appropriate financing. The other side deals with finding a *source* of funds that matches the needs and uses which have been described. There are four general types of funding that the CLT may seek in attempting to acquire and develop real property: grants, loans, venture capital, and internally generated capital. We briefly discuss these, indicating various conventional and nonconventional sources for each.

**Grants.** Grants are gifts that require neither the payment of interest nor eventual repayment of the original sum. While any institution may be the source of a grant—corporations, unions, voluntary associations, universities, and the like—CLTs have been most successful in obtaining grants from foundations, churches, individuals, and government agencies.

Although our focus here is on gifts of cash, we should note that grants frequently take the form of property or labor, offered to the CLT free of charge. Gifts of labor, in particular, are frequently overlooked by organizations in search of financing. A number of state and federal agencies offer direct technical assistance to organizations engaged in housing, agriculture, conservation, or economic development. CLTs should also look to technical schools, colleges, professional associations, unions, and county extension agents for skilled assistance, provided without charge.

Except for grants from government, the CLT would be well advised to look always to *local* sources first. The temptation is great for the new CLT to seek funding from institutions and individuals who are the most well known and the most well off; hence, grant proposals are often sent to the largest foundations, to national religious organizations, and to wealthy individuals throughout the country *before* they are sent to similar sources in the CLT's own backyard. We believe this to be a mistake. There are at least three reasons for initially concentrating on local sources of grants. First of all, local foundations, churches, and individuals give the CLT an opportunity to personalize the request for funds by cultivating face-to-face relationships with persons who manage or own these funds. Secondly, local grantors are more likely to be familiar with, and concerned about, some of the problems the CLT is attempting to address. Finally, local grantors are able to enjoy one of the few direct rewards of being a donor of cash—appreciation and praise from members of their own community. For institutions and individuals alike, the public relations potential of a local grant is sometimes irresistible.

As for grants from government, the sources of funds change as frequently as the programs and agencies which provide them. We shall not discuss specific sources of public funds. We will, however, make the claim that CLTs are among the most effective and appropriate vehicles for public investment in local communities. This is a point that should be stressed whenever CLTs approach public officials with requests for funding. The CLT is an *effective* vehicle because, in a time of rising social needs and declining public budgets, the CLT maximizes the impact of social expenditures. It does this by minimizing the transfer costs of passing subsidized housing from one owner to the next. (Subsidies include low-interest loans and loan guarantees, homeowner deductions for mortgage interest and property taxes, accelerated depreciation for owners of rental housing, energy rehabilitation grants, and various types of rent subsidies such as HUD's Section 8 program.)

Public subsidies for housing are designed, for the most part, to control the cost of buying a home. If the owners of subsidized units are permitted to sell their equity interest for whatever the market will bear, then the price of a dwelling will rise for each successive owner—necessitating a higher subsidy to bring the property within the financial reach of the next generation of buyers. The CLT, by limiting the equity return that each owner can realize on the sale of his or her dwelling, keeps the purchase price of the property lower and within the reach of other families with modest means. The original subsidy, which kept the price low in the first place, is retained in the property instead of removed as private profit.

The CLT is an *appropriate* vehicle for public investment because the appreciation in value of the subsidized property accrues to the community, rather than to a private developer or private landlord. Equity created through public investment remains in the public domain (via the CLT). It is used to maintain the stock of moderately priced housing and to enhance the quality of community life, not to enrich a few individuals.

Effective and appropriate as the CLT may be as a recipient of grants, it is well to remember that grants are one-shot deals. They are usually given on a one-time basis for a single aspect of a specific project. To qualify for such funding, the CLT may need to tailor its project in such a way that it meets the guidelines for the gift of funds, but no longer meets the needs and expectations of the persons for whom the project was intended. Grants are also seldom given to sustain an ongoing project. Consequently, many a project begun with grants has eventually folded for lack of operational funds. Grants can be used to acquire property, launch a project, or to meet immediate crises, but dependence on them for the long run is risky.

Finally, while on the subject of grants, we should not neglect the small contributor. Stalking the elusive million-dollar grant, many community-based organizations fail to coax more modest contributors into their circle of support. Aside from the obvious loss of funds, such disregard needlessly squanders an opportunity to widen the CLT's social base. Fund-raising and community organizing—like research and organizing—can be made to go hand-in-hand. Launching a project via small, broad-based contributions can have a social and political benefit that goes far beyond their financial return.

**Loans.** As the *New York Times* observed in 1981, "People in America no longer shop for homes; they shop for financing." Loans for the acquisition and development of real property are available from conventional or nonconventional sources, on a short- or long-term basis, at various rates of interest, with a bewildering array of payback provisions. Even for banks and savings-and-loans—the most conventional, conservative lenders of mortgage money—the demise of the long-term, fixed-rate mortgage has ushered in a new era of "creative financing," giving rise to a veritable jungle of new mortgage types and terms.

The goal of such creative financing is to bring the monthly payments on a mortgage loan down to a level that can be tolerated by the buyer—without the seller having to reduce the sales price of the property. The buyer's *initial* financing cost is pushed lower than the market interest rate (which has run as high as 19 percent in recent years), making a property immediately affordable for many buyers who could not otherwise meet exorbitant requirements for interest and cash down payments. The problem with most of these financing schemes, however, is that after the first few years the buyer's costs can escalate rapidly. These new schemes shift the risk of inflation and economic instability from the lender to the borrower, making the borrower extremely vulnerable to downturns in the larger economy. Unless the CLT expects to be in much better financial shape in future years than it is at present, such "creative financing" should be approached with some caution. This does not mean that the CLT should avoid it altogether, for such mortgage financing may fit the CLT's circumstances quite nicely.

These new forms of financing are being developed not only by lenders, but by the sellers and builders of housing as well. There are over a hundred new ways in which the cash of the buyer, the funds of the lender, and the equity of the seller are being put together to finance the acquisition of housing and land. Here are five of the most common:

1. *Variable rate.* Interest rates are tied to prevailing market rates. If market rates are steady or in decline, the buyer will do very well; if market rates climb, the buyer's monthly payments can skyrocket. Long-term, variable rate mortgages are now offered by most major lenders.

2. *Contract for deed.* The buyer assumes the existing mortgage on a piece of property, originally financed at a rate of interest considerably below the current rate. To cover the balance between the earlier mortgage price and the selling price, the buyer contracts *with the seller* to pay off the balance in three to five years. During that time, the buyer agrees to pay interest on the balance at three or four percentage points below the current market rate; the balance is paid in a lump-sum "balloon" at the end.

3. *Wraparound.* The seller of a piece of property keeps whatever mortgage he or she already holds—one that was probably financed at a low rate of interest a number of years before—and provides the buyer with a long-term contract for deed, covering the price of the property (less the down payment). The buyer is charged an interest rate that is several points higher than the rate of the mortgage held by the seller.

4. *Shared appreciation.* The lender provides a long-term, fixed rate mortgage on bargain terms—i.e., at a rate of interest that is lower than the current market rate—but claims a percentage of the appreciation whenever the property is eventually sold. (Unless a CLT is willing to abandon the limited equity provision in its lease agreement, a shared appreciation mortgage will be inappropriate.)

5. *Reverse annuity.* A reverse annuity mortgage (RAM) allows homeowners to convert the equity in their homes into a steady stream of income, while retaining the right to live in the house until death. When the house becomes vacant, due to the death or departure of the original owner, the buyer (the one who has paid the annuity) claims the property. Though RAMs were originally developed by commercial lenders, several nonprofit organizations have begun

to use them to aid the elderly and to acquire property for low-income housing. This may be a method of long-term financing that the CLT may want to explore—both to acquire property in the future and to prevent displacement of elderly residents now.

Another conventional source of loan financing has been the federal government. Since the creation of the Federal Housing Administration (FHA) in 1934, the federal government has been in the business of insuring home mortgage loans or, under other programs, issuing loans directly. These programs, administered by the Department of Housing and Urban Development (HUD) and the Farmers Home Administration (FmHA), come and go with remarkable frequency, and are too numerous (and changeable) to name. The CLT that wishes to learn more about the terms and availability of such publicly funded loans must contact the local or regional offices of the agencies which offer them.

Before leaving these conventional sources of funding, we should note a special problem that CLTs have encountered in seeking mortgage loans. Lenders have been reluctant to approve a mortgage for houses on land that is leased from a CLT. Where the property serves as security for the loan, the conventional lender wants the freedom to seize the property and sell it at the highest possible price in the event of default. If the CLT owns the land, and if the lease limits the equity that the homeowner may realize from the sale of the house, then the lender is restricted in his or her ability to reclaim and resell the property should the need arise. Conventional lenders will not tolerate such interference of their legal right to recover their funds and, if possible, make a profit. Under such circumstances, they will not loan to a CLT or to a CLT leaseholder.

CLTs have found two ways around this problem—both of which, we should acknowledge, somewhat violate the "pure" idea of the CLT. The first option is to subordinate the *lease* to the mortgage, so that the lender will not be bound by all of the provisions of the lease should the lender need to seize the house. This is the tack that has been taken by the Covenant Land Trust in Maine, in their attempt to obtain a home mortgage loan from FmHA. (The quest of the Covenant CLT for FmHA funding has had at least one consequence that may be of use to other rural CLTs. The FmHA's central office in Washington, D.C., has ruled that there is nothing in FmHA's regulations that forbids issuing a mortgage for a house leased from a CLT.) The second option is to subordinate the *land* to the mortgage, so that the lender may claim both the house and the land, should the homeowner default on his or her loan. A leaseholder of the Valley CLT in Massachusetts has recently obtained a loan from a local bank on these terms. Under either option, the CLT would be well advised to interject a clause in the loan agreement between the lender and the leaseholder giving the CLT the *option* of assuming any loan that is threatened by default. Such a provision might be written to give the CLT 30 or 60 days to assume the loan *before* the lender may seize the property.

Should a number of its leaseholders negotiate loans from conventional sources, a CLT might consider establishing a "mortgage insurance fund" of its own. The CLT would require each leaseholder who borrows mortgage money to borrow 110 percent of what is actually needed. The extra 10 percent would be placed in an escrow account as an emergency fund to cover default by any leaseholder. Whenever the borrower reached the point of completing repayment of the original loan, this extra 10 percent would be returned. In this way, the CLT might increase the security of the individual leaseholders, while reducing the risk of CLT land being lost through foreclosure.

**Nonconventional sources of loan capital.** The staggering cost and tortuous terms of conventional loans—combined with the kind of biases already discussed—have pushed conventional sources of mortgage money beyond the reach of many organizations like CLTs. Rural CLTs, such as those in Clairfield, Tennessee, and Hancock County, Maine, face an additional problem. Banks are reluctant to finance basic, inexpensive houses—precisely *because* they are basic and inexpensive (and possibly owner-built as well). Consequently, local grass-roots organizations have been forced to seek alternative sources of mortgage and home improvement money.

One important source of nonconventional financing can be found among a growing number of institutions and individuals who wish their pension funds, trust funds, inheritances, or extra income to be used in ways that promote social justice and social welfare. Sometimes described under such headings as "socially responsible investment," "ethical investing," or "faith and finance," this approach to lending represents an important source of loan capital for organizations with purposes and projects like those of a CLT.

Even as the will to invest in such projects has increased, however, the way to do so has remained obscure. Socially responsible investors and socially committed borrowers have experienced enormous difficulties in even finding each other, let alone working out loan agreements that are mutually beneficial. Few conventional lenders have either the desire or the know-how to place social investments in community projects that will yield a satisfactory return for the investor and a social dividend for the borrower. A different kind of intermediary is needed to bring these parties together, acting as a "broker" to package loans that are satisfactory to both.

In 1979 a community investment fund was created by the Institute for Community Economics to play precisely this role. Established as a revolving loan fund, this pilot project was intended to bridge the gap between investors with social concerns and communities, organizations, and low-income families with pressing financial needs. Depositing a cash amount with the loan fund, the investor/lender may designate the terms under which the money may be borrowed, the schedule of repayment, and the rate of return. Loans are then made to community-based groups like CLTs on a short-term basis, for five years or less, so that assistance can be provided to as many communities as possible.

The growth potential of such a fund is great. There is no reason, however, why ICE should be the only organization acting to establish a fund of this type. Indeed, because its ultimate concern lies in fostering cooperative economic development in local communities, ICE is presently working with several community groups to develop revolving loan funds of their own. The CLT in Cincinnati has already created such a financial mechanism for aiding its own leaseholders. The most reliable long-term source of loan capital for CLTs may eventually be found in a diverse, decentralized, highly organized network of community-based revolving loan funds, set up to support local development.

Another nonconventional way of developing loan capital is the technique used by the Ottauquechee Regional Land Trust in acquiring the South Woodstock Country School property. As explained in Chapter 9, the Ottauquechee trust was able to borrow $565,000 from a local bank by getting a number of community residents to co-sign for the loan—each of them submitting a personal financial statement and pledging collateral for a portion of the total loan. Though few communities will be able to borrow such a large amount, there can be important opportunities for CLTs to assemble this kind of financial support from sympathetic members of their communities.

**Venture capital.** The declining availability of public funds and the increasing competition for limited foundation funds have led community-based groups like CLTs to explore new methods of private funding for local projects. One technique, designed to attract private investment in property acquisition and development, is *syndication.* There are other ways that venture capital might be obtained, but syndication deserves special mention.

Syndicated financing begins with a legal entity known as a limited partnership. In a limited partnership, there are one or more "general partners" and any number of "limited partners." The general partners are usually the ones who initiate the project (for example, the acquisition and rehabilitation of an apartment building) and create the partnership. They tend also to have the dominant voice in controlling the partnership once it is formed, and to assume primary responsibility for managing any property that is acquired (though the management function may be subcontracted to another firm). The general partners sell shares in the partnership to persons who wish to receive a portion of the real revenues and "paper losses" of the intended project. These shareholders, from whom most of the capital is raised to undertake the project, are known as limited partners.

The limited partners are usually more interested in the project's losses than in its revenues, for it is the project's usefulness as a tax shelter which makes it attractive to wealthy investors. Owners of a real asset like an apartment building are allowed four types of tax deductions: expenses for operation and repair of the building, property taxes, interest on the building's mortgage, and depreciation. It is this last deduction which is the most attractive to private investors, because depreciation can result in a substantial "paper loss" that may entail no real loss of capital whatsoever. The partnership's total "loss" is divided among the limited partners, in proportion to the share of the project's original cost which was paid by each. The limited partners can then use their share of this loss to reduce their taxes on other income.

It should be emphasized that depreciation cannot be claimed for land; it can only be claimed for structures on the land. Syndication, therefore, cannot be used to finance the acquisition of land as such, but it can be important as a way of financing development or redevelopment projects. In Minneapolis, for instance, it has been used by the West Bank CDC in developing the Seven Corners area. For the CLT that is involved in development, it may give access to substantial amounts of capital, although it may be necessary to work out the potential complications that arise from the CLT's interest in limiting equity. Since the technique depends on changeable tax laws—and interpretations of those laws—its advantages and disadvantages will have to be explored in terms of specific future situations. More than any of the other financing schemes mentioned in this chapter, syndication requires the expert advice of a trusted attorney to lead the CLT safely through this financial forest.

**Internally generated capital.** The most obvious source of internally generated capital available to the CLT is the pool of funds created by the collection of lease fees. Some CLTs set their fees high enough to meet the annual cost of retiring the debt on any land that is leased. Others, recognizing that such a policy may exclude most low- and moderate-income families, set their lease fees at a much lower rate. (More on this in the next chapter.) Regardless of whether these fees are large or small, the long-term prospect is that a large CLT, with a certain proportion of its property free of debt, will eventually have a small capital surplus from its annual collection of lease fees.

The second source of internally generated capital is the labor that leaseholders put into property which is leased, owned, or shared in common with other members of the CLT. Such labor, which creates "sweat equity" for the leaseholders themselves, may play an important part in the financing of development projects. It may actually be required as a condition of each lease. Covenant CLT, for instance, requires each leaseholder to put at least 700 hours of labor into the construction of his or her house. Other CLTs expect leaseholders to contribute a certain amount of time to maintaining shared resources, buildings, or equipment.

Finally, there is "bootstrapping," a source of capital that is both potentially important and controversial. Bootstrapping is the practice of selling (or swapping) a parcel of land in order to retain or acquire another parcel that is preferable to the one that is sold. As in the case of New Communities, a CLT *may* sell off part of its holdings to raise whatever funds are necessary to retain possession of the rest. When it is possible, however, a more desirable alternative is the one mentioned by Charles Sherrod of New Communities (Chapter 3)—the possibility of selling some of the land's resources, or crops produced by these resources, if it can be done in accordance with sound land-use policies. Rather than selling the land that they did, New Communities would have preferred to sell the timber and develop the land agriculturally so that, like the rest of their land, it would continue to generate income for them while remaining under their control. When bootstrapping does involve the resale of land, the CLT may retain the development rights for some or all of the land—as the Ottauquechee trust did in South Woodstock—or it may retain full title to some land while selling selected parcels for commercial development.

Bootstrapping holds great financial promise because of its ready availability, ease of execution, and lucrative return. It may, in fact, be the fastest way for a CLT with limited financial resources to expand its holdings and generate capital for needed improvements. As a conscious strategy, however, the resale of land also plays rather fast and loose with some of the basic principles underlying the CLT model. Land is treated as a commodity that may be bought and sold to raise capital for future projects. Bootstrapping resembles, to an uncomfortable degree, the kind of speculative trading in real property that the CLT is supposed to discourage. It is, therefore, a method of financing that some CLTs will reject out-of-hand. However, although we do not recommend that CLTs begin behaving like real estate brokers in their own communities, we must concede that opportunity or necessity may lead a CLT to consider selling some of the property that it holds. The founding bylaws of a CLT should make the sale of land difficult, but may still allow the trust to make whatever financial decisions are needed to achieve its long-range goals.

# CHAPTER 14

# Land-Use Planning and Development

The fact that this chapter follows chapters on acquisitions and financing should not suggest that land-use planning and development are matters to be considered only after land has been selected and purchased. In general, a concern with how land is to be used and developed will pervade every acquisition process—as well as most other activities of the CLT. At some point, of course, detailed plans must be made, but the timing of this specific planning process will vary from one situation to another. It may be done after the land is acquired, as in the case of the CLA's land in Tennessee, or before it is acquired, as in Cedar Riverside; or it may take place as the acquisition process is being completed, perhaps following the acquisition of an option or right-of-first-refusal. But regardless of when planning takes place, it is a process in which a wide range of factors must be considered. In this chapter, we want to sort out the most common and most important of these factors and to suggest some basic ways of dealing with them.

## THE CLT'S ROLE AS PLANNER AND AS DEVELOPER

In performing its essential function of holding land for the benefit of a community, a CLT will necessarily place some restrictions on the use of the land; it will at least generally prohibit uses that are not in the best interests of present and future members of the community. Beyond these general restrictions, however, the roles played by individual CLTs will vary. In many cases, the CLT will be the organization directly responsible for specific land-use planning. In some cases, it will also play the role of developer—that is, it will plan and carry out the building of roads, the construction or rehabilitation of housing, and so on. However, it is quite possible for a CLT to delegate or share these roles with other parties. In Cedar Riverside, for instance, the Project Area Committee is the primary planning agency for the community, and the West Bank CDC is the community developer. The Cedar Riverside CLT will be limited to the essential function of holding the land. In this case the CLT's role has, of course, been shaped by preexisting community organizations. But most CLTs will have to decide for themselves how extensively they will be involved in planning, and whether they will be actively involved in developing the land.

In making these decisions, a CLT will need

to evaluate its own resources and capabilities and decide how these can most effectively be applied; it will also need to consider the resources and capabilities of other community organizations with which it might cooperate; and it will need to consider both the interests and the resources of its potential leaseholders. Some CLTs have refrained from getting involved in development activities because they have felt that they lacked the necessary resources, preferring instead to concentrate what they had on basic acquisition and trusteeship functions. This policy, however, may mean that the CLT's land can only serve the interests of leaseholders who can afford to develop it themselves, and thus cannot serve those most in need of it—*unless* another nonprofit organization can develop the land, or help leaseholders to develop the land, in affordable ways. For this reason, cooperative arrangements between CLTs and such organizations as community development corporations and nonprofit housing development corporations can be extremely important. Where such organizations do not already exist, a CLT may want to initiate an effort to establish one; or, at least temporarily, it may want to perform development functions through its own organization.

Land-use planning is a somewhat different matter. Since planning activities are far less expensive than actual development, and since land-use planning can never be completely separated from the CLT's basic trusteeship function, most CLTs do make specific plans for their own land. In doing this, however, they may still draw on the expertise of other organizations, and they will want to work closely with both potential leaseholders and members of the community generally. The Community Land Association in Tennessee, for instance, has received expert planning assistance from the East Tennessee Community Design Center and, to a lesser extent, from the Tennessee Valley Authority. It has also made good use of the community's own immediate knowledge of the land.

## LAND-USE PLANNING: BASIC CONSIDERATIONS

Regardless of how land-use planning is done or who does it, there are some basic questions that should be considered in every case. The relative importance of these questions will vary from one situation to another—particularly between urban and rural situations—but their potential relevance should never be completely ignored.

**For what uses is the land itself best suited?** For a CLT that is dealing with undeveloped rural land, this may be the primary question that will need to be answered; and if a large tract of rural land is being considered, the answer may have many parts. The best use for particular pieces of land may depend on a wide variety of natural features. Some of the more commonly important ones are:

- Type and depth of topsoil. What agricultural uses is it best suited for?
- Subsurface structure. What effect will bedrock and subsoil conditions have on

potential construction of roads, buildings, septic systems?

- Slope of the land. Is it too steep to cultivate, or to build houses on, or to allow access? What direction does it face? How much sunlight does it receive? How much is it exposed to prevailing winds?
- Moisture conditions and drainage patterns. Is the land too wet for some uses in the spring, too dry for some uses in the summer or fall? Will runoff from melting snow or heavy rains interfere with certain uses?
- Resources. Is there a usable supply of water? In what quantity and of what quality? Are there existing forest resources? Mineral resources? (Mineral resources may include such modest advantages as a supply of gravel suitable for building a needed road.)

If a CLT is dealing with already-developed urban land—such as the land beneath a 50-unit apartment building—its concern with natural features such as these will probably be minimal (but it might still want to find out if the cellar fills up with water in the springtime).

**For what uses are existing improvements best suited?** What condition are they in? What will be needed to rehabilitate them or to modify them for other uses? For many urban CLTs, such questions concerning existing buildings will be obviously important. In the case of land already fully utilized for housing, the question may immediately become, "Housing for whom?" Is it best suited for elderly people? For families with children? Who can afford it and for whom can it be made affordable? In urban situations where land is not fully utilized—as in Cedar Riverside—the question may be how to preserve the usefulness of existing buildings while making greater use of the land around them.

Rural CLTs will be less likely to acquire existing housing but may be concerned with existing infrastructure, such as roadways and power lines, which may have a major bearing on how the land can best be used.

**What effect will neighboring land use have on a particular piece of land?** The range of possible effects may include such things as overcrowded streets and parking facilities, noise pollution as well as other forms of pollution, and a wide range of other influences on the environment. On the positive side, it may include such things as attractive views and access to markets, sources of supply, transportation, educational and health facilities, and parks or other forms of open space. In Cedar Riverside, housing in the Seven Corners neighborhood was judged to be not suitable for families with children because of the nearness of an expressway and a business district. On the other hand, housing in the Riverside Park neighborhood, which adjoins a spacious park, is eminently suited for such families.

No piece of land can be completely isolated from surrounding land—and particularly not by the ownership boundaries that we create. All CLTs will want to avoid the narrow focus that is typical of much private ownership.

**What effect would particular uses have on the community and the environment generally?** Just as it must consider the effect that neighboring uses have on its land, a CLT will, of course, consider the effect that its own use of land will have on the surrounding environment and the people in it—a consideration that stems directly from the CLT's concern with community interests and that involves not only efforts to prevent harmful effects on the community but efforts to promote beneficial effects.

Kerry Mackin

*Covenant CLT in Maine will preserve the shoreline of Patton Pond in its natural state. Houses are being built some distance from the pond.*

**How is the use of the land affected by public policies?** Zoning ordinances, building codes, urban renewal plans, and subdivision regulations all have an effect on how land can be used legally. So do other local, state, and federal regulations designed to protect the environment and to conserve natural resources. It is important to know what legal restrictions apply to every piece of land with which the CLT is concerned. It is also important to know what government assistance may be available for particular uses—whether it is technical assistance in agriculture or forest land management, guaranteed loans or subsidies for housing, or help from local government in developing and maintaining infrastructure.

## STAGES OF THE PLANNING PROCESS

These stages can be seen generally as the major steps of a process that naturally begins with gathering information and ends with the community's consideration of one or more detailed land-use proposals. It should be recognized, however, that there will be a good deal of overlap among the stages. One state will not necessarily be complete when others are initiated.

**Gathering information.** Obviously a sound land-use plan must be based on a thorough knowledge of the land and of the community that will affect and be affected by it. The kind of community research discussed in Chapter 10 and the "scouting" activities discussed in Chapter 12 will be important parts of the information-gathering process. At this point, however, we focus on the basic means of acquiring further information about the land itself.

1. *Study the land directly.* Direct observation is an obvious source of information which should not be treated casually. On-site observation should be thorough and objective. Acquiring and planning the use of land is an exciting process, and this excitement can be an important stimulus to a CLT's efforts, but it can also interfere with a thorough and objective study of the land. People's dreams for the land can easily lead them to see those features that fit their

dreams while failing to notice features that may present problems or that suggest a different use. For this reason, the opinions of experienced and objective observers—perhaps local contractors or farmers, depending on the kind of use being considered—can be especially useful. On the other hand, do not let the planning process be prematurely limited by what may be the very conventional experience of such people. The aim at this point is to gather information. For the long run, what the dreamer sees may be as important as what the contractor sees.

In addition to studying the land itself, you will want to note existing improvements—the size, location, and condition of roads, houses, and other structures. You will also want to note other current or recent uses of the land. If the land is being used for agriculture, what crops are grown on what areas, and with what success and what effect on the land? Significant neighboring land uses should be noted, too.

The use of maps to organize information will shortly be discussed, but it should be emphasized here that some sort of mapping will be a necessary means of recording information from the start. In the course of doing community research, the CLT may already have acquired or developed a map that will serve this purpose, particularly in urban areas where the first concern will probably be with lot boundaries and the positioning of buildings and infrastructures on and adjacent to the lot. In rural areas, the early acquisition of aerial photographs of the land in question will save the trouble of mapping the positions of roads, buildings, bodies of water, cultivated land, hedgerows, woods, and so forth.

2. *Talk to people who know the land.* In some cases, the best source of information may be the previous owner or previous or current tenants. Neighbors and other long-term residents of the area may also be important sources. What any of these people report should not be a substitute for what can be directly observed, but there may be some things that you will not have an opportunity to observe. Has the well ever gone dry during a drought? Does the meadow, or the cellar, flood in the springtime? Do the pipes freeze in the winter? Where is the septic tank located (or is there one)? When was the roof last worked on? What goes on in the neighborhood that will affect the lives of residents? Are public services dependable?

3. *Consult official public sources of information.* Previous research may already have put the CLT in touch with some of these sources. Some that may be particularly useful during the planning process are:

- U.S. Soil Conservation Service: can provide information on local soil types, subsurface structures and their permeability, water tables.
- Agricultural Extension Service: will perform soil tests and provide other technical assistance.
- Municipal and regional planning agencies and local zoning boards: may supply information about the land itself, as well as current use and legal restrictions.
- Local environmental groups: may have done research that will prove useful.
- Departments of state and local governments concerned with streets and highways, water and sewage systems, and other public services; also, privately owned utilities: can supply information concerning local service, location of water and sewer lines, power and telephone lines, and easements held in connection with these services. (*Note:* It is also important to inquire about the future plans of such departments—for example, whether the highway department plans new construction or improvements of existing roadways which may, sometimes drastically, affect the land in question.)

**Organizing information, mapping.** As noted above, maps will probably have been used in the process of collecting information. As this information accumulates, maps will also be important as a means of organizing it and communicating it to everyone involved in the planning process. For this purpose, a large base map of the area may be drafted—large enough so that detailed information can be recorded on it. If multiple copies of such a map are available, different types of information can be recorded on different copies, and other copies can serve as a base on which to draft specific land-use proposals. (Engineering and architectural firms normally have facilities for copying large documents of this sort. You can probably find one that will make copies for you for a modest fee.) It may also be possible to map information on a series of transparent overlays that can be superimposed on a base map or on an aerial photograph.

The aim at this point should be not only to record all information accurately but to arrange it so that it can be perceived and understood by all interested members of the community. Information that is accessible only to experts, or only to the few who have gathered it, cannot facilitate democratic community-based planning.

**Seeking professional assistance.** Professional help may already have been sought in the course of gathering information. Now, as the planning process proceeds, further assistance may be needed. If tentative plans call for development of the land, it may be wise to bring in any professionals, such as engineers and architects, who will later be involved in the development process—since it is often impractical to isolate land-use planning from the development through which particular plans will be realized.

The fact that it may be wise to involve these professionals in the early stages of planning does not mean, however, that the whole process should be handed over to them at this point. It is important not to ignore the expertise of professionals, but it is also important not to allow them to take over what should be a community-based planning process. Cedar Riverside architect Tim Mungavan's comments on the tendencies of architects to bring their own "agendas" to the process (presented later in this chapter) are worth noting.

**Involving the community in planning.** If the community organizing efforts have been effective, there should already be a good deal of interest and participation in the planning process. It remains now to familiarize as much of the community as possible with the information that has been gathered, and to involve as many community members as possible in the shaping of specific plans. It is particularly important to see that current occupants and any other people directly affected by the planning are involved. For these purposes, public meetings or workshops may be held. Depending on the extent of the planning to be done and the range of its possible effects, these

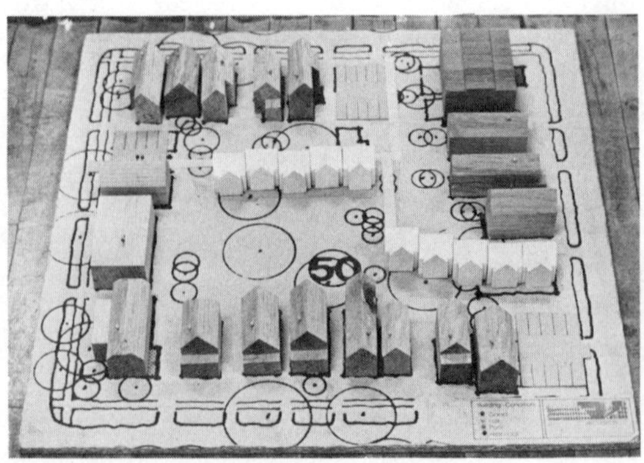


Charlotte Fisketti

*Block model used in Cedar Riverside neighborhood planning workshops.*

may be large, community-wide meetings, or they may be smaller meetings held on a building-by-building or block-by-block basis. In some cases, both types may be needed. In every case, though, it will be important both to communicate all relevant information clearly to the community and to encourage genuine community participation.

The Cedar Riverside PAC's use of three-dimensional block models in their block-by-block planning workshops is an excellent example of a technique that not only presents necessary information clearly but also facilitates participation by all concerned. Whether such models are used or not, the approach should be one that allows people to begin with basic considerations and does not rush them toward someone else's preconceived conclusions. As is emphasized in the case studies—most specifically in the Clairfield and Cedar Riverside cases—most people are capable of responding realistically and creatively to the challenge of planning the use of land in their own communities. These people are not only affected by what happens to the land, they are experts on the ways this land has been and can be used. No land-use plan should ignore this kind of expertise.

**Seeking approval from zoning boards and other use-regulators.** Getting approval from a public agency may be, in fact, the final step in the planning process, but this does not mean that you should wait until the very end to approach such an agency. Early in the process, information should be gathered concerning the legal requirements and limitations that may be imposed on the use of the land. If it appears that a plan will require special approval, it may be important to work closely with such agencies throughout the entire planning process.

The Hearthstone Community, in planning its residential community on land it was to lease from the Monadnock CLT, met frequently with the local zoning board and other local officials over a nine-month period. This process not only resulted in eventual approval of Hearthstone's plans (which called for a locally unfamiliar type of development and might have been denied approval), but helped to broaden community understanding of their goals and the CLT's goals. It may also have been useful in structuring the planning process itself.

## DEVELOPMENT

As should be clear from the previous discussion, land-use planning is not always clearly separable from the planning of development. Any development is a specific use of land, and many of the factors that have been discussed in connection with land-use planning are also relevant to development. Nevertheless, development does involve a distinct set of problems.

Embracing many of these problems is the question of affordability. Like the decision to acquire a particular piece of land, the decision to develop it in a particular way will usually involve a substantial commitment of money. It is therefore important to calculate carefully the real costs of the project and the real benefits that can be expected from it. It is also true, however—and again, there is a parallel with acquisition decisions—that some balance must be struck between a cautious approach to financial commitments on the one hand and, on the other, a willingness to act, to take some risks.

In this book we cannot provide detailed advice on even a single type of development project. However, we will comment briefly on several matters that may be of particular concern to CLTs involved in either building new housing or rehabilitating old housing. (The question of financing such developments is dealt with in Chapter 13.)

**Professional designers.** Architects, engineers, and other professionals can be expensive, yet in the long run their advice may save time and money. Few groups will want to undertake development projects of any size or complexity without professional help. Even Covenant CLT and HOME Co-op, which together have been quite self-reliant in their approach to development, have utilized professionally conceived designs—though it is worth noting that they now have one such design that can be adapted for various sites and various families without bringing in an architect for each individual house.

The question of how to find the right architect for a particular project is a difficult one to answer. We asked Tim Mungavan, architect and staff person for the Cedar Riverside PAC, for his advice on the matter.

*

*TIM MUNGAVAN:* If someone is willing to work for you, for the amount of money that you have to pay and with the kind of difficulty that you have to face in order to work for a community group, then they have to be pretty committed to the whole process to begin with. I think that's a good indication. There is something about architectural training that encourages people who have gone through it to impose their own agendas on the events that occur. It's good to have an architect involved in the process early, if you have somebody that you trust, but I would be very leary of unrelated agendas that they might have. Sometimes when we talk about hiring architects we talk about what their political inclinations are. Well, that may not be the most important thing. The most important thing is how willing they are to accept your goals and to stick with those. But it's difficult, because you can also get someone who will agree to anything you say but will design something that doesn't look at all attractive.

One of the weaknesses we have had is that we tend to hire architects that do a great job of talking. In one case, we had an architect who was so endearing in the way he talked that he ended up talking all the time. It's very hard for someone who is not involved in it to distinguish between someone who just talks a good show and someone who is going to produce something, so you want to look at the products that the architect has produced in the past and see if that's the kind of thing you want.

*

**Volunteer labor.** Just as money spent on professional building design may result in long-term savings, wages paid to skilled workers may often save money in the long run. Nevertheless, volunteer labor can play an important part in many community-based development projects if the right kind of role is designed for these volunteers in the first place. Covenant CLT and HOME Co-op have developed a successful building program that relies heavily on volunteer labor. Several important factors seem to be involved in their success. First, they have two very dedicated full-time construction supervisors who are competent builders and are skillful in working with volunteers, and the whole building process is designed around the use of these volunteers. Second, the basic house design is relatively simple and does not require a great deal of fine finishing work—and the leaseholders who are being helped to build these houses do not expect a great deal of fine finishing work. Third, the houses now being built do not have to meet the conventional expectations of banks or government agencies. The first house that was built did have to meet such expectations in order to qualify for FmHA financing; in that case, the quality of volunteer work (among other things) did cause a problem, even though the house was sound and satisfactory to the people living in it.

Rehabilitation projects may also lend themselves to volunteer labor if the work can be planned and supervised by experienced people and if informed judgments are made in matching volunteers' various skill levels to particular jobs. Similarly, there are opportunities for residents of old buildings to earn sweat equity by doing at least some of the rehabilitation work themselves. In some cases—when resident leaseholders will own the building, when they have some basic skills, and when major structural rehabilitation is not required—residents may carry out the work more or less on their own. In other cases, the CLT will need to take responsibility for calculating the extent and probable expense of the needed work, and will need to help residents decide what they can realistically undertake themselves.

**Frequently unanticipated costs.** Certain construction costs often are not fully anticipated by less-experienced developers. Site development is one area that is sometimes treated too casually when probable costs are estimated. In rural areas, the cost of building an access road, doing excavation work, installing a septic system, drilling a well, and bringing in electric power can add up to more than the cost of actual construction. A realistic land-use plan can limit the costs, but it is important nevertheless to estimate these costs carefully for each building project. They can vary drastically from site to site.

Another area where costs are difficult to anticipate and are often underestimated is in the basic structural work that may be required in rehabilitation projects. Structural problems are often not the most visible problems and may have been obscured by superficial repairs.

## Grading Old Houses

As mentioned in Chapter 8, the Cedar Riverside PAC, with the help of a local contractor, developed a system for grading the condition of old houses. It was used to determine which houses were worth rehabilitating, and serves as a starting point for more specific redevelopment planning. The point system used in the evaluation sheet was designed specifically for the Cedar Riverside situation and may need to be modified for other localities.

| | *GRADING* | | |
|---|---|---|---|
| | Good | Fair | Poor |
| A. STRUCTURAL | | | |
| 1. Foundation | 20 | 10 | 0 |
| 2. Windows | 15 | 10 | 0 |
| 3. Siding | 10 | 7 | 4 |
| 4. Roof/soffets | 10 | 7 | 2 |
| B. MECHANICAL | | | |
| 1. Heating | 10 | 7 | 2 |
| 2. Electrical | 10 | 7 | 7 |
| 3. Plumbing | 10 | 7 | 2 |
| C. DESIGN/INTERIOR CONDITION | | | |
| 1. Floor plan | 7 | 6 | 5 |
| 2. Ingress/egress | 7 | 6 | 5 |
| 3. Wall surfaces | 10 | 7 | 2 |
| D. SITE | 7 | 6 | 5 |

*Range:*

| | | | |
|---|---|---|---|
| Poor | *34 to 75* | Fair+ | *90 to 95* |
| Fair− | *76 to 82* | Good− | *96 to 100* |
| Fair | *83 to 89* | Good | *101 to 106* |
| | | Good+ | *107 to 116* |

For this reason, it is important to have experienced guidance in calculating the full need for rehabilitation and in estimating its cost.

## LONG-TERM LAND MANAGEMENT

After the land-use planning process and initial development have been completed, a CLT continues to be generally responsible for seeing that its land is not misused. However, certain specific management rights and responsibilities will normally be turned over to leaseholders. The lease arrangement itself should describe the basic division of responsibility between the CLT and the leaseholder (discussed in the next chapter), but it will not contain a detailed long-term management plan. Depending on their situations, many CLTs will want to develop such a long-term plan. They will at least want to develop a clear strategy and an effective set of procedures for dealing with questions of land use that may arise in the future.

Rural CLTs—especially those holding undeveloped or lightly developed land—should be particularly concerned with long-term management, since sooner or later someone will probably want to develop the land in some way. A basic land-use plan will regulate such future development, but it will not regulate it in all of its details. Furthermore, it is impossible to anticipate all future situations. The needs of the community and of the leaseholders may change; economic factors affecting the land may change. The uses to which the land *might* be put—and the problems and opportunities related to these uses—may eventually differ from what they are when initial planning is done. There is an obvious need both for a continuing concern with land use and for a flexible approach.

As mentioned in Chapter 4, the Clairfield Community Land Association has developed with the help of the Tennessee Valley Authority, a land management handbook which serves as a detailed guide for its leaseholders. This handbook can be cited in a lease as the criterion for determining what land uses and management practices are allowable; but unlike the lease itself, the handbook can be amended by the CLT membership as unanticipated problems and opportunities are discovered. Such a handbook seems to be a very good way of assuring responsible control while providing the necessary flexibility.

In Greenfield, Massachusetts, the Valley Community Land Trust has created a land-use committee that is not only responsible for basic land-use planning for each piece of land acquired, but is also empowered to approve or disapprove all major developments proposed by leaseholders. They thus have the same kind of control over the CLT's land as is held by local government agencies that issue, or refuse to issue, building permits for developments within their jurisdictions.

In the case of HOME Co-op and Covenant CLT, the Self Help Family Farms program continues to work closely with leaseholders after they have moved into new homes on CLT land. The emphasis is not on regulating the use that people make of their leaseholds but on educating and assisting them in appropriate land uses. However, the CLT does reserve timber rights on all the land it holds, which is in fact mostly wooded. Forest resources are managed for a sustained yield of timber and firewood, and leaseholders are guaranteed a supply of firewood to heat their houses.

Whatever approach is taken to long-term land management, all CLTs will want to maintain that essential balance between individual and community interests, and in doing so they will want to keep both individual leaseholders and the community as a whole involved in the process.

CHAPTER 15

# Leasing and Leaseholders

Our final chapter is concerned with the question of who will use the land and with the relationship between the user and the CLT. These are extremely important considerations. No amount of technical sophistication or financial support will assure the success of a CLT if there are basic misunderstandings between the landowning CLT and the leaseholders who use the land. Developing a genuine understanding and basis for agreement with potential land-users may take some time, but it can be very important not to rush the process.

In some cases, the question of who will use the land will not be specifically answered until after land has been acquired and its use planned, as is true with the 17 acres acquired by the Clairfield Community Land Association. In other cases, the question will be answered before acquisition takes place, either because the land is acquired to meet the needs of already-identified people—like the Maxwell family in Cincinnati—or because the property is already occupied when it is acquired. The latter situation—the acquisition of already-occupied property—involves a special range of considerations that can be particularly important to urban CLTs.

## OCCUPIED PROPERTY

If a CLT is eventually organized in Columbia Heights to hold the land on which tenant-owned apartment buildings are situated, it will not, at least initially, have to face the question of whether to acquire occupied property: Its essential purpose will be to do precisely that. In other urban situations, however—and Cincinnati's West End is a good example—this question can be significant, for there can be both important advantages and important disadvantages in acquiring occupied property.

Robert O'Keefe

*Vivian Maxwell and children (CLT leaseholders in Cincinnati).*

**Advantages.** When the current tenants are already organized and are interested in the CLT and willing to work with it, and when the existing use of the land is consistent with the CLT's goals, the acquisition of occupied property can be the best way for a CLT to have an immediate and visible impact on the community. If the CLT can help these tenants to keep their established homes in the community, it will not only perform an immediately important service but may gain a base of support for further action. As was suggested in the discussion of "targeting" in Chapter 12, this sort of acquisition can be especially advantageous if the tenants of the building include some who are potential community leaders; but even without extraordinary leadership potential, any group of tenants that is willing and able to work together to do something about their housing situation offers a good starting place for a CLT's activities.

**Disadvantages.** The primary disadvantage of acquiring occupied property is that it does not allow the CLT to select the users of the property (until vacancies occur later on), and thus may not allow it to provide for those most in need of land or housing. It does not provide a home for the Mrs. Maxwells or other displaced people. There may also be other important drawbacks, depending on the existing tenants. Just as there are advantages in working with interested and well-organized tenants, there are disadvantages in acquiring property where there are established problems with or among the tenants.

In many cases, of course, advantages and disadvantages will be mixed. The existing tenants in a building may include some who are enthusiastic about the CLT and some who are indifferent. In weighing pro and con in such situations, the CLT must consider its own organizing capability—and the time available for this organizing—as well as the needs of existing tenants and the consequences for the community of *not* acquiring the property. The Columbia Heights case study (Chapter 6), as well as information in Chapter 10, may provide some help for those approaching this sometimes difficult question.

**Introducing tenants to the CLT.** Once a CLT has decided to acquire an occupied building—or at least seriously to pursue acquisition—it must deal with the question of how to introduce tenants to the CLT concept and to the particular situation that would result from CLT acquisition of their building. Three things seem particularly important.

1. The CLT should know the *history of the building* and of previous landlord-tenant relationships. It should know what problems the tenants have faced and what attitudes have resulted. It is especially important to know the tenants' attitudes concerning ownership. Are they interested in owning the building, individually or as a co-op or tenants association? Can they accept the idea of limited equity tenant ownership of the building combined with CLT ownership of the land?

2. The *consequences of CLT ownership* should be made clear. The CLT should, itself, thoroughly understand the economics of the purchase and should communicate this understanding clearly. It is quite common for an owner who has not maintained a building properly, and has let its condition deteriorate, to decide to sell out at the point when major repairs become unavoidable. The necessary repairs will have to be made and tenants' payments may have to be increased to pay for them. If this situation is not clearly understood by the tenants beforehand, the CLT may find itself blamed as just another landlord that has come in and raised the rent. The starting point in discussing such situations with the tenants

*Handbook designed by CLCC to introduce tenants to the CLT concept.*

should be the fact that *the building is for sale* and that *someone is going to buy it.* The consequences of purchase by the CLT can then be looked at in relation to the probable consequences of purchase by other possible buyers.

3. Tenants should be given a clear *description of the rights and responsibilities* of CLT members and leaseholders. For this purpose, some sort of handbook will be very useful. The Community Land Cooperative of Cincinnati has created such a handbook in the form of a small comic book—a simple, basic introduction to what it means to belong to and lease from a community land trust.

**Buildings where existing tenants may not become leaseholders.** A CLT should never get involved where there is active resistance to CLT ownership. However, there may be situations where tenants do not oppose the CLT, and may even welcome its acquisition of their building, but are still not interested in assuming ownership of the building or becoming active members of the CLT. Older tenants especially may simply want to keep their homes as renters. Though the CLT generally will want to encourage tenants to take responsibility for ownership and maintenance of their own buildings—and thus develop equity in their homes—it should not necessarily avoid situations where tenants prefer to rent. If the price is right and if ownership of the property will serve the long-term goals of the CLT, then it may still be wise to acquire the property.

In Cincinnati, a two-unit building in acceptable condition was offered to CLCC for $9,000 by an owner who did not want to see the existing tenants displaced. One of these tenants was elderly, and neither was interested in buying the building. Though initially preferring to wait and conserve their resources for properties where there was more tenant interest, CCLC did eventually decide that it was best to accept this offer. The price was an extremely good one; the landlord-tenant relationship was not difficult. Acquisition meant that the property would be removed from the market and would be affordable for other low-income people in the future. In situations such as this, most CLTs should be open to the possibility of acquiring the property and either managing it (at least for the present) as a traditional rental situation, or spinning off ownership of the building to a nonprofit housing corporation for rental management—if this arrangement will secure the future availability of the building as low-income housing.

## SELECTING LEASEHOLDERS FOR VACANT PROPERTY

In many cases the CLT will, of course, have the responsibility to select those people with whom it will enter into lease agreements. The situation may be one in which vacant housing has been acquired and is being (or will be) rehabilitated, as was the case with the Columbia Heights Community Ownership Project; or it may be that a vacancy has opened up in previously occupied housing; or it may be that new housing is to be made available, or that vacant land is to be made available to leaseholders, with or without some assistance in developing it. Several basic considerations are relevant to the selection process in all of these situations—though specific selection criteria will vary with the CLT's goals and the nature of the property.

In every case, the CLT should make sure that its criteria for accepting leaseholders are clearly stated, reasonable, and fair, and that the process for considering applicants is clearly understood and workable. The process may require that applicants provide certain information about themselves—for example, an account of their skills or financial status. It may require an interview. It may be a process that is handled by a committee—probably with the board giving final approval to the committee's decisions. But regardless of how the decision is made, there should be a clear accounting of the process to all applicants. People who are not selected should understand why. If these people are left feeling that they have been treated unfairly or with indifference, then the position of the CLT can be seriously weakened, no matter how much it may be helping those it has selected as leaseholders.

When possible, it is best to line up potential leaseholders before acquisition takes place, so that the people who will use the land can help in selecting and acquiring it, can participate in planning for use, development, or redevelopment, and will be in a position to develop sweat equity through the development process. If a number of qualified applicants have been identified, there will be a better chance of matching a particular property with the needs and capabilities of a particular user. In fact, the question of who will receive the next lease may be determined by what property next becomes available. In other words, it may not be a question of who is at the head of the list, but of which people on the list can best be helped with the property that it is possible to acquire—though the priority of some applicants may still be recognized as higher than that of others. The CLT should be careful, however, not to raise the hopes of more people than it can possibly provide for. On the other hand, it

Kerry Mackin

*The Burpee family and their new home on Covenant CLT land in Maine.*

should recognize the danger of closing itself off from potential applicants and addressing only the needs of a small group of friends. Again, a balanced, realistic, and honest approach is called for.

**Criteria for selection of users.** Each CLT will establish its own specific criteria, as well as its own way of applying them, but generally the following factors will be considered:

- Applicant's need.
- Special skills and resources necessary for productive use of the land (an important criterion when agricultural or forest land is being leased).
- Applicant's ability to handle the necessary costs of the arrangement.
- Applicant's history in the community: length of residence, record of service or involvement in community affairs.
- Applicant's commitment to CLT principles, and prior involvement with CLT.
- CLT's broader concern with supporting some diversity within the community—with meeting the needs of different age groups, ethnic groups, etc.
- When other factors are equal: a first-come, first-served criterion, or some sort of lottery, so that people will feel that they have been fairly treated.

Normally, users of the land are expected to become members of the CLT and to remain members in good standing. Active participation in CLT efforts should be encouraged but is usually not required—though it *might* be required on the same basis that a certain number of hours of work are required of food co-op members.

## BASIC LEASE AGREEMENTS

As noted in the first part of this book, the CLT concept rests on the proposition that individuals, as well as communities, have legitimate interests in the use of land. We have defined these basic interests as security, earned equity, and a reasonable legacy. The lease is the means by which these individual interests are protected. It is the specific agreement in which individual and community interests are balanced.

**CLT leases as distinct from traditional leases.** The CLT lease is in fact very different from traditional leases, and it is important to distinguish it clearly from the kind of conventional agreement between landlord and tenant that most people have had some experience with. For most people, the word *lease* conjures up images of apartment rental, tenant farming, or low-income neighborhoods where landlords sell buildings and displace long-term residents. In such situations a lease represents very limited security, conflict with profit-motivated landlords, no control over future uses of the property or over the rental cost of its use, no equity in improvements, and no rights for descendants. There are some exceptions to these conditions—in some commercial leases; in the historical land leases in Baltimore County, Maryland, and several other localities; and in a number of new private developments involving land-lease arrangements—but the CLT lease is different in important ways from all of these. The relationship between a CLT and a leaseholder is not a traditional landlord-tenant relationship. The CLT is a nonprofit corporation designed to benefit the community and individuals within it. Leaseholders are members of the CLT and are represented on its board. The situation is thus more similar to cooperative ownership than to a traditional rental situation. The CLT lease will contain a number of unusual specific provisions designed to benefit leaseholders while protecting community interests.

**CLT leases compared to deeds.** We are used to thinking that the rights of ownership come only with a deed. However, once we conceive of property as a bundle of separate rights, we can recognize that a lease, like a deed, is a way of conveying certain rights from one party to another. The deed normally conveys the bundle as a whole, permanently. The lease conveys certain specified rights for a limited period of time. In the case of a traditional lease, these rights are usually very limited, and the period of time very short. But a lease can—and the CLT lease does—convey substantial ownership rights to the leaseholder for an extended period of time. Furthermore, it does this with as much legal force as a deed. In other words, from a legal point of view, the rights defined and conveyed by a properly drawn lease are as fully protected during the term of the lease as the same rights would be if they were conveyed by a deed.

The lease is a very flexible legal instrument. It can be drawn to provide for almost any division of rights and responsibilities between landowner and leaseholder. It can be adapted to almost any purpose, circumstance, and term. In the hands of the CLT, the lease is the critical tool which creates an alternative to conventional public or private ownership. It enables the CLT to differentiate between land and improvements, use value and market value, earned and unearned value, and between the legitimate interests of individual land-users and the legitimate interests of the community.

**Key issues in the CLT lease.** Because the lease is such a flexible instrument and because CLTs will want to adapt it to deal with a variety of special circumstances and purposes, we cannot discuss every issue that will have to be confronted in drawing up a particular lease. However, we can note the most basic and commonly confronted issues and the most practical ways of dealing with them.

The *term* of most CLT leases is the lifetime of the leaseholder, or its equivalent (limited to a specified number of years but automatically renewable). The lease is inheritable. The CLT agrees to issue a similar lease to a designated heir.

CLT leases will contain a *general state-*

*ment of how the land is to be used.* Such a statement is a means of implementing the CLT's basic land-use plans and its basic assessment of what is best for the community as a whole, but it should not overly restrict the leaseholder's freedom to make specific choices within broad categories of use. In other words, the lease may state that the land will be limited to residential use, or agricultural use, or commercial use, or some combination of these, but it will not tell leaseholders what they can and cannot do with their own residences and it will not tell farmers what crops to plant. Leaseholders who might want to use the land in some way that is not covered by the general statement of purpose—for instance, opening a shop on land limited to residential use—will need to seek specific permission from the CLT.

Normally the leaseholder is required to pay a *fee* to the CLT. This requirement rests on the idea that the leaseholder has a basic responsibility to provide a fair return to the community for the use of the land. The fee not only covers the CLT's expenses (including taxes on the land) and provides needed capital, but also discourages individuals from trying to hold (and thus withhold from the community) more land than they can really use. Most CLTs make an effort to base the amount of the fee on the "use value" of the land rather than on its market or speculative value.

In the case of land used for residential purposes, use value is usually calculated with reference to what others pay for the use of comparable land in the community—which is, of course, determined by the market (though sometimes it is a regulated market, as when rent controls apply.) In practice, most CLTs also consider what the leaseholder can afford and/or what the CLT must receive in order to pay the cost of acquisition.

To meet land acquisition costs, a CLT may have to set a relatively high fee (if the leaseholder can afford it) until the land is paid for, then either eliminate all lease fees thereafter or credit the additional amount already paid against future payments. Covenant CLT, for instance, combines financing for land acquisition and house construction in a single mortgage loan on which the leaseholder makes regular monthly payments. Once the mortgage is retired, these leaseholders have no further financial obligation to the CLT. The disadvantage of this simple arrangement is that it blurs the distinction between land leasing and traditional private purchase. When possible, it is better to isolate the lease fee as representing the leaseholder's underlying and continuing responsibility to the community.

When leaseholders are made directly responsible for paying off the costs of a relatively expensive acquisition, the burden on them can be heavy. Occasionally a CLT will hold some land for which acquisition costs and perhaps taxes are high and some comparable land for which they are low (perhaps because it has been acquired through bargain sale or with grant funds). In these situations it is possible to equalize the burden of these costs on the leaseholder by adjusting lease fees on the basis of average costs of all land.

Some CLTs have set up different kinds of fee structures for land used for different purposes. The Valley Community Land Trust, for instance, distinguishes between the fee paid for land used for residential purposes and the fee paid for the use of productive land. The residential fee is required only for the first 25 years of the lease, at which time leaseholders are considered to have paid fully for a secure place to live. The fee paid for productive agricultural land, however, is paid for the full term of the lease, on the assumption that the community should continue to receive a return for the value that the user continues to derive from the land. Other such distinctions may be made in the case of commercial and industrial use, and in some cases it may even be reasonable to distinguish between various kinds of commercial and industrial use, depending on their real benefits and costs for the community.

When people wish to donate their land to a CLT and then use it as leaseholders, there may be no lease fee; or they may sell the land on paper and hold a mortgage with payments set to balance the amount of the lease fee, and with provision for some payment to them if they leave before their equity has been fully used.

Because CLTs are concerned with providing land to those who will use it themselves, the lease usually prohibits *subleasing* except with special approval from the CLT. In some cases, however, the original lease may grant the right to sublease on specified terms. Monadnock CLT, for instance, leases land to Hearthstone Community with the right to sublease residential plots to the community's individual members. In Cincinnati, as mentioned in Chapter 7, CLCC leases the Vine Street property to Barbara Kyser with the right to sublease rental housing units and a storefront (to the Contact Center), but with the requirement that at least 75 percent of the rental units go to people who are eligible for Section 8 subsidies, and that any net income from the property above $1,000 per year be split with the CLT.

In establishing the *responsibilities of leaseholders,* the CLT lease will normally require that leaseholders occupy or use the land themselves and that they maintain the land in a socially and ecologically responsible manner. The occupancy requirement for residential land is often stated as occupancy for at least six months out of every year. The lease will not usually spell out in detail what does and does not constitute socially and ecologically responsible use. It may, however, refer to specific guidelines (like those in Clairfield's land-use handbook) established outside of the lease itself. Where there is a particular concern with the harmful effects of specific uses, these uses may be specifically prohibited in the lease.

The CLT lease agreement should allow for *termination* of the arrangement by the leaseholder at will (at any time, for any reason), with reasonable notice to the CLT. The CLT may terminate the lease only for legal cause (failure of the leaseholder to live up to the terms of the agreement).

Questions may arise concerning the rights and responsibilities of the CLT and/or the leaseholders. Since it is impossible to anticipate all of these questions, the lease will provide for an *arbitration procedure* to deal with them. Typically, the procedure will involve an arbitration panel for which each party appoints one member, with these two members then agreeing on a third. Both parties agree in the lease that the decision of the arbitration panel shall be final. Attorneys have advised that should a dispute eventually be taken to court, a judge will be likely to respect the findings of a fairly constituted panel rather than rehearing the issues in dispute.

## BUILDINGS AND IMPROVEMENTS

In the first section of the book, we discussed the distinction between land and natural resources on one hand and buildings and other human improvements on the other. The CLT typically puts this distinction into effect by separating ownership of land from ownership of improvements. Retaining ownership of the land, the CLT leases it to others on terms which allow them to own buildings and other improvements themselves. They may own them as individuals or as co-ops or through other types of corporation, and the property may be structured as individually owned single units, common property, condominiums, or rental housing (as long as the rental arrangement serves the purposes of the CLT). A basic advantage of the CLT over many other development models is that it can accommodate these varied ownership structures while providing a firm, unified, community-based foundation for any or all of them.

Regardless of which ownership structure is utilized, the separation of land from improvements allows leaseholders to build and maintain equity that results directly from their investments, while preventing them from capturing unearned value by selling the land. In actual practice, however, they might still capture some or all of this unearned value if they were free to sell their improvements, with the long-term lease attached, in the open market, since the property with the land to which it gives access may be desirable enough to cause prospective buyer-leaseholders to pay considerably more for the improvements than the previous owner-leaseholder had invested in them. In such cases, the price of the improvements comes to reflect neither what they have cost their owner nor their replacement cost, but the market value of the irreplaceable land to which they provide legal access. In some instances, the efforts of the CLT to protect and enhance the community may actually increase the market value of improvements on leased land.

**Limiting equity.** To avoid this indirect effect of land speculation, the CLT typically retains an option to purchase any buildings or other improvements owned by the leaseholder, at a fixed price or at a price fixed by an agreed-upon formula, should the leaseholder or his or her heirs decide to terminate the lease and sell the improvements. If the CLT chooses not to exercise this option (perhaps because it lacks the resources or prefers to use them elsewhere), the usual agreement is that the leaseholder may market the improvements and that the CLT will grant a similar leasehold interest to the purchaser of the improvements. In the event that the leaseholder in this situation is unable to find a buyer within a reasonable period of time, the typical lease will permit the CLT to take possession of the improvements, sell them, and convey the proceeds, minus the cost of the sale, to the leaseholder.

Ed Wierzbowski

*Pam Roberts, founding member of the Valley CLT, at home on CLT land.*

**Calculating earned equity.** In this matter, the aim of the CLT is clearly to guarantee to leaseholders a fair return for their actual investment of labor and capital. However, the value of this investment cannot be accurately represented by a simple calculation of dollars originally invested. Some measurement of depreciation of the property should be factored into the calculation of the leaseholder's equity. An adjustment may also be made for monetary inflation or deflation since the time of investment. Yet in times of rapid inflation, even this adjustment may price some properties out of reach of many low- or moderate-income people whose incomes have not kept up with the rate of inflation. For this reason, some CLTs, in an effort to keep housing affordable, have chosen to measure equity in terms of original dollar investment, adjusted only for depreciation. Others, to protect the leaseholder's interest, have chosen to appreciate the equity by a full inflation factor. Still others have worked out compromises between these two approaches, allowing for some but not all inflation.

**Alternative ways of guaranteeing security, equity, and legacy.** It is actually possible to provide security, equity, and legacy for the user of the land either through the combination of land lease and homeownership that we have been describing or through a single lease arrangement, in which buildings as well as land are owned by the CLT and leased to the land-user, with a provision for rebating a portion of the fees when the lease is terminated (so that the leaseholder still builds equity). Some CLTs are exploring the second of these alternatives because their attorneys believe that local laws may create legal complications for the land lease/homeownership arrangement. It does not seem that these complications are insurmountable, but the situation does suggest that some CLTs may find that the single lease arrangement is more practical for them.

The most important thing, in any case, is the result that the arrangement has for the leaseholder and the community, not the legal means by which it is achieved. However, there are some advantages to the land lease/homeownership arrangement when it can be implemented without undue complication. For one thing, it gives an obvious form to the distinction between land and improvements, and in the long run it is important to encourage an appreciation of this distinction. For another, it more clearly permits and requires maintenance responsibility on the part of leaseholders and thus frees the CLT to concentrate on other matters. But, as with other issues, CLTs should recognize the variety of options available under their state and local laws, and be prepared to utilize different arrangements when they are more appropriate.

**The need for fundamental agreement.** As we have suggested, the assumptions commonly associated with words like "ownership" and "lease," can interfere with a CLT's efforts to balance individual and community interests. For many in our society, ownership has come to be associated as much with the opportunity to profit from market increases and speculative gains as with basic aspirations for a secure home and livelihood. Leasing, as we have noted, suggests to many people an insecure and disadvantaged position. Because of this, and because of the additional confusion that can be generated by the sometimes complicated legal forms in which agreements must be embodied, it is extremely important to have a fundamental agreement among CLT members and prospective leaseholders.

Discussion of the basic interests of individuals and communities should take place at the very beginning of the process. The group should come to a full agreement about what rights and responsibilities the individual land-user should have, and what rights and responsibilities the community should have through the CLT. This agreement should be reached *before* there is any discussion of the particular legal means that will be used to secure and enforce these rights and responsibilities.

It may even be a good idea to draft a document that states in the plainest possible language the agreed-upon goals of the CLT and prospective leaseholders as they begin their relationship. To our knowledge, no CLT to date has drawn up such a document, but a basic "covenant" of this sort might be negotiated, describing the agreed-upon rights and responsibilities of both parties. It might then be signed by all concerned before any specific lease agreements are negotiated. The document might have no legal standing at all, or it might be attached as an appendix to the lease agreement with a provision in the agreement that the spirit of the document shall govern both parties in the performance of the lease. But in any case, such a document could be useful in setting the right mood, clarifying the nature of the relationship, and avoiding the tension, suspicion, and misunderstanding that so easily arise when people approach negotiations and contracts regarding property.

**Legal and technical assistance.** In Chapters 11 and 12, we discussed the process of choosing and working with attorneys in connection with incorporation and acquisition procedures. Generally what was said in those contexts applies as well to the matter of drafting lease agreements and arranging for the leaseholder's ownership of improvements. As a matter of fact, these arrangements will often be closely interrelated with acquisition procedures, and it will be useful to have the same attorney working on all aspects of the overall situation. However, several things should be emphasized. Since the CLT lease is radically different from conventional leases in what it is designed to accomplish, and since the attorney's previous experience may be confined to conventional leases, you will need to be sure that you do not get a more conventional lease agreement than you really want. It should be recognized, too, that lawyers are accustomed to approaching such agreements as the representative of just one of the two parties involved. They are used to protect the interests of one party against the other; they are not used to balance the interests of two parties. It may therefore take a special effort to steer your legal advisor toward working out a balanced agreement.

It will also be important to get technical assistance from a source that does have experience with CLT leases. Such assistance is not usually a substitute for a local attorney who is familiar with local and state laws, but it may be important in helping to clarify issues for both the CLT and the leaseholders.

## LEASEHOLDER SERVICES

While the CLT expects responsibility and a positive commitment from leaseholders, it also has a moral responsibility to them above and beyond the lease agreement, and a practical need to help them use their leaseholds appropriately and well. This is particularly true with low-income leaseholders, who have only limited access to the credit and services that may be needed for such things as emergency repairs to their buildings. There are a number of ways that CLTs can provide supplementary services for their leaseholders, depending on the resources available and the needs to be met. The following seem to us to be particularly appropriate and useful ideas.

**Homeowners training program.** Especially for leaseholders without previous experience in maintaining their own homes (because they have been renting), a basic training program can be very useful, and may in fact be required as a condition for granting the lease. Training may deal with such things as the fundamentals of heating, electrical, and plumbing systems, simple repairs, materials, tools and service resources, energy conservation, and budgeting. In providing this sort of training, a CLT may be able to get help from local organizations that have already established such programs for others. In Cincinnati, for instance, the Better Housing League has provided this service for a number of years to new homeowners who have purchased homes on their own, and is now providing similar training to CLCC leaseholders. It is also assisting the CLCC in evaluating the financial and practical capabilities of applicants.

It may also be possible to recruit experienced volunteers from local churches and community groups to teach and counsel leaseholders on maintenance matters—either individually or in groups. Group sessions of this sort may have the advantage of building relationships among leaseholders and developing a base for later cooperative activities.

**Maintenance co-op.** A CLT may want to create a cooperative maintenance program as an integral part of its organized effort (with leaseholder participation perhaps required, perhaps optional, and with the participation of other members also possible), or it may want to

*A new generation can enjoy the benefits of their parents' labor and of their own—on land leased from Covenant CLT in Maine.*

Kerry Mackin

encourage leaseholders to organize their own co-op. Among the specific possibilities are tool co-ops, through which basic tools are owned collectively and used by individuals as needed; skills exchanges, through which individuals trade their special skills for those of others; and simple labor co-ops in which people work together on each other's homes.

**Joint contract for management or services.** Leaseholders may want to join together to contract with local tradespeople or businesses for various maintenance services, or they may want to hire, collectively, a management company to provide basic comprehensive maintenance service. They may also want to look into the possibility of buying insurance collectively for the sake of lower premiums and/or coverage for families who would have a difficult time obtaining it on their own.

Robert O'Keefe

*CLCC leaseholders, members, and other community residents in front of the Contact Center in Cincinnati.*

**Emergency loan fund.** Because leaseholders who are otherwise capable of maintaining their homes and meeting regular monthly expenses may be unable to finance large unexpected repairs (such as major furnace repairs), the CLT may establish an emergency fund to make low- or no-interest loans for these repairs. Capital for the loan fund may come from a surcharge on regular lease fees, or through a sum added to the cost of acquisition and included in the leaseholder's loan, or by voluntary subscription or grants.

**Personal services.** The CLT may wish to provide personal counseling for leaseholders in relation to lease performance and other personal problems. It may also work to organize, or encourage leaseholders to organize, cooperative arrangements for babysitting and other personal services. Such efforts can be important not only in meeting immediate needs but in strengthening the sense of community within the CLT group and in promoting the overall success of the leasehold arrangement. There may be difficulties, however, if the CLT's role in providing counseling is not separated from its role as landlord and fee-collector. The person who has the job of seeing that fees are paid and other lease obligations met is not always in the best position to be a friend and counselor to leaseholders—and the person involved in counseling is not in the best position to enforce the terms of the leases. For this reason, the Cincinnati CLT has a part-time staff person whose job is solely to help and counsel leaseholders, while the business side of the CLT-leaseholder relationship is handled by the director. In Maine, HOME Co-op is able to provide a wide range of services to Covenant CLT leaseholders through its outreach program, the various programs of the learning center, and the family farms program. HOME has also sponsored "retreats" for leaseholder families in an effort to strengthen the sense of community among them.

As the people in the Maine and Cincinnati CLTs are very much aware, it is not enough to provide low-income people with land and financing for homes and then leave them to their own resources. If the CLT is to succeed in the long run, there must be a strong base of support involving both leaseholders and other members.

For any CLT, the development of cooperative programs around the interests of leaseholders and their friends and neighborhoods is a way to strengthen the sense of community that is as essential to the CLT as it is to the community as a whole. No community can flourish if the interests of its individual members are neglected. And no person can flourish in isolation, without community. The strength of the community land trust lies in its ability to serve the interests of both individuals and communities—and to serve each through the other.

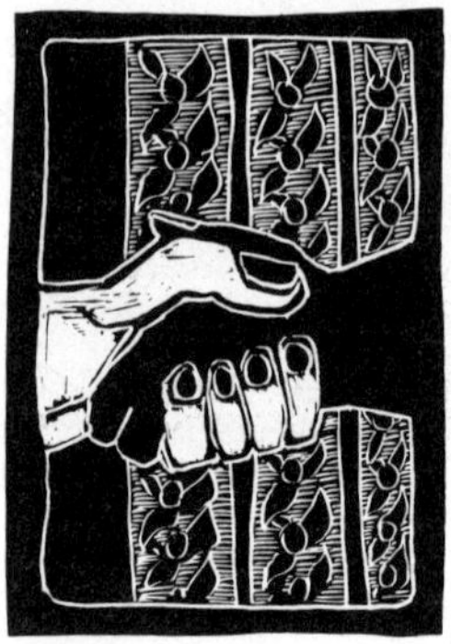

# Bibliography

## BACKGROUND


Barnes, Peter, ed. *The People's Land.* Emmaus, Pa.: Rodale Press, 1975.

Borsodi, Ralph. *Flight from the City.* New York: Harper and Row, Harper Colophon Paperback, 1972.

——. "Trusterty and Property, the Possessional Problem." In *Seventeen Problems of Man and Society.* Anand, India: Charotar Book Stall, 1968. Available from: School of Living, Route 7, York, PA 17402.

Fisher, Steve. *A Landless People in a Rural Region: A Reader on Land Ownership and Property Taxation in Appalachia.* 1979. Available from: Highlander Center, Route 3, Box 370, New Market, TN 37820.

George, Henry. *Progress and Poverty.* 1962 (1st ed., 1880). Available from: Schalkenback Foundation, 50 East 69th Street, New York, NY 10021.

Hartman, Chester. "Displacement: A Not-So-New Problem." In *Social Policy,* Vol. 9, March/April 1979.

Hartman, Chester; Keating, Dennis; and LeGates, Richard. *Displacement: How to Fight It.* 1982. Available from: Legal Services Anti-Displacement Project, 2150 Shattuck Avenue, No. 300, Berkeley, CA 94704.

Heartland Project. *Strangers and Guests: Towards Community in the Heartland.* 1980. Available from: Midwest Bishops, 220 South Prairie Avenue, Sioux Falls, SD 57104.

Highlander Center. *Appalachian Land Ownership Study.* 1981. Available from: Highlander Research and Education Center, Route 3, Box 370, New Market, TN 37820.

Laska, Shirley, and Spain, Daphne, eds. *Back to the City.* New York: Pergamon Press, 1980. (A collection of essays dealing with residential reinvestment and gentrification.)

Levin, Marc. "Neighborhood Development and the Displacement of the Elderly." In *Urban Law Annual,* Vol. 18, 1980.

McClaughry, John. *Expanded Ownership.* Available from: The Sabre Foundation, P.O. Box 1114, Fond du Lac, WI 54935.

Meyer, Peter. "Land Rush." In *Harpers,* Vol. 258, January 1979.

National Association of Home Builders. *Housing at the Turning Point: A Reassessment of America's Shelter Needs for the 80s.* 1980. Available from: NAHB, 15th and M Streets NW, Washington, DC 20005.

Strong, Ann L. *Land Banking: European Reality, American Prospect.* Baltimore, Md.: Johns Hopkins Press, 1979.

United States Department of Agriculture. *National Agricultural Lands Study: Final Report.* Washington, D.C.: USDA, Government Printing Office, Order No. 344-842, 1981.

——. *A Time to Choose: Summary Report on the Structure of Agriculture.* Washington, D.C.: USDA, Government Printing Office, Order No. 723-560/686, 1981.

Waite, G. Graham. "The Long-term Lease as an Alternative to Home Ownership: A Proposal." In *Urban Law Annual,* Vol. 15, 1978.

Weiler, Conrad. *NAN Handbook of Reinvestment Displacement.* Washington, D.C.: National Association of Neighborhoods, 1978.

## THE CLT MODEL (RECENT APPLICATIONS)

Blackmore, John. "Community Trusts Offer a Hopeful Way Back to the Land." In *Smithsonian,* Vol. 9, No. 3, June 1978.

Davis, John E.; Geisler, Charles C.; and Matthei, Charles. "The Role of Alternative Land Institutions in Employment and Local Economic Development." In *Economic Democracy and Locally Based Development Strategies,* William F. Whyte, ed. Washington, D.C.: U.S. Department of Labor, 1982.

Eshman, Rob. "In Land We Trust." In *New Roots,* No. 17, July/August 1981.

Geisler, Charles C. "In Land We Trust." In *Cornell Journal of Social Relations,* Vol. 15, Fall 1980.

Heart, Sarah. "Improving Our Use of the Land." In *Living Alternatives Magazine,* Vol. 1, No. 6, February 1980. (An interview with Robert Swann, lead author of the 1972 book on community land trusts, published under the name of the International Independence Institute.)

International Independence Institute. *The Community Land Trust: A Guide to a New Model for Land Tenure in America.* Cambridge, Mass.: Center for Community Economic Development, 1972.

Matthei, Chuck. "Community Land Trusts as a Resource for Community Economic Development." In *Financing Community Economic Development,* Richard Schramm, ed. Ithaca, N.Y.: Program in Urban and Regional Studies, Cornell University, 1981.

——. "Stormy Economy Alters American Dream." In *Catholic Rural Life,* Vol. 31, No. 7, 1981.

——. "The Earth in Common." In *Sojourners Magazine,* November 1979.

Matthei, Chuck, and Davis, John. "Community Land Trusts: A Response to Tenant Displacement." In *Shelterforce,* Vol. 7, March 1982.

Swack, Michael. "For Economic Development, the Future Is Now." In *Reporter,* Vol. 6, No. 3, July/August 1981.

## ORGANIZING, RESEARCH, AND OUTREACH

Alinsky, Saul. *Rules for Radicals.* New York: Random House, 1971. (A practical guide to community organizing, written by America's most famous community organizer.)

Bluestone, Barry, and Harrison, Bennett. *Capital and Communities: The Causes and Consequences of Disinvestment.* Washington, D.C.: The Progressive Alliance, 1980. (An investigation of plant closings and capital flight).

Community Publications and Research Group. *People before Property: A Real Estate Primer and Research Guide.* 1972. Available from: The Midwest Academy, 600 West Fullerton, Chicago, IL 60614.

Fishbein, Allen, and Zinsmeyer, Jeffrey. *A CRA Guidebook: Neighborhood Reinvestment Strategies* and *A CRA Guidebook: Assessing Community Credit Needs.* 1979. Both guidebooks are available free of charge from: Department of Housing and Urban Development, Office of Neighborhood Development, Washington, DC 20410.

Kahn, Si. *Organizing.* New York: McGraw-Hill, 1982.

Levy, Clifford. *A Primer for Community Research.* San Francisco: Far West Research, 1972.

National Training and Information Center. *Home Mortgage Disclosure Act and Reinvestment Strategies.* 2d ed. Washington, D.C.: Department of Housing and Urban Development, Order No. 0023-000-00554-9, 1979.

Trust for Public Land. *Neighborhood Land Revitalization Manual.* Washington, D.C.: U.S. Department of the Interior, Government Printing Office, Order No. 1981-0-523-478/173, 1981. Also available from: TPL, 95 Madison Avenue, Suite 1407, New York, NY 10016. (A guide to local land inventories and land-based organizing in urban areas.)

Villarejo, Don. *Research for Action.* 1980. Available from: California Institute for Rural Studies, P.O. Box 530, Davis, CA 95616. (A guide for organizers and researchers interested in property.)

Warren, Rachelle B., and Warren, Donald I. *The Neighborhood Organizer's Handbook.* Notre Dame, Ind.: University of Notre Dame Press, 1980.

## INTERNAL ORGANIZATION

Connors, Tracy. *The Nonprofit Handbook.* New York: McGraw-Hill, 1979.

Institute for Community Economics. *Model By-Laws for a CLT* and *Model Lease Agreement for a CLT.* Greenfield, Mass.: ICE, 1982.

Internal Revenue Service. *How to Apply for Recognition and Exemption for an Organization.* IRS Publication No. 557. Available free from nearest IRS office. (Also ask for forms SS-4, 1023, 1024, and 990.)

## FINANCING

Architectural Conservation Trust for Massachusetts. *The Revolving Fund Handbook.* Boston: ACTM, 1979.

Bowe, Gerald G. *Where Do All the $$ Go? What Every Board and Staff Member of a Nonprofit Organization Should Know about Accounting and Budgeting.* Concord, N.H.: New Hampshire Charitable Fund, 1975. Available from: New England Charitable Fund, P.O. Box 1335, Concord, NH 01101.

Department of Housing and Urban Development. *Funding Sources for Neighborhood Groups.* Washington D.C.: Office of Neighborhoods, Voluntary Association, and Consumer Protection.

Ehrmann, Michael. *Financial Leveraging in Community Development Rehabilitation.* Washington, D.C.: Department of Housing and Urban Development, Office of Urban Rehabilitation and Community Reinvestment. (Available free of charge.)

Flanagan, Joan. *The Grassroots Fund Raising Book.* Chicago: Swallow Press, 1977.

Gross, Malvern J., and Warshauer, William. *Financial and Accounting Guide for Nonprofit Organizations.* 3d ed. New York: Ronald Press, 1979.

Henke, Emerson O. *Introduction to Nonprofit Organization Accounting.* Boston: Kent Publishing Company, 1980.

Kurzig, Carol M. *Foundation Fundamentals: A Guide for Grantseekers.* New York: Foundation Center, 1980.

Long, David F. *How to Organize and Raise Funds for Small Nonprofit Organizations.* South Plainfield, N.J.: Groupwork Today, Inc., 1979.

Mitiguy, Nancy. *The Rich Get Rich and the Poor Write Proposals.* Amherst, Mass.: Citizen Involvement Training Project, 1978.

Shellow, Jill R. *Grantseekers Guide: A Directory for Social and Economic Justice Projects.* 1981. Available from: Network of Grantmakers, 919 Michigan Avenue, Fifth Floor, Chicago, IL 60611.

"Surviving Nonprofit Accounting," Parts I and II. In *Grantsmanship Center News.* Los Angeles: Grantsmanship Center.

## ACQUISITION, PLANNING, AND DEVELOPMENT

Applegate, Rick. *"Public Trusts: A New Approach to Environmental Protection."* 1976. Available from: Exploratory Project for Economic Alternatives, 1519 Connecticut Avenue NW, Washington, DC 20036.

Bolton, Charles. *Citizen's Action Manual: A Guide to Recycling Vacant Property in Your Neighborhood.* Washington, D.C.: Heritage Conservation and Recreation Service, U.S. Department of the Interior, 1979. (Prepared for HCRS by the Trust for Public Land.)

Carney, William. *A Citizen's Guide to Maintaining Neighborhood Places.* Washington, D.C.: Heritage Conservation and Recreation Service, U.S. Department of the Interior, 1981. (A sequel to the *Citizen's Action Manual,* cited above.)

Community Land Association. *Community Land Association Handbook.* 1982. Available from: White Oak Community Center, Duff, TN 37729. (Prepared by a local CLT with assistance from the Tennessee Valley Authority, this booklet illustrates basic principles of site planning and environmental protection for members and leaseholders of a rural CLT.)

Couglin, Robert E., et al. *The Protection of Farmland: A Reference Guidebook for State and Local Governments.* Washington, D.C.: Government Printing Office, 1981.

Fenner, Randee Gorin. "Land Trusts: An Alternative Method of Preserving Open Space." In *Vanderbilt Law Review,* Vol. 33, No. 5, 1980.

Francis, Mark; Cashdam, Lisa; and Paxson, Lymon. *The Making of Neighborhood Open Spaces: Community Design, Development and Management of Open Spaces.* 1981. Available from: Center for Human Environments, City University of New York, 33 West 42nd Street, New York, NY 10036.

Hendler, Bruce. *Caring for the Land: Environmental Principles for Site Design and Review.* Planning Advisory Service Report No. 328. Chicago: American Planning Association, 1977.

Hoose, Phillip M. *Building An Ark: Tools for the Preservation of Natural Diversity through Land Protection.* Covelo, Calif.: Island Press, 1981.

Lynch, Kevin. *Site Planning.* 2d rev. ed. Cambridge, Mass.: M.I.T. Press, 1971.

School of Living Land Committee. *The Ecological Use of Land.* 1982. Heathcote Center, 21300 Heathcote Road, Freeland, MD 21053.

Seldin, Maury, and Swesnick, Richard. *Real Estate Investment Strategy.* 2d ed. New York: John Wiley and Sons, 1979.

Smith, Herbert. *The Citizen's Guide to Planning and Zoning.* 1979. Available from: American Planning Association, 1313 East 60th Street, Chicago, IL 60637.

Trust for Public Land. Technical bulletins for land trusts. Available from: TPL, 82 2nd Street, San Francisco, CA 94105; or TPL, 95 Madison Avenue, Suite 1407, New York, NY 10016. (TPL publishes a number of useful bulletins dealing with land acquisition techniques, tax issues, and the protection of agricultural and other open space lands.)

## PERIODICALS

*Conservation Counselling Service.* Kingsbury Browne, Hill and Barlow, 225 F Street, Boston, MA 02110. (A subscription service, costing approximately $400 per year, that provides current information and analysis on pending tax legislation, current regulations, and recent rulings affecting the preservation of open space lands.)

*Cooperative Housing Bulletin.* National Association of Housing Cooperatives, 2501 M Street NW, Suite 451, Washington, DC 20037.

*Neighborhood Conservation and Reinvestment.* Preservation Reports, Inc., 1016 16th Street NW, Suite 275, Washington, DC 20036. (A twice-monthly publication that monitors federal, state, and local policies and programs affecting urban rehabilitation, historic preservation, and community reinvestment.)

*Planners Network.* 1901 Q Street NW, Washington, DC 20009. (A national organization of progressive planners, academics, and community activists that publishes a regular newsletter dealing with issues of housing, planning, social services, and development.)

*Rural America* and *The RHA Reporter.* 1346 Connecticut Avenue NW, Washington, DC 20036. (Both publications report on policies and programs affecting family farmers and other people living in small towns and rural areas. The *Reporter* deals specifically with rural housing issues.)

*Shelterforce.* 380 Main Street, East Orange, NJ 07018. (A national publication which analyzes housing problems from the point of view of tenants and housing activists.)

*Southern Neighborhoods.* 1879 Columbia Drive, Decatur, GA 30032. (A bimonthly publication that reports on the "community control movement in the South.")

# Contributors

*Bonnie Acker* is a self-employed typesetter and graphic designer who has lived in southeastern Massachusetts for the past five years. Working as a community organizer as well, she has a special interest in producing images which "express our day-to-day longings for a violence-free life, good health, supportive work, and a future for all children."

*Marie Cirillo* has worked as an organizer and local developer in four Appalachian communities during the past 30 years. She has recently returned to Clairfield, Tennessee, after a year in Washington, D.C., serving as co-director of Rural American Women.

*John Davis* joined the staff of ICE in 1981 after doing graduate work in development sociology and city and regional planning at Cornell University. He worked previously for five years as a community organizer and social services administrator in Tennessee.

*Rob Eshman* is a free-lance journalist with a primary interest in issues of hunger, land, and draft registration. He was co-founder of the Dartmouth Wood Crew, a project which helps to furnish fuelwood to low-income, elderly, and handicapped persons.

*Charles Geisler* is an assistant professor of rural sociology at Cornell University with an interest in landownership, local control, and community. He is president of the ICE board of trustees.

*Harvey Jacobs* is a doctoral candidate in city and regional planning at Cornell University. He previously worked as a planner with Vermont's Ottauquechee Regional Planning and Development Commission and was co-founder of the Ottauquechee Regional Land Trust.

*Andrea Lepcio* is land projects coordinator for the Hanover Consumer Cooperative in Hanover, New Hampshire. She was formerly an intern for Congressman George Brown (D-California) and principal organizer of the first Congressional Hearing on the Family Farm Development Act.

*Kerry Mackin* is a professional photographer residing in Boston. She also teaches photography for the Appalachian Mountain Club in the White Mountains of New Hampshire.

*Chuck Matthei* has been a member of the ICE board of trustees since 1978; he has served as a full-time member of the ICE staff since 1980. He has spent over 15 years organizing around civil rights, peace, energy, and housing issues.

*Bob O'Keefe* currently works for a housing rehabilitation construction company in Boston. He also works as a free-lance photographer.

*Perk Perkins* has served as director of the Sojourners Housing Ministry and has worked as an organizer for the Southern Columbia Heights Tenants Union in Washington, D.C. He has recently returned home to Mississippi to become associate director of the Southern Woodcutters Assistance Project.

*Kirby White* has worked as a part-time college English teacher and, on occasion, as a free-lance editor. He has an active interest in rural housing, CLTs, and land issues. He lives near Cambridge, New York.

# THE INSTITUTE FOR COMMUNITY ECONOMICS

The Institute for Community Economics (ICE) is a nonprofit corporation committed to the principle that communities should have a significant role in planning their own economic development and should be the beneficiaries of that development. ICE is particularly concerned with communities facing problems of access to land and housing for low- and moderate-income people. It developed the CLT model as a means of dealing with these problems.

ICE helps community groups identify and analyze their land and housing problems and evaluate the potential of the CLT and other cooperative models of local development to address these problems. The institute provides technical assistance to local groups on a range of subjects: community organization and education; legal incorporation and the formulation of bylaws, lease agreements, and other necessary documents; property acquisition, development, and rehabilitation; financing and organizational fund-raising; and negotiation with local, state, and federal agencies and private organizations.

Recognizing that the lack of access to capital is a major barrier to community acquisition and development of property, ICE has established a revolving loan fund to provide start-up loans for community-based projects. The fund is capitalized through loans from a growing number of individuals and organizations who want to invest their money in socially constructive efforts. ICE has also assisted a number of groups in locating alternative sources of financing within their own communities.

The institute is also engaged in documenting the efforts of CLTs and other cooperative local development organizations around the country, and is working to make the experience of these groups more widely available. The present book is a product of this effort. Some members of the group that came together to write the book are continuing to prepare and update CLT case studies and other informational material for distribution by ICE.

The work of the institute is carried out by a full-time staff, an active board of trustees, and a network of co-workers who contribute a wide range of skills and experience. ICE's first priority is to help those community groups whose needs are greatest. Members of ICE's staff receive only basic living expenses in return for their work—a fact reflecting both practical necessity and a moral commitment by the staff. Financial support for the institute comes from individual contributions, church and foundation grants, and fees for services to community groups. Fees are based on a sliding scale so that what a group pays depends on its resources. Authors' royalties from the sale of this book will also go to support the work of the institute.

*The Institute for Community Economics*
*151 Montague City Road*
*Greenfield, MA 01301*
*(413) 774-5933*

# Index